Managing Change and Innovation in Public Service Organizations

Managing Change and Innovation in Public Service Organizations is the first textbook in the Routledge Masters in Public Management series.

The context and environment of public services is becoming increasingly complex and the management of change and innovation is now a core task for the successful public manager. This text aims to provide its readers with the skills necessary to understand, manage and sustain change and innovation in public service organizations.

Key features include:

- The use of figures, tables and boxes to highlight ideas and concepts of central importance.
- A dedicated case study to serve as a focus for discussion and learning and marry theory with practice.
- Clear learning objectives for each chapter with suggestions for further reading.

Managing Change and Innovation in Public Service Organizations provides future and current public managers with the understanding and skills required to manage change and innovation. This groundbreaking text is essential reading for all those studying Public Management, Public Administration and Public Policy.

Stephen P. Osborne is Professor of Public Management and Head of the Public Management Group at the Aston Business School, UK. **Kerry Brown** is Associate Professor in the School of Management and Director of the Work and Industry Futures Research Program at Queensland University of Technology, Australia.

ROUTLEDGE MASTERS IN PUBLIC MANAGEMENT

The **Routledge Masters in Public Management** series is an integrated set of texts. It is intended to form the backbone for the holistic study of the theory and practice of public management as part of:

■ a taught Masters, MBA or MPA course at a university or college;
■ a work-based, in-service, programme of education and training; or
■ a programme of self-guided study.

Each volume stands alone in its treatment of its topic, whether it be strategic management, marketing or procurement and is co-authored by leading specialists in their field. However, all volumes in the series share both a common pedagogy and a common approach to the structure of the text. Key features of all volumes in the series include:

■ a critical approach to combining theory with practice which educates its reader, rather than solely teaching him/her a set of skills;
■ clear learning objectives for each chapter;
■ the use of figures, tables and boxes to highlight key ideas, concepts and skills;
■ an annotated bibliography, guiding students in their further reading; and
■ a dedicated case study in the topic of each volume, to serve as a focus for discussion and learning.

The series editors are:
Stephen P. Osborne, Professor of Public Management, Aston Business School, Aston University, UK (editor-in-chief).

Owen Hughes, Professor of Public Management, Monash University, Australia.

Walter Kickert, Professor of Public Management, Erasmus University, Rotterdam, The Netherlands.

Managing Change and Innovation in Public Service Organizations

Stephen P. Osborne
and Kerry Brown

Routledge
Taylor & Francis Group

LONDON AND NEW YORK

Stephen P. Osborne:
In loving memory of my father, Frank, for all his inspiration
and guidance

Kerry Brown:
For Neal and Rachel

First published 2005
by Routledge
2 Park Square, Milton Park, Abingdon, Oxon OX14 4RN

Simultaneously published in the USA and Canada
by Routledge
270 Madison Ave, New York, NY 10016

Transferred to Digital Printing 2007

Routledge is an imprint of the Taylor & Francis Group, an informa business

© 2005 Stephen P. Osborne and Kerry Brown

Typeset in Perpetua and Bell Gothic by
Florence Production Ltd, Stoodleigh, Devon
Printed and bound in Great Britain by
TJI Digital, Padstow, Cornwall

British Library Cataloguing in Publication Data
A catalogue record for this book is available from the British Library

Library of Congress Cataloging in Publication Data
Osborne, Stephen P., 1953–
　Managing change and innovation in public service organizations/Stephen P. Osborne
　and Kerry Brown.–1st ed.
　　p. cm. – (Routledge masters in public management series; 1)
　Includes bibliographical references and index.
　1. Public administration.　2. Organizational change.　I. Brown, Kerry.　II. Title.　III. Series.
　JF1525.073078　　2005
　658.4'06–dc22　　　　　　　　　　　　　　　　　　　　　2004012505

ISBN 10: 0-415-32897-7 (hb)　　　　ISBN 13: 978-0-415-32897-5 (hb)
ISBN 10: 0-415-32898-5 (pb)　　　　ISBN 13: 978-0-415-32898-2 (pb)

Contents

CONTENTS

Figures, tables and boxes

FIGURES

TABLES

BOXES

FIGURES, TABLES AND BOXES

Acknowledgements

Chapter 7 of this volume, on understanding and managing innovation, is expanded and developed from material in S. Osborne (1998) *Voluntary Organizations and Innovation in Public Services*. London: Routledge.

Thanks to Stacy Ridge, Jennifer Waterhouse and Jennifer Frahm for their assistance.

Abbreviations

EU	European Union
IT	Information Technology
NPM	New Public Management
PEST Analysis	Political-Economic-Social-Technological Analysis
PSO	Public Service Organization
PSS	Personal Social Services
SWOT Analysis	Strengths-Weaknesses-Opportunities-Threats Analysis
UK	United Kingdom
VNPO	Voluntary and Non-profit Organization

Part I

Introduction

Chapter 1

Change and innovation in public service organizations

Planned and emergent phenomena

LEARNING OBJECTIVES

By the end of this chapter you should:

- be clear about the approach of this text and its structure;
- understand the difference both between innovation and change and between planned and emergent phenomena; and
- have developed clear objectives for your own learning.

KEY POINTS OF THIS CHAPTER

- The nature of public services, and of public service organizations (PSOs), have changed substantially around the world over the past twenty years. This has been a result in part of the increasingly volatile societal and political environment that they exist in and in part of the growing scarcity of public resources.
- This changing environment has made it increasingly important for public service managers to engage in the management of change and innovation – and to be clear about the difference between these two phenomena.
- Change and innovation can also be both planned and emergent phenomena – and again these two variants require different approaches to their management.

KEY TERMS

- **New Public Management (NPM)** – an approach to managing public services that prioritizes managerial, as opposed to professional, skills and which includes resource and performance management at its heart.
- **Change** – the gradual improvement and/or development of the existing services provided by a PSO and/or their organizational context. It represents continuity with the past.
- **Innovation** – the introduction of *new elements* into a public service – in the form of new knowledge, a new organization, and/or new management or processual skills. It represents *discontinuity* with the past.
- **Planned phenomena** – events that PSO managers can foresee and make strategic or tactical contingencies for.
- **Emergent phenomena** – events that PSO managers cannot foresee and which arise because of unexpected changes in the environment.
- **Discontinuity** – a characteristic that differentiates innovation from change and that represents a break from prior or existing service configurations and/or professional skills.

CHANGE AND INNOVATION IN PUBLIC SERVICES AND IN PUBLIC SERVICE ORGANIZATIONS

For much of the last century, public service organizations (PSOs) were the embodiment of stability. Invariably integrated as part of government as a whole, these organizations were classical Weberian hierarchical bureaucracies. The organizational emphasis was upon incremental growth and development and upon a planned approach to the administration of public services.

However, as the twentieth century drew to a close, this picture began to change. These classical public service bureaucracies had been well suited to a stable and slow-changing environment. A range of factors in the late twentieth century, though, conspired to change this environment. These factors are analysed in more detail in Chapter 2. However, the key changes included:

- global economic changes which meant that PSOs could no longer rely upon steady incremental growth, and had instead to focus on the efficient and effective use of increasingly scarce resources;
- a consequent growth of a managerial, rather than administrative, approach to the provision of public services, often called the *New Public Management*, or *NPM* (McLaughlin *et al.* 2002);
- demographic changes, particularly the ageing of the population in most countries;

- changes in expectations as citizens became more sophisticated, requiring greater focus on choice and quality in the provision of public services; and
- political changes, which marked a paradigmatic change against the hegemony of the state in meeting expressed public needs and towards more complex approaches which increasingly required the governance of multiple relationships between service providers.

These factors led to a change in nature of public services provision. Far from this role being the assumed priority of the state, it became increasingly a task undertaken by a range of organizations in what has become known as the *plural state* (Osborne and McLaughlin 2002). This comprises a range of PSOs from the government, non-profit and business sectors that need to collaborate in the provision of public services. The evolution of this plural state has also seen a shift, first from the administration of public services to their management – and then from their management to their governance, where the governance of plural relationships has become the central task for the provision of effective public services (Kickert *et al.* 1997).

All these developments have put a premium upon the skills of managing change and innovation in public services.

Change and innovation in public services

Change and innovation are over-lapping phenomena. However, it is important from the outset to be clear about where they converge and where they diverge – as well as their impact upon the management and delivery of public services (Box 1.1).

Change is a broad phenomenon that involves the growth and/or development of one or more of a number of elements of a public service. These include:

- the design of the service;
- the structure of PSOs providing it;
- the management or administration of these PSOs; and/or
- the skills required to provide and manage the public service.

By contrast, *innovation* is a specific form of change. Its nature is explored in more detail in Chapter 7. Put simply, however, innovation is *discontinuous change*.

Rather than representing continuity with the recent past it represents a break with the past. What had been acceptable or adequate for the provision of public services in the past will no longer be so – their provision will require new structures or skills that mark a break with this past experience. This discontinuity might involve the creation of a new organization, the meeting of a newly established need (such as HIV/AIDS in the 1980s and 1990s) or the development of new skills or a new technology to meet an established need (many information technology changes in both the administration and provision of public services come under this heading).

Clearly, there are many common skills involved in managing innovation and change. These include the predicative skills discussed in Chapter 3, the skills of managing individual staff members through the change process discussed in Chapter 5, and the issues of sustainability discussed in Chapter 11. However, there are also distinctive skills and issues – such as managing cultural change and encouraging and supporting innovation in PSOs. To make an obvious point, it is one thing to encourage staff to develop their work-based skills. It is a task of a highly different order, however, to persuade staff that innovation has rendered their existing skills base redundant and that they need to retrain. This volume explores both the common skills of managing change and innovation and the distinctive ones for each task. Before doing this, however, it is important to establish one other key concept for managing change and innovation – that is the difference between *planned* and *emergent* change and innovation.

Planned and emergent change and innovation

In an ideal world, a manager of a public service should be able to scan their environment for changes, assess their impact upon their organization and services, and develop appropriate changes or innovations to respond to these environmental changes. In reality, though, managing change and innovation in public services is more complex than this. In addition to such *planned change*, public service managers also need to be able to deal with *emergent change*. This change is thrust upon an organization by circumstances that it can neither control nor, sometimes, predict.

BOX 1.1 CHANGE AND INNOVATION IN PUBLIC SERVICES

Change is the *gradual* improvement and/or development of the existing services provided by a PSO or their organizational context. It represents *continuity* with the past.

Innovation is the introduction of *new elements* into a public service – in the form of new knowledge, a new organization, and/or new management or processual skills. It represents *discontinuity* with the past.

For PSOs there are two significant sources of emergent change and innovation. *First it may be required by a sudden unforeseen crisis.* This might be environmental (such as an earthquake or forest fire), health related (such as the SARS outbreak of 2003 in Hong Kong) or a man-made crisis (such as major fire in an underground railway, as occurred in London in the 1990s). Now public services have always had to expect such sudden crisis and much energy is expended on trying to reduce the likelihood of such a crisis, to predict the likely timing or locality of it, and/or to develop skills to deal with it (hence the development of such professions as risk and crisis management). However, the very nature of emergent change means that it can never be entirely planned for.

The Great Hanshin-Awaji earthquake in Japan in 1996 is a good example of an emergent phenomenon and its impact on public services. Such earthquakes are a constant risk in Japan. This fact is known and planned for. However, this did not prevent a major and profound earthquake devastating the town of Kobe in 1996. Such was the extent of this devastation, and its location, that it created both a massive surge in the need for crisis care of its victims (including a significant number of elderly people, because of the location of the epicentre of the earthquake in a neighbourhood populated by a large elderly community) and a collapse of the local infrastructure, including transport and communications (because of the physical impact of the earthquake).

Both the central and local governments in Japan were paralysed by the size of this tragedy and the subsequent care needs of the population. The machinery of public services ground to a halt in the face of this event. As a result of this paralysis, many civil and volunteer organizations emerged in the Kobe area to help care for the earthquake survivors. The success of these civil organizations provided a trigger for the development of a profound innovation in Japan – the development of a locally based non-profit sector which has come to be seen as a major provider of public services (Imada 2003).

The second source of emergent change, although less profound than such crises, is probably more common for public services managers. *This derives from the political context of public services and PSOs.* Most public service managers have little or no control over the policy process at a national or local level. Thus changes engendered at this political level can impose the need for innovation and/or change in public services – and sometimes over very short time-scales.

This form of emergent change is especially challenging for public service managers. It can be unpredictable and can often seem as much related to the short-term political advantage of a ruling political party as to a substantive change in public need. Nonetheless it is a fact of life for public services.

This theme of planned and emergent change and innovation is a recurrent one throughout this volume. It is also returned to in more detail in Chapter 10, when the sustainability of change and innovation in PSOs is considered.

7

THE APPROACH ADOPTED IN THIS BOOK

This volume is intended for students of public management, often public managers themselves, who want to develop a critical understanding both of the processes of change and innovation in public services and of approaches to their management. It is neither a handbook that is prescriptive about how to manage innovation and change nor a theoretical text. Rather it seeks to provide readers with three elements:

- a critical understanding of the nature of change and organizations in public services and PSOs;
- a range of skills which can be applied in directing and managing change and innovation in public services; and
- the potential to develop their understanding and development further in the future.

Put simply, it is about *educating* public managers rather than simply *training* them. As well as the core text, each chapter in this volume will include:

- learning objectives for each chapter;
- an initial summary of the key points to be covered in the chapter;
- definitions of key terms used in the chapter;
- boxes, figures, bullet points and tables to present essential material;
- case examples and vignettes drawn from actual practice;
- discussion questions and/or exercises;
- notes, where appropriate;
- references; and
- an annotated bibliography for further reading.

The appendices to this volume also offer two longer case studies of change and innovation management in practice in public organizations, written by practitioners, together with key questions for consideration and/or discussion.

Structure of the book

Chapter 2 explores *the current volatile environment of public services and PSOs* and considers the triggers for innovation and change within that environment. Chapter 3 then considers the *issue of assessing the need for change and innovation.* It reviews the strengths and weaknesses of a number of key tools in this area. Chapters 4 to 6 explore the *management of change in PSOs.* Chapter 4 reviews critically *the extant literature on managing change.* Chapter 5 explores *the actual process of implementing*

3, 4, 5, 6

and managing change in PSOs. Finally Chapter 6 considers *the important issue of managing cultural change in PSOs*.

Chapters 7 to 9 then turn to the issue of *the management of innovation in PSOs*. Chapter 7 reviews critically *the innovation studies literature*, whilst Chapter 8 discusses *the support of innovative individuals within PSOs*. Finally Chapter 9 explores *how the innovation process can be managed within these organizations*.

The conclusions to this book cover two issues. Chapter 10 discusses the issue of *the sustainability of change and innovation in public services*. The book concludes with Chapter 11 which considers the key issues for PSO managers in managing change and innovation, as well as possible emergent issues for the future.

DISCUSSION QUESTIONS

1   Consider a public service or PSO that you are familiar with. Audit its development over the last decade and draw up a list of the key ways in which it has changed. Then consider the extent to which these changes were examples of incremental change or discontinuous innovation.

2   Using the list developed in question 1 above, now classify both these changes and innovations as planned or emergent phenomena. Consider:
- if there is any pattern that emerges about the relationship between innovation and change, and planned and emergent phenomena, in this service or organization; and
- what the environmental triggers have been that initiated the need for this change or innovation.

REFERENCES

Imada, M. (2003) The voluntary response to the Hanshin Awaji earthquake: a trigger for the development of the voluntary and non-profit sector in Japan. In S. Osborne (ed.) *The Voluntary and Non-profit Sector in Japan: the Challenge of Change.* Routledge, London, pp. 40–50.

Kickert, W., E.-H. Klijn and J. Koppenjan (1997) *Managing Complex Networks – Strategies for the Public Sector.* Sage, London.

McLaughlin, K., S. Osborne and E. Ferlie (2002) *The New Public Management. Current Trends and Future Prospects.* Routledge, London.

Osborne, S. and K. McLaughlin (2002) From public administration to public governance: public management and public services in the twenty first century. In S. Osborne (ed.) *Public Management – Critical Perspectives Vol. I.* Routledge, London, pp. 1–10.

FURTHER READING

On the changing environment of public services and PSOs

Four books are particularly useful here. Both N. Flynn (2002) *Public Sector Management*, Prentice Hall, Harlow and O. Hughes (2003) *Public Management and Administration*, Palgrave Macmillan, Basingstoke, provide good basic introductions to the changing nature of public management in the twenty-first century. K. McLaughlin, S. Osborne and E. Ferlie (2002) *The New Public Management. Current Trends and Future Prospects*, Routledge, London, offers a more sophisticated analysis of these changes and their impact upon a range of elements of PSOs. Finally S. Osborne (2002) *Public Management – Critical Perspectives Vol. I*, Routledge, London, offers a strong collection of the seminal papers from the recent past which have both tracked and evaluated the changing nature of public management.

On the nature of change and innovation

This topic is explored in more detail throughout this book. However, readers may also want to make an initial exploration of the perspectives available in the 'mainstream' management literature. On the management of change, C. Carnall (1990) *Managing Change in Organizations*, Prentice-Hall, New York, and D. Wilson (1992) *A Strategy of Change*, Routledge, London, both still offer good introductions – the former is more strong on the tactics of managing change within organizations whilst the latter is more strong on a critical understanding of managing change.

On the management of innovation, the edited collections by M. Tushman and W. Moore (1988) *Readings in the Management of Innovation*, Harper Business, New York and A. Van de Ven, H. Angle and M. Doole (1989) *Research on the Management of Innovation*, Harper & Row, New York, despite their age, remain the best introductions to this topic. A more concise collection, though less comprehensive, is that edited by J. Henry and D. Walker (1994) *Managing Innovation*, Sage, London.

Chapter 2

The volatile environment of public service organizations

LEARNING OBJECTIVES

By the end of this chapter you should:

- have a clear understanding of some of the key forces promoting and requiring change and innovation in PSOs;
- have developed your skills in considering the key environmental forces affecting your organization and/or services; and
- have considered the specific forces driving change and innovation in your organization or service.

KEY POINTS OF THIS CHAPTER

- It is useful to understand the changing nature of the environment of PSOs by exploring their political, economic, social and technological dimensions.
- A useful approach to such an understanding is through the development of a PEST Analysis.

KEY TERMS

- **PEST Analysis** – This is a tool to encourage the systematic analysis of the political, economic, social and technological changes occurring in the environment of a PSO.
- **The contract state** – an approach to the provision of public services that emphasizes the use of contracts as the key governance mechanism used by government in order to ensure the efficiency, effectiveness and accountability of public services.
- **The plural state** – a description of the state that emphasizes its role as the planner and purchaser of public services but with their provision coming from a plurality of sources, including the state itself, the business sector and the voluntary and non-profit sector.
- **Globalization** – the increasingly global context and impact of both national states and their public services.
- **Sustainable communities** – communities which are able to maintain themselves both in terms of their economic and social coherence and in terms of their identity in the wider society.

THE PEST ANALYSIS

The first chapter of this volume gave a brief overview of the factors requiring change and innovation in PSOs. This chapter will take this analysis further, whilst also introducing one specific technique for structuring your analysis of the environment – *the PEST Analysis* (Box 2.1).

A PEST Analysis is not a substitute for your scanning or researching your environment. This is still required and some key approaches to this are included

BOX 2.1 THE PEST ANALYSIS

PEST stands for 'Political-Economic-Social-Technological'. A PEST Analysis is a structured way of analysing factors in the environment that may be requiring change or innovation by your organization. In this context, the environment is considered not simply as a physical entity rather than as a mixture of man-made and physical environments. You should brainstorm out the factors either which have impacted upon your organization in the recent past or which are going to influence the course of your organization over the next five years. Once you have done this you need to group these factors under each of these four headings to map out the factors controlling the course of your organizational development.

in the next chapter. However, it does provide a framework for structuring how you think about your changing environment. A development of this approach (the Aston Matrix) is presented in the next chapter, which provides a more sophisticated approach for your own organization or service.

A PEST ANALYSIS FOR PUBLIC SERVICES IN THE UNITED KINGDOM (UK)

This chapter will develop a PEST Analysis for PSOs specifically in relation to the UK. In reality, though, there can be no such thing as a generic, 'one size fits all' PEST Analysis. A key task for you, therefore, will be to consider which of these factors is relevant both to your national/regional context and to your specific organizational context – and which other new factors you would want to include (see Exercise 2.1, below).

Political factors

Not surprisingly, political factors are an essential element to be considered when scanning the future development of PSOs. Their environment is, after all, a fundamentally political one.

Taking a longer view, seven political factors have required change and innovation by PSOs in the UK over the past decades:

- the move from a rationing to a user-responsive mode of public service;
- the introduction of markets and contracting into public services;
- the election of the 'New Labour' government in 1997 (and its subsequent re-election), with its focus on 'community governance';
- the development of the plural state and the move from government to governance;
- the impact of the European Union;
- the twin forces of globalization and regionalization; and
- the ongoing process of policy change.

The changing mode of public services delivery. In the immediate post-war period, public services in the UK were dominated by the need to ration scarce public services and to provide a basic level of service for all users. In this situation the model of public administration, and its emphasis on the rule of law and the administration of public services, dominated. However, as British society developed over the late twentieth century, this concern changed. Rationing scarce resources remained a priority (indeed originally increased from the late 1970s onward). However, societal culture changed from one of seeing service users as dependent upon the state and as only eligible for a uniform level of service, to one where increasingly service users required and expected choice and quality in their public services. This was also associated with the concern to deal with the problem of scarce resources not by *public administration* to a basic level but by *the management of public services* and PSOs – and which development became known as the 'New Public Management' or NPM (Osborne 2002, McLaughlin *et al.* 2002). This is discussed further below.

The introduction of markets and the contract state into public services. One of the first manifestations of the growing managerialism related above was the introduction in the 1980s and 1990s by the Thatcher and Major governments, of the use of contacts and market mechanisms, rather than hierarchical line management, for the governance of services. This quite profound paradigmatic change required a host of innovative approaches from PSOs to the delivery of public services and which were genuine examples of innovation as 'discontinuous change marking a break with the past', as discussed above. It required PSOs

- to develop managerial skills, as opposed to professional ones;
- to develop new organizational forms both in the government and in the non-profit and business sectors; and
- to promote a change of culture towards using markets to allocate scarce resources rather than hierarchical line management.

These profound changes, which affected PSOs across the world, have been analysed in more detail in McLaughlin *et al.* (2002) and Flynn (2002).

The New Labour government. The election of 'New Labour' in 1997 in the UK certainly did not signal the end either to the marketization of public services or to the trend to public management rather than administration. It did represent a sizeable shift of emphasis, though. The almost obsessive concerns of the prior Conservative government were replaced by a more pragmatic 'what works where' approach. Also the NPM was developed further through the concept of 'community governance' (Clark and Stewart 1998). This required not only the effective management of public services, but the involvement of the community in the planning and management of these services – though the debate continues as to the extent to which this approach was rather more rhetorical than real (see, for example, Johnson and Osborne 2003 on this debate in the context of local strategic partnerships in England).

The plural state. A key element of the new environment of public services that has been embedded further in the UK by the New Labour government has been the concept of the 'plural state'. Whilst under public administration, the focus had been upon the planning and provision of public services through unified governmental organizations (such as local government), increasingly under New Labour, this has been replaced by a plural model of service planning and provision. A range of partners from the government, non-profit and business sectors have become involved in the planning and management of public services. This had a number of implications for PSOs that have required significant change and innovation, discussed further below.

The European Union (EU). Whilst the UK has been notoriously slow to enhance the concept of a 'United States of Europe', nonetheless it has increasingly become embedded with its other European members in the EU. In particular the structural funds for the regeneration of deprived and marginal countries within the EU have become a prime source of regeneration funding in the UK – especially in rural areas (Shucksmith 2000). The distinctive institutional and organizational context of the EU has had a profound effect upon the need for change and innovation in PSOs.

Globalization and regionalization. The EU itself is just one example of the growing impact of global factors upon PSOs in the UK. On the one hand, the models and experience of public management in other countries (such as Osborne and Gaebler's (1993) concept of 'reinventing government' from the US) have impacted upon the UK. Its own experience of the NPM has also influenced developments elsewhere – and especially Australia and New Zealand (Pollitt 2002). On the other hand, the 'free market' of the EU has seen the introduction, albeit slowly, of significant mainland European partners into the UK plural state.

Regionalization has played a significant part in promoting divergence between public services and their management *within* the UK. Self-government in Northern Ireland and Scotland (and to a lesser extent in Wales) has seen the structures, processes and expectations of public services and PSOs diverge dramatically across the UK, once again requiring significant organizational change (see Osborne *et al.* 2003 for further discussion on this). Further, especially within England, there has been the growth of the regional level of government, with the increasing influence of such bodies as the Government Offices of the Regions and the Regional Development Agencies. This trend is expected to deepen.

Ongoing policy change. Finally within this broader political context there has been ongoing policy change in the UK which not surprisingly has had a massive effect upon PSOs. The development of community care and the notion of the 'mixed economy of care' (Wistow *et al.* 1996), of the Local Agenda 21 for sustainable community (Whittaker 1995) and of new approaches to health care (Flynn and Williams 1997) are just three examples from the recent past of this phenomenon. Such policy change is endemic to PSOs although its content varies across fields and user groups tremendously. However, whatever the context, this process of public policy development is invariably a source of the need for change and innovation within PSOs.

This brief section has emphasized the point of understanding the political context of PSOs and how this can force emergent change upon such organizations. The practical inputs of many of these factors are found below, in the 'technology' section of this PEST Analysis.

Economic factors

Inevitably, economic factors play a part in the provision of public services. The pre-eminent task for the management of PSOs is the allocation of scare resources – often itself a definition of economics. Five economic factors are especially noteworthy for PSOs in the UK:

- the global economic situation;
- the changing funding structures of PSOs;
- the marketization of public services;
- the introduction of charging for public services, and a focus on the costs and revenues of public services; and
- the issue of economic sustainability.

The global economy. Global economic factors impact upon the economics of nation states – which in turn impact upon the ability of governments to fund public services. The global and economic changes of the late twentieth century (including the increasing costs of fuel, the rise of multi-national corporations and the growth of cheap(er) labour costs in the developing transitional nations have all impacted upon the Western market economies – including the UK. These factors should not be overlooked in understanding the economic environment of PSOs.

Funding structures. There have been significant changes in how PSOs are funded in the UK over the past two decades that have appreciably changed the face of public services. Three examples will make this point. First, the funding structure of local government has undergone several changes from the traditional system of rates through the ill-fated 'poll tax' to the present community charge. Moreover the regulations governing what levels of charging local government can set, and how they can allocate money have also changed, presenting significant challenges both for the structure of local government itself and for services that it (part) funds.

Second, the health service has seen the growth of internal and 'quasi' markets (Le Grand 2002) as a means to allocate resources, along with the growth of generic management posts within these services. This has fundamentally changed the relationships between primary care practitioners and hospitals and within hospitals themselves.

Third, the EU has become a major source of funding for area regeneration in the UK over the past two decades. However, the impending accession of a number of transitional nations from Eastern Europe has led to the abolition of many of the structural funds in order to allocate money eastwards. This has itself posed challenges to PSOs involved in regeneration.

The marketization of public services. The growing trend towards marketization has led many public services either to decide to, or to be required to, commence managing the costs of their services and also to begin to charge for public services. For non-profit organizations, they have also found themselves in an increasingly competitive situation, with regard either to their generic fund-raising work or to their bidding for government contracts. This changing focus both towards cost awareness and control and towards revenue generation has required new approaches to the management of PSOs.

Economic sustainability. Finally, sustainability has become an imperative issue for PSOs. This may be in terms of their work in relation to developing economically sustainable communities through area regeneration programmes. However, it may also be in terms of the sustainability of the services of a PSO itself. Many public funding schemes are notoriously reluctant to commit to organizing revenue provision for a programme or service. A core task for a new PSO is thus to secure ongoing funding from alternative sources or to develop its income base.

Social factors

Public services are inevitably influenced by social factors – and themselves are often addressing new or emerging social needs. The key social factors for PSOs in the UK in the recent past have been:

- the ageing of the population;
- changing expectations of the population;
- the social inclusion agenda;
- the growth of new forms of social need and the redefinition of existing ones; and
- the need for sustainable communities.

The ageing of the population. Populations around the world are becoming older. This affects PSOs in two ways. On the one hand it poses new challenges for their services, to meet the needs of this increasing elderly population – though it also imposes increased costs in doing so (another economic factor!). On the other hand, it poses a specific issue for PSOs in relation to the recruitment and retention of good staff. As the population ages, the employable population has shrunk. PSOs

17

can be at a disadvantage in trying to recruit staff compared to private sector organizations that can often offer more attractive remuneration packages. This requires an innovative approach to recruitment for PSOs.

Changing expectations. As the twenty-first century has begun, the expectations of the users of public services have changed. They are now less prepared to accept 'given' public services passively and increasingly expect greater choice and quality in the public services that they use.

This change has also been reflected in the terms used to describe the users of public services. For much of the twentieth century, such users were often described as 'clients', with an expectation that public service professionals would 'do' things to 'them' on the basis of their (i.e. the professionals) assessment. Increasingly now though, public service users are being described, and describe themselves, as 'consumers', 'customers' and even 'citizens'. Each of these terms carries its own connotations for public services in terms of the expectations of the users.

Social inclusion. The language of the disadvantaged with which public services often work is also changing. Increasingly the focus is upon social exclusion and social inclusion. This focuses the attention of PSOs upon the structural ways in which people are excluded from the community. Critics have argued that this is at the expense of more substantive terms of analyses (such as class or income). Nevertheless the 'social inclusion agenda' (SEU 1998) is a central one for PSOs in the UK and has required them to take new and innovative approaches to their work.

New and changing needs. Inevitably, need in society changes and develops. Genuinely new needs are perhaps less common nowadays but they do arise. The needs of people who are HIV positive or have AIDS is one of the most prominent examples of the last decades. Equally though, as technology develops (see below) the needs which were thought impossible to respond to in the past have now become more possible to address (the development of medical technology, such as in heart transplants and surgery is a good example here).

In addition, existing needs can get reframed, requiring services to change to meet the requirements of the new discourse. The best example of this is the changing nature of the needs of people with disabilities. In previous decades, the needs of 'handicapped' people were often premised on their passivity and upon images of disempowerment. However, social changes in how disability is viewed have led to the development of services which deal directly with the issue of disempowerment and where people with disabilities are more active, and equal, partners in meeting their own needs than in the past.

Sustainable communities. Finally, just as sustainability was identified as a key economic goal, so it is in social terms also. Local Agenda 21 has highlighted the importance of developing local communities that not only have a sustainable economic base but which also are sustainable in terms of their structure and governance (Whittaker 1995). This challenge of sustainability has changed the task of many PSOs working with local communities.

Technological factors

In the field of public services, technology can be thought of in two ways: *hard technology* (which involves the structures and equipment of public services) and *soft technology* (which involves the processes and skills for delivering public services). Both have changed over the past two decades.

In terms of *hard technology*, three developments in particular are important. The first, not surprisingly, is the impact of *information technology (IT)* upon the delivery of public services (see for example, Luck and Golden 1996). This has had an impact in terms of:

- the administration of public services;
- the use of management information systems;
- as a tool for service users; and
- the analysis and dissemination of information about public services (for service user, PSOs and their funders).

Thus, IT has been both an input into change and innovation in PSOs, by changing how services are provided, and on output, in terms of being an element of new forms of public services.

The second hard technology has been the development of *new organizational forms* for PSOs. This too has had an impact in a variety of ways. New organizational structures have been necessary, either as a result of the political, economic and social changes detailed above, or prompted by the IT developments just detailed. These new structural forms have themselves become spurs to change and innovation inside organizations and significant changes and innovation themselves. Important structural changes have included:

- the purchaser–provider split within local authorities;
- the use of quasi-market structures in the health service;
- the increasing use of public–private partnerships for the provision of public services;
- the development of new legal entities for PSOs (such as Development Trusts – see DTA 1997); and
- the growth of hybrid forms of PSOs (Joldersma and Winter 2002), which incorporate elements from both the public and private sectors.

19

The final hard technological factor has been the development of *new service delivery technologies* – such as new equipment or drugs in medicine, or new technology for supporting people with disability in the communities. Inevitably such new technology requires change and innovation within PSOs.

Moving to the *soft technologies*, it is possible to highlight three key developments. The first of these is the development of new skills for the delivery of public services. These may either be new professional skills (in terms of social work or education, for example) or new managerial skills (the development of the NPM brought with it a whole host of new managerial skills into the public sector, such as marketing and strategic planning). These new professional and managerial skills have unquestionably changed the face of PSOs in the twenty-first century.

The second soft technological change has been the *changing nature of accountability*. This has been both in terms of a shift from traditional models to plural ones (Cutt and Murray 2000) and in terms of the tools of performance management (Boyne 2000).

The final soft technological change has been in *the role of professionals* in PSOs. Changes over the past two decades have privileged the growing managerial cadre in PSOs of the expense of traditional professional autonomy (Broadbent and Laughlin 2002). However, this is an ongoing case of change and is continuing to be contested within PSOs.

CONCLUSIONS

This brief PEST Analysis of PSOs in the UK should have made several points. First, change is endemic in the context of public services. Second, such change has major consequences for the provision and management of public services and of PSOs and is itself a significant source of change and innovation in the planning, management and provision of PSOs and of public services. Whether the change is planned or (usually) emergent, it is vital to take a proactive approach to it. Third, tools such as the PEST Analysis, and the others discussed in the next chapter, are essential elements in helping the public services manager to confront and engage with these challenges.

Needless to say, the changes and innovations that they require and stimulate can be of different ilk. They can involve:

■ the development of new organizational structures and forms for PSOs;
■ the development of new public services, 'per se';
■ the development of new managerial and/or professional skills/processes;
■ the development of new administrative systems and skills;
■ the development of new ways of engaging with service users; and
■ the development of new forms of performance management and accountability.

This chapter has given an overview of the types of challenges leading to change and innovation within PSOs and given an example of how a PEST Analysis can be used to structure your thinking about these changes. Exercise 2.1 now gives you an opportunity to test out this approach either in relation to your own PSO or a PSO that you are familiar with. You should complete this exercise before moving on to Chapter 3.

EXERCISE 2.1

This chapter has used a PEST Analysis to explore the changing context of PSOs in the UK. Inevitably this has been developed at the most general level of analysis. It is time now to undertake your own PEST Analysis of the changing context of public services in your own community – either specifically in terms of the PSO that you work for or more generally in terms of PSOs in your community. You should do this even if you are based in the UK. Environmental factors can change over time or be seen differently from the context of different services.

Once you have undertaken the analysis, consider what the impact of these changes is for your chosen field of public services. Summarize in a couple of paragraphs what you see as the key challenges that your service has to confront and engage with over the next two to three years. You will be able to use this analysis as the starting point for mapping the need for change and innovation in your chosen service or PSO. This will be pursued further in the following chapter.

DISCUSSION QUESTIONS

1   How useful do you think the PEST Analysis approach is, for mapping the changing environment of public services and PSOs? What are its strengths and limitations?

2   To what extent is it realistic to separate out the political, economic, social and technological factors driving change and innovation? How might you go about developing a more integrative approach to their understanding?

REFERENCES

Boyne, G. (2000) External regulation and Best Value in local government, *Public Money & Management* 20(3): 7–12.

Broadbent, J. and R. Laughlin (2002) Public services professionals and the New Public Management: control of the professions in the public services. In K. McLaughlin,

S. Osborne and E. Ferlie (eds) *The New Public Management. Current Trends and Future Prospects.* Routledge, London, pp. 95–108.

Clarke, M. and J. Stewart (1998) *Community Governance, Community Leadership and the New Labour Government.* YPS, York.

Cutt, J. and V. Murray (2000) *Accountability and Effectiveness Evaluation in Non-profit Organizations.* Routledge, London.

Development Trusts Association [DTA] (1997) *Here to Stay: a Public Policy Framework for Community Based Regeneration.* DTA, London.

Flynn, N. (2002) *Public Sector Management.* Prentice Hall, Harlow.

Flynn, R. and G. Williams (1997) *Contracting for Health. Quasi-markets and the National Health Service.* Oxford University Press, Oxford.

Joldersma, C. and V. Winter (2002) Strategic management for hybrid organizations, *Public Management Review* 4(10): 83–100.

Johnson, C. and S. Osborne (2003) Local strategic partnerships, neighbourhood renewal and the limits to co-governance, *Public Money & Management* 23(3): 147–54.

Le Grand, J. (2002) Quasi-markets and social policy. In S. Osborne (ed.) *Public Management. Critical Perspectives* [Volume II]. Routledge, London, pp. 9–22.

Luck, M. and P. Golden (1996) What is 'IT'? Information technology management in voluntary and non-profit organizations. In S. Osborne (ed.) *Managing in the Voluntary Sector.* International Thomson Business Press, London, pp. 167–86.

McLaughlin, K., S. Osborne and E. Ferlie (eds) (2002) *The New Public Management. Current Trends and Future Prospects.* Routledge, London.

Osborne, D. and T. Gaebler (1993) *Reinventing Government. How the Entrepreneurial Spirit is Transforming the Public Sector.* Plume, New York.

Osborne, S. (2002) Public management across the twentieth century: a review of practice and research. In S. Osborne (ed.) *Public Management – Critical Perspectives Vol. I.* Routledge, London, pp. 11–14.

Osborne, S., A. Williamson and R. Beattie (2003) The national context of local governance: does it matter? Evidence from rural regeneration initiatives in England, Northern Ireland and Scotland, *Local Governance* 29(1): 1–13.

Pollitt, C. (2002) The New Public Management in international perspective: an analysis of impacts and effects. In K. McLaughlin, S. Osborne and E. Ferlie (eds) (2002) *The New Public Management. Current Trends and Future Prospects.* Routledge, London, pp. 274–92.

Social Exclusion Unit [SEU] (1998) *Bringing Britain Together.* SEU, London.

Shucksmith, M. (2000) *Exclusive Countryside? Social Inclusion and Regeneration in Rural Areas.* Joseph Rowntree Foundation, York.

Whittaker, S. (ed.) (1995) *First Steps: Local Agenda 21 in Practice.* HMSO, London.

Wistow, G., M. Knapp, B. Hardy, J. Forder, J. Kendall and R. Manning (1996) *Social Care Markets: Progress and Prospects.* Open University Press, Buckingham.

FURTHER READING

The best books which chart the changing nature of public service and PSOs, and their roots in the environment, are N. Flynn (2002) *Public Sector Management*, Prentice Hall, Harlow; O. Hughes (2003) *Public Management & Administration*, Palgrave Macmillan, Basingstoke; and the edited collection by D. Farnham and S. Horton (1996) *Managing the New Public Services*, Macmillan, Basingstoke – though this latter collection is really only relevant to UK based readers.

For an exploration of the impact of these changes upon the nature of public management itself then the collection edited by Kate McLaughlin and her colleagues – K. McLaughlin, S. Osborne and E. Ferlie (2002) *The New Public Management. Current Trends and Future Prospects*, Routledge, London – is highly recommended as *an essential text*.

For readers wishing to put the UK based developments discussed here into international perspective then the following chapter is highly recommended: C. Pollitt (2002) The New Public Management in international perspective: an analysis of impacts and effects. In K. McLaughlin, S. Osborne and E. Ferlie (eds) (2002) *The New Public Management. Current Trends and Future Prospects*, Routledge, London, pp. 274–92.

Finally an early, but important, examination of the use of a PEST Analysis within a PSO (in this case, in voluntary and non-profit organizations) is provided by S. Jain and S. Surendra (1977) Environmental forecasting and nonprofit professional organisations, *Long Range Planning* (10).

Chapter 3

Assessing the need for change and innovation

LEARNING OBJECTIVES

By the end of this chapter you should have:

- understood the difference between the planned and emergent models for assessing the need for change;
- learned a range of approaches to assess need; and
- considered how they might best be applied within your own service or PSO.

KEY POINTS OF THIS CHAPTER

- The planned and emergent approaches to change and innovation provide quite different slants upon their management.
- Planned approaches concentrate upon scanning the environment through the gathering of data and its analysis.
- Emergent approaches concentrate upon developing the ability of staff at all levels of the organization to respond to changes in its environment.

KEY TERMS

- **Planned change** – change that is the result of a systematic process of scanning the environment and determining the ways in which an organization must change.
- **Emergent change** – change that is thrust upon an organization by changes in its environment that are outside of its control.
- **Learning organization** – an organization that encourages continuous learning and adaptation at all organizational levels.
- **Market research** – the planned acquisition and analysis of data measuring some aspect either of the needs that a PSO is addressing or of the ways in which it addresses these needs, for the purpose of improving the organization's ability to meet those needs more effectively.
- **Community profiling** – a comprehensive description of the needs of a population that is defined, or defines itself, as a community, and the resources that exist within a community, carried out with the active involvement of the community itself, for the purpose of developing an action plan or other means of improving the quality of life in the community.
- **SWOT Analysis** – A systematic approach to assessing the internal strengths and weaknesses of an organization and the opportunities and threats existing in its environment.

PLANNED AND EMERGENT CHANGE MODELS

In Chapter 1 we introduced the concepts of *planned* and *emergent* innovation and change. In this chapter we look at approaches to assessing the need for change and innovation. The planned and emergent models offer different trajectory for this task.

Planned approaches to change and innovation assume that it is possible to scan the environment in order to assess the need for change. On this basis it is then possible to use one of several techniques to plan the change required (Zaltman *et al.* 1973).

Beckhard (1969) suggests a four-stage process, moving from assessing need to planning change (Box 3.1). In this chapter we are concerned primarily with stages I and II of this model – the latter two stages are dealt with in more detail in the subsequent chapters of this volume.

It should be added that a core element of such planned approaches to change and innovation is that of defining the future state required *after* the change. Planned approaches are chary of vague change statements such as 'improving organizational performance' or 'instilling greater motivation in staff'. These planned approaches require the manager to ask: 'how exactly will the organization (and its components) be different once the change has been achieved?' Planning is then in

BOX 3.1 THE FOUR STAGE MODEL OF PLANNED CHANGE

I   Setting goals and defining the future state required after the change.
II Diagnosing the present condition in relation to these goals and setting a 'desired future state'.
III Defining the transitional activities and commitments required to reach this desired future state.
IV Developing strategies and an action plan to manage this transition and reach the desired future state.

Adapted from Beckhard (1969)

relation to this 'desired future state'. You should try Exercise 3.1, to help your understanding of this concept, before moving on.

Emergent approaches to change and innovation, by contrast, assume that it is not possible to plan for change. This is because, as suggested in Chapter 1, the environment is too complex and is itself changing too rapidly to allow for a planned approach (Wilson 1992). From this starting point, the emergent school of thought advocates the model of the *learning organization* (Argyris and Schon 1996). In this model, rather than attempt to plan for change and innovation, the intention is to develop an organizational culture where all levels of the organization are equipped to confront and deal with the emergent change arising out of this environment. This is explored further below.

EXERCISE 3.1 DESIRED FUTURE STATES FOR CHANGE

Take your own PSO, or one that you are familiar with. Identify a simple area of its work that requires change or improvement (such as staff car parking, waiting room arrangements or something similar). Write down a clear statement of what the problem is – and then a clear statement of how things will be better once the situation has been changed. This is a statement of your 'desired future state'.

For example, your problem might be 'lack of staff car parking and poor motivation for staff to arrive in work on time as a result of this'. It might well be that it is impossible to increase the car parking available for your staff. Your desired future state could then be 'a rotational system for allocating car parking spaces that allows all staff an opportunity to use the car park and leading to all staff arriving on time at work'.

PLANNED APPROACHES TO ASSESSING THE NEED FOR CHANGE AND INNOVATION

Three common approaches to assessing the need for change and innovation are discussed here:

- the Market Research approach;
- the Managerial approach; and
- the Social Audit approach.

The Market Research approach

In their seminal text on marketing for non-profit organization, Kotler and Andreason define Market Research (MR) as:

> . . . the planned acquisition and analysis of data measuring some aspect or aspects of the marketing system for the purpose of improving an organisation's marketing decisions.
>
> (1987: 201)

In this volume, we are using the term more broadly. We would reframe this definition as:

> The planned acquisition and analysis of data measuring some aspect either of the needs that a PSO is addressing or of the ways in which it addresses these needs, for the purpose of improving the organisation's ability to meet those needs more effectively.

The underlying assumption of this model is thus that a PSO needs to constantly monitor and evaluate both the needs that it should be addressing and how it addresses these needs in order to improve its performance – *either* by modifying the target needs that it should address *or* by improving its existing approach/ developing new approaches to meeting these target needs.

The key steps of the MR process can be summarized as:

- defining the sort of information required to address a question about the needs that a PSO is addressing;
- deciding on the balance between costs and sophistication, and determining a budget for the MR exercise;
- designing a MR package to provide the information required within the budget agreed;

BOX 3.3 USES OF MARKET RESEARCH

1   **Assessing patterns of use**   How are the services of a PSO used and what trends are there/how will these change?

2   **User perceptions of services**   What are the beliefs/cultural attitudes of service users to that service and how might it better relate to these beliefs and attitudes?

3   **User experience of services**   Irrespective of its effectiveness, what is the experience of using a public service for its beneficiaries, and how might this be improved?

4   **User motivation**   What is the relationship between a public service and the needs of a user, and how might these impact upon the take-up of a service?

5   **Type of users**   What is the profile of the users of a service (such as in terms of their age, ethnic background, geographic location, family structure, etc.) and what are the implications of this for service delivery?

6   **Competition/collaborators**   Who else is providing a service to meet the identified need and what would your relationship with them be?

Adapted from Chapman and Cowdell (1998)

- Panel studies (the views of the same panel of people are assessed over time).
- Experimentation (often difficult in human services or public services for vulnerable people).

Low cost options

- Focus groups (interview users in groups with specific terms of reference).
- Convenience sampling (sampling people who are easily accessible).
- Snowball sampling (asking initial participants who else should be contacted, and so on, in an iterative fashion).
- Piggy-backing (including your MR questions in someone else's survey).
- Volunteer researchers (using volunteers to conduct surveys).
- Students (engaging students from local colleges or universities to undertake a MR project for you as part of their course).
- Secondary sources (use existing data from elsewhere).
- Board of Directors (appoint experienced researchers to the Board of the PSO and utilize their experience).

EXERCISE 3.2 DEVELOPING A MARKET RESEARCH PLAN

Take a PSO that you are familiar with. Consider the following issues:

1   What potential sources of primary and secondary data are available, in order to assess how successful this organization is in meeting the needs of its target user group?
2   What potential difficulties might arise in gathering this data, and how might they be resolved?
3   What would be the potential cost(s) of accessing this data – and how might IT be used to reduce these?

On the basis of your answers, draw up an initial MR plan and budget for this PSO.

Evaluations of MR

MR is an essential element of the planned approach to change and innovation. It can provide a PSO with the information about user need(s) that is needed to improve its performance and effectiveness. It need not be prohibitively expensive, so long as a little time is taken to discover what information already exists in the public domain. Where primary research is required, then a PSO needs to be pragmatic about what can be achieved with its budget.

However, MR is not the answer to all planned change. By its nature, MR deals with the existing needs of existing service users. It can tell you little, for example, about needs that do not presently exist (but which may do in the future) or about the views of people that do not presently use a service – but who may require it in the future. As such it is fundamentally rooted in the 'status quo'. To consider the need for more fundamental changes or innovation for a PSO, then a more 'broad-spectrum' approach is required – such as that of social audit discussed below. An effective PSO needs to decide which of these models of research it needs – or perhaps more accurately, which model it needs at what stage in its organizational life.

The Managerial approach

This approach to assessing the need for change and innovation draws on strategies and tools from strategic management. The focus here is upon using these techniques:

31

- to predict key elements of the organizational environment that might need addressing (*the PEST Analysis* and/or *Aston Matrix*);
- to assess the strategic position of the organization in relation to its environment (*the SWOT Analysis*); and/or
- to evaluate the potential costs and benefits of a desired change or innovation (*Cost–Benefit Analysis*).

The Aston Matrix

In the previous chapter we were introduced to the concept of the PEST Analysis as a tool for exploring the environment factors influencing a PSO. The Aston Matrix takes this process a stage further, by positioning these factors across three dimensions – the meta, the macro and the micro:

- *Meta-level factors* are those that concern the broadest societal level of the organizational environment – the national political environment, national demographic changes and long-term technological changes, for example;
- *Macro-level factors* are either those that concern the industry-level features of the environment (the make-up of organizations involved in a particular public service or the current state of professional knowledge about an identified need, for example) or those that concern the geographic region that a PSO is located within (the demography of a region or its socio-economic profile, for example);
- *Micro-level factors* are those that concern the internal environment of a PSO (its staff mix, organizational culture or its use of IT, for example).

Table 3.1 presents an Aston Matrix for a hypothetical non-profit organization in an inner city area of the West Midlands in the UK, involved in an area regeneration partnership. This matrix allows its manager to track the extent to which the different levels of factors are congruent or not. In this case, it highlights:

- the need to pursue EU funding;
- the need to engage in regional partnerships and with the new local office of the Developments Trust Association; and
- the need to change its staffing profile to increase its ability to engage with the local Black and ethnic minority population.

As a result of this initial analysis, the PSO concerned can then develop a more specific analysis of its relationship to its local environment and in relation to these identified factors. A good way to approach this task is through a SWOT Analysis.

The SWOT Analysis

SWOT Analysis stands for 'Strengths-Weaknesses-Opportunities-Threats Analysis'. It is a very common technique within strategic management for assessing the position of an organization in relation to its environment. The technique is simple. The Analysis is used to assess the *internal* strengths and weaknesses of an organization and its *external* opportunities and threats. Taking the example of the area regeneration non-profit organization from the previous section, Table 3.2 presents a SWOT Analysis of this organization in relation to the three factors identified through the previous Aston Matrix.

This analysis allows the agency to decide how it is going to build upon its strengths and opportunities. This could be by:

- using the EU experience and contacts of the CEO to secure EU funding;
- using its good local networks to build funding partnerships with other agencies, around a Local Strategic Partnership; and
- emphasizing its inner city position and partnership involvement in any future funding applications.

By contrast, this analysis also allows the PSO to highlight the weaknesses and threats that it faces and to develop a plan to deal with them. This might be by:

- developing a recruitment strategy to increase the number of Black and ethnic minority staff and/or staff experienced in working with these local communities;
- building links to the Development Trusts Association locally; and
- using the profile identified in the strengths/opportunities element of this analysis to secure its medium-term funding base.

Cost–Benefit Analysis

The focus of a Cost–Benefit Analysis (CBA) is, not surprisingly, upon balancing the costs of a potential change or innovation against its potential benefits (Sugden and Williams 1978; see also Knapp 1984). Inevitably this is not a mechanistic process, but rather involves the exercise of managerial judgement.

It is also important to differentiate between three types of costs in such an analysis:

- *resource costs*, in terms of finance, staffing, capital or other such costs;
- *transaction costs*, in terms of the costs of managing the change process; and
- *opportunity costs*, in terms of what alternative opportunities are forgone by pursuing one particular opportunity ('If I do A, then I cannot do B').

Table 3.1 Example of an Aston Matrix

Factors	Level		
	Meta	Macro	Micro
Political	Development of Local Strategic Partnerships (LSPs) New EU policy on regeneration funding New policy focus on linking social inclusion and regeneration	Development of new regional regeneration partnership (regional) New District Council (no overall control) elected in major conurbation (regional)	Appointment of new CEO with experience of successful EU funding applications
Economic	Regeneration funding to be targeted at inner city areas Funding to be linked to organizational involvement in public–private partnerships	Declining employment in major conurbation in regional (regional) Development of network of LSPs nationally (industry)	Need to find replacement for regeneration funding ending in ten months' time
Social	Decline in inner city residential population in UK	Deterioration in local relations between Black and Asian populations (regional)	Lack of Black and ethnic minority staff
Technological	Growth in use of LSPs and Development Trusts in regeneration Encouragement of use of Parish Councils in urban areas to increase social inclusion	Establishment of new Development Trusts Association office in region	Existing staff of the PSO come primarily from a traditional community development background – with a professional rather than community orientation

Table 3.2 *Example of a SWOT Analysis*

Strengths	Weaknesses
Appointment of new CEO with EU experience	Traditional 'community development' background of many staff
Established name in the region	Lack of Black and ethnic minority staff and of staff with experience of working with these communities
Good links to existing regeneration agencies	Impending end of current funding programme to leave the PSO economically exposed
Member of embryonic local LSP	Lack of links to emerging Development Trusts Association in region
New EU funding to become available	Lack of credibility of the PSO with the local Black and ethnic minority population
Possibility of learning from national LSP network	Lack of links to potentially influential local Development Trusts Agency office
New national framework for LSPs	Worsening local economy may impose further strain on limited (and reducing) resources of the PSO
Government funding to be targeted at inner city areas and PSOs working in existing public–private partnerships	Lack of clarity about the future policy directions of the newly elected Council
Opportunities	Threats

There are five stages of a CBA. These are:

Stage I   Identify the possible change options for an agency to meet to an identified need or performance gap.

Stage II   Estimate the resource, transaction and opportunity costs for each option.

Stage III Estimate the potential benefits of a change for (i) the agency (ii) its users (iii) the wider community, and (iv) any other key stakeholders (NB this process should also include a no-change option – what might happen if the PSO does nothing).

Stage IV   Evaluate these potential benefits against the costs estimated in Stage II.

Stage V   Select the appropriate change option that offers the PSO the optimal balance between its costs and benefits, and develop an implementation plan to progress this option.

Inevitably, this model combines some objective data collection (perhaps about costs) with subjective decision making in the evaluation of options. This is perfectly acceptable – as long as the subjective element is acknowledged and CBA is not used simply to provide a gloss of respectability to an already agreed decision process.

Evaluation of Managerial approach

The strength of this approach lies in its practical focus upon the PSO itself and how it meets expressed need. It provides pragmatic tools for assessing the relationship of the organization to its environment.

However, as with the MR approach, it is often limited by its focus on the 'here and now'. It emphasizes continuity and incremental growth, by concentration on developing existing strengths and opportunities, rather than discontinuity and innovation, which may require a 'leap of faith' beyond what is known. You can help develop your own view of this managerial approach now, by undertaking Exercise 3.3.

The Social Audit approach

Both the above approaches have been critiqued for their dependence upon responding to changes in the existing environment and for their top-down approach to the change and innovation approach. To an extent, the Social Audit approach responds to these criticisms, whilst still being rooted firmly within the planned change paradigm.

Social Audit includes a cluster of techniques, including *needs assessment*, *community consultation* and *community profiling*. Hawtin *et al.* (1994) describe a community profile as:

> A *comprehensive* description of the *needs* of a population that is defined, or defines itself, as a *community*, and the *resources* that exist within a community, carried out with the *active involvement of the community* itself, for the purpose of developing an *action plan* or other means of improving the quality of life in the community.
>
> (Hawtin *et al.* 1994: 5, their emphases)

In this context, *community* can refer to either 'a community of place', such as a village or urban neighbourhood (a common approach in this case is that of the *village appraisal* – see Osborne and Tricker 2000) or 'a community of interest', such as a shared need (perhaps a disability) or cause. Whichever definition of community is used, though, the key elements of these approaches to needs

EXERCISE 3.3 APPLYING THE MANAGERIAL APPROACH TO CHANGE AND INNOVATION

Take your own PSO, or one that you are familiar with, and identify a specific need or performance gap that must be addressed. Conduct a progressive series of an Aston Matrix, a SWOT Analysis and a CBA around this issue. On the basis of these develop recommendations for what changes and/or innovations the PSO needs to introduce.

Once you have conducted this exercise, consider the strengths and weaknesses of the process. In particular consider:

1   How constraining or enabling did you find the process, in helping you to develop plans for change or innovation by the identified PSO?
2   To what extent did you have, or could you access, the information required for these analyses?
3   Did you feel that these approaches helped you develop ideas for changes and innovations to improve the performance of your PSO or not (and why)?

assessment are drawn from the discipline of *social research* (Wadsworth 1997). Unlike the two prior methods, this approach does not work from the existing needs of a community, or the services that a PSO provides. Rather it focuses upon the holistic needs of a community and the full range of options for meeting these.

Hawtin *et al.* (1994) describe six stages to the community profile process:

Stage I   Preparing the ground.
Stage II   Setting aims and objectives.
Stage III   Deciding on methods.
Stage IV   Fieldwork.
Stage V   Reporting.
Stage VI   Action.

They also highlight a number of key issues to be resolved in undertaking a community profile:

■   In what way, and to what extent, is the local community (however defined) to be involved in the process?

- To what extent is it possible to make use of existing information sources and what new information needs to be collected?
- What methods should be used in gathering new information about needs in the community?
- How is the information gathered to be analysed?
- How are the findings of the research to be reported – and to whom?
- In what way is this information to be used to bring about change or innovation in public services?

Evaluation of the Social Audit approach

As should be apparent, social audit does share many of the strengths and weaknesses of the MR approach discussed above. However, it is perhaps a more radical and fundamental approach to needs assessment, in the sense that it does not start from any preconceived definition of need or services. Rather it invites the community to define its own.

This does allow the most open approach to predicting the need to future change or innovation by a PSO. However, it does also run the risk of raising unrealistic expectations amongst the target community of a PSO or of identifying potential changes that are indeed needed – but that are beyond the resources of a PSO. Consequently, it is important for any organization undertaking such a fundamental review both to be aware of these dangers and to set the bounds of the exercise, perhaps in resource terms, prior to it beginning.

Conclusions on the planned change approaches to change and innovation

These approaches do offer concrete and clearly delimited techniques for planning change in public services. However, they tend to stress a number of points that are not necessarily to the benefit of a PSO:

- They assume that you can plan for change and innovation, yet it may emerge unexpectedly from the environment or be thrust upon you by a higher-level institution (such as a change of policy by government).
- They usually assume a top-down process to change management that focuses on managerial action rather than the active involvement of frontline workers or the community – though this is not the case for social audit.
- They minimize ongoing organizational learning.

The latter point is particularly important. It is the starting point for the alternative approach to change and innovation – the emergent approach.

EMERGENT APPROACHES TO INITIATING ORGANIZATIONAL CHANGE AND INNOVATION

We have already been introduced to the concept of emergent change and innovation – phenomena that are not planned but which emerge from the external environment – and for PSOs that includes their political environment in particular. To recap, the emergent approach to change and innovation argues that:

- the environment is too complex and is now changing too quickly for traditional models of planned change to be effective, and
- top-down, planned change minimizes the learning that goes on across the organization and which could enable it to change and innovate more effectively in the future.

This approach is sometimes called 'groping along' (Golden 1990). This is the concept that you cannot plan for change and innovation, because of the above reasons, so you have to learn and develop by trial and error.

Senge (1990) has argued that learning is the key to organizational survival and growth. This approach to organizational change and innovation does present a fundamentally different role for managers, though, compared to the planned approaches discussed previously. Far from being the leaders of change, a learning organization approach requires managers to be *the enablers* of organizational learning, creating an environment where staff can learn from their experience, and use this themselves to stimulate change and innovation. Senge (1990) has gone so far as to argue that effective organizations should be creative entities that are skilled at obtaining information, processing it, and modifying their behaviour as a result of this information. Such organizations need to be prepared to experiment, to learn from their own experience and to learn from other organizations. Finally, Brodtrick (1998) makes an explicit connection between organizational learning and innovation in PSOs.

The basis of the organizational learning approach

The basis of this approach to organizational change and innovation is within learning theory, and particularly in the model of the *learning cycle* developed by Kolb (1979). He argued that learning is a continuous and cyclical process of testing theory by experience and vice versa. The learning cycle is shown in Figure 3.1. It is possible to start this cycle at its bottom or top. *Deductive learning* starts with a theory about how something works. This is then developed into hypotheses that are tested out in practice. This experience is subsequently evaluated and becomes the basis for modifying the original theory – or developing a new one.

39

Inductive learning, in contrast, starts with the actual practical experience of doing something. This is evaluated and is used to build a theory about the particular activity concerned. This is then turned into hypotheses and used to guide future action – where it may again become modified by experience.

Argyris (1991) has developed this theory of learning further, through the twin concepts of *single loop learning* and *double loop learning*. Single loop learning is sometimes called 'problem solving' and is best associated with the ability to respond to change in a specific set of circumstances. It is usually associated with incremental development and change. Double loop learning is more complex, involving the ability for individuals to reflect upon their experiences and learn from them – changing their behaviour as a result. It is usually associated with innovative development.

The learning organization

Pitts and Lei (1999) argue that a learning organization has the ability to respond to change because its staff are more prepared to experiment and adapt. Salaman (1995) suggests therefore that learning organizations need to embed a cyclical learning process into their organizational behaviour (Figure 3.2).

A range of models exists to suggest how this learning environment can be inculcated within organizations. All of them emphasize the need to prevent the 'routinization' of organizational behaviour and to encourage differing perceptions of problems and needs to come up against each other. Pitts and Lei (1999), for example, argue for six elements of a learning organization:

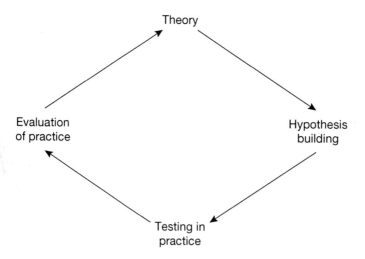

Figure 3.1 *The learning cycle.*

Source: Based on Kolb *et al.* (1979).

Figure 3.2 *The organizational learning cycle.*

Source: Based on Salaman (1995).

- the frequent rotation of managers;
- the continual training of personnel;
- the decentralization of decision making;
- the encouragement of multiple experiments by staff;
- a high tolerance for failure; and
- an openness with the organization towards a diversity of viewpoints.

The frequent rotation of managers exposes them to new experiences and perspectives and prevents them from becoming too wedded to one perspective. Continual training encourages staff to see learning as a key organization skill and to be less fearful of obsolescence if the skills-demands of the organization change. Decision-making decentralization encourages all staff to participate in key decisions, improving organizational responsiveness. Experimentation and a tolerance of failure promote the development of innovative ideas and support a culture where staff are encouraged to look for new responses to organizational tasks — even if they do not always prove effective. Organizational openness allows staff to put forward new points of view, whilst diversity brings differing perspectives to the same issues, promoting organizational learning and development.

Evaluation of the learning organizational approach

The learning organization model undoubtedly has much to offer to PSOs. Their environments are complex and prone to unexpected changes, due to their political nature. This approach encourages organizations to see change and innovation as a core task of all staff, on a continuous basis, rather than a discrete managerial function. It is thus a very empowering approach to innovation and change.

However, it does have significant potential drawbacks. These are particularly significant for PSOs. First, the 'learning organization' concept can be at odds with the actual nature of many PSOs. Historically these have been hierarchical organizations, where information is often jealously guarded (and sometimes rightly so, to protect the confidentiality of their service users) and where the culture has been one of professional dominance rather than openness. The learning organization model thus requires significant cultural change for many PSOs (the issue of cultural change is discussed further in subsequent chapters of this volume).

Second, there can be a real danger of burnout for staff expected to change continuously. Working in PSOs can be a highly stressful job in its own right and many staff, rightly or wrongly, look for stability in their organizational life, not constant change. This can make staff wary of this approach to organizational development.

Finally, some of the characteristics of learning organizations are very hard for PSOs to adopt. In particular, PSOs are notoriously 'risk-aversive' – for good and bad reasons. On the one hand, they are often dealing with vulnerable people and sensitive issues. This can make it very difficult to encourage risk taking. The family of a patient who dies when a doctor experiments with a new form of surgery are not likely to be sympathetic to the need for risk-taking inside a hospital for example. On the other hand, public services tend to be very high profile in the media, because they deal with issues fundamental to society. Once again, staff are unlikely to want to take risks if it means that they may end up the focus of a media campaign.

EXERCISE 3.4 THE ORGANIZATIONAL LEARNING CYCLE

Consider your own PSO, or one that you are familiar with. Compare it to the model of the learning organization discussed above. Ask yourself:

1   What elements of this model are embedded in this organization, if any?
2   How would you go about shifting the culture of this organization from its current one towards that of a learning organization?
3   What could be the potential pitfalls and barriers to this process and how might you resolve them?

CONCLUSIONS

It seems unnecessary to try to counterpoise the planned and emergent approaches to change. It is possible to plan for change and innovation in public services – and where possible, gathering information to feed this process is sensible. Equally it is important that the organization as a whole learns from this process and that mechanisms are in place to promote and support such learning.

DISCUSSION QUESTIONS

1   Consider a PSO that you are familiar with. To what extent do you believe that it is possible for this organization to plan for change? What factors make it more or less likely that a planned approach to change and innovation will succeed for it?

2   The planned approaches to change all tend to assume a certain rationality in decision making within PSOs. Do you believe that this is a justified assumption? How might some of the irrational, or arational, elements of organizational behaviour impact upon the ability of a PSO to plan for change?

3   What would be the key issues in introducing a learning organization approach to a PSO that you are familiar with? To what extent do you believe that this would equip it with the ability to change and innovate – or what factors might prevent this?

REFERENCES

Aaker, D., V. Kumar and G. Day (1995) *Marketing Research*. John Wiley & Sons, New York.

Argyris, C. (1991) Teaching smart people how to learn, *Harvard Business Review* (May/June) pp. 99–109.

Argyris, C. and D. Schon (1996) *Organizational Learning 2, Theory Method and Practice*. Addison Wesley, Reading, MA.

Beckhard, R. (1969) *Organization Development, Strategy and Models*. Addison Wesley, Reading MA.

Brodtrick, O. (1998) Organizational learning and innovation: tools for revitalizing public services, *International Review of Administrative Sciences* 64(1): 83–96.

Chapman, D. and T. Cowdell (1998) *New Public Sector Marketing*. Pearson, Harlow.

Chisnall, P. (1992) *Marketing Research*. McGraw-Hill, London.

Golden, O. (1990) Innovation in public sector human service programs: the implications of innovation by 'groping along', *Journal of Policy Analysis and Management* 9(2): 219–48.

Hawtin, M., G. Hughes and J. Percy-Smith (1994) *Community Profiling. Auditing Social Needs*. Open University Press, Buckingham.

Knapp, M. (1984) *Economics of Social Care*. Macmillan, London.

Kolb, D. (1979) *Organizational Psychology*. Prentice Hall, New York.

Kotler, P. and A. Andreason (1987) *Strategic Marketing for Non-profit Organizations*. Prentice Hall, New Jersey.

Osborne, S. and M. Tricker (2000) Village appraisals, *Local Economy* 14(4): 346–56.

Pitts, R. and D. Lei (1999) *Strategic Management – Building and Sustaining Competitive Advantage*. South Western College Publishing, Cincinnati.

Salaman, G. (1995) *Managing*. Open University Press, Buckingham.

Senge, P. (1990) *The Fifth Discipline*. Doubleday, New York.

Sugden, R. and A. Williams (1978) *The Principles of Practical Cost Benefit Analysis*. Oxford University Press, Oxford.

Wadsworth, Y. (1997) *Do It Yourself Social Research*. Allen & Unwin, St Leonards, NSW.

Weisbrod, B. (1981) Benefit cost analysis of a controlled experiment: treating the mentally ill, *Journal of Human Resources* 16: 523–50.

Wilson, D. (1992) *A Strategy of Change*. Routledge, London.

Zaltman, G., R. Duncan and J. Holbek (1973) *Innovations and Organizations*. John Wiley, New York.

FURTHER READING

Planned approaches to change

Market research – There are a plethora of books in this field. The most easily accessible are probably D. Aaker, V. Kumar and G. Day (1995), *Marketing Research*, John Wiley & Sons, New York and P. Chisnall (1992) *Marketing Research*, McGraw-Hill, London.

Managerial approaches – No one text is the clear leader here. P. Joyce (1999) *Strategic Management for the Public Services*, Open University Press, Buckingham and J. Bryson (1995) *Strategic Planning for Public and Non-profit Organizations*, Jossey-Bass, San Francisco, both give good introductions to the skills and techniques in this field – and with a useful critical edge.

Social audit – The best introduction to this is undoubtedly M. Hawtin, G. Hughes and J. Percy-Smith (1994) *Community Profiling. Auditing Social Needs*, Open University

Press, Buckingham. This is a lucid and well-written text. Yoland Wadsworth (1997) *Do It Yourself Social Research*, Allen & Unwin, St Leonards, NSW is also a good 'no frills' guide to practice. S. Osborne and M. Tricker (2000) Village appraisals, *Local Economy* 14(4): 346–56 provide a critical evaluation of one particular type of social audit – the village appraisal. Finally, in a Health Services context, I. Crombie, H. Davies, S. Abraham and C. du V. Florey (1993) *The Audit Handbook. Improving Health Care Through Clinical Audit*, John Wiley, Chichester, is a good introduction to this specific framework.

Emergent and post-modern approaches to change

Peter Sege's (1990) popular book *The Fifth Discipline*, Doubleday, New York, is a good introduction to this approach and is accessible. The seminal works here – and still very important – are C. Argyris and D. Schon (1978) *Organizational Learning*, Addison Wesley, Reading, MA, and the paper by B. Leavitt and J. March (1988) Organizational learning, *Annual Review of Sociology* 14: 319–40. Finally, much useful material is brought together by R. Kanter, B. Stein and T. Jick (1992) *The Challenge of Organizational Change: How Companies Experience It and Leaders Guide It*, Free Press, New York.

Part II

Managing change in public service organizations

Chapter 4

The processes of change in public services and public service organizations

LEARNING OBJECTIVES

By the end of the chapter you should be able to:

- understand the different processes of change in public services and public service organizations;
- categorize the different levels at which change occurs in public services and public service organizations;
- distinguish the different models of change relating to public services and public service organizations; and
- identify the drivers of change within public services and public service organizations.

KEY POINTS OF THIS CHAPTER

- Changes in public services have been transformational and continuous.
- Convergence theory is characterized by universality of changes to public services but there has been debate about the appropriateness and applicability of the translation of New Public Management (NPM) into the global arena.
- The context for change comprises different layers across global, national, institutional, organizational and sub-organizational settings.
- A multi-layered governance framework is a useful device for understanding the different levels at which change occurs in public services and public service organizations.

KEY TERMS

- **Transformational change** – change that is fundamental, large-scale, radical and dramatic. It radically alters existing configurations of power relations, organizational structures and value sets.
- **Convergence theory** – this hypothesizes that disparate elements and themes gradually merge to become a singular, common entity. Universal trends in the ideology, operation and management of public services have resulted in public services across the globe becoming similar.
- **Public choice theory** – this posits that public services should separate management and policy from the delivery of public goods and services to avoid self interest and 'empire building'.

This chapter explores the processes of change across public services. It proceeds by outlining a framework for identifying a hierarchy of contexts in which change occurs. Identifying diverse change contexts aids understanding the different impacts of change across public services and public service organizations. An overview of the different models of change in public services and public service organizations is provided. The chapter identifies the forces for change within the public service and public service organizations and analyses how these drivers shape the outcomes of change. Understanding the processes of change and managing change are critical elements of the roles of leaders and managers in public service organizations. Restructuring, reform and change initiatives have been devised and implemented in public service organizations as a result of a range of influences. Public service organizations undergo change as the external environment of the public sector alters and the public service responds to changes in the political, economic and social context, and as internal operational requirements vary.

UNDERSTANDING THE CONTEXT OF PUBLIC SERVICE CHANGE

Chapter 2 explored some of the specific triggers for change and innovation in PSOs. This chapter now takes a step back and explores some of the more conceptual ways in which to understand the pressures for change, in particular, in PSOs and in public services. It takes the specifics triggers for change identified previously in Chapter 2 and places them within a framework of governance in order to better understand their relationship and import. The conceptualization of change in public services over the last decades of the twentieth century is that it has been extensive, far-reaching and continues at an increased pace into the twenty-first century. The scope of public service change has been equated to a paradigm shift

(Kettl 2000). There is acknowledgement that the scale of reform and restructuring has changed the character, operation and ideological underpinnings of public services to such an extent that the model of change is identified as transformational (Worrall et al. 2000, Osborne and Gaebler 1992). The type and degree of adjustment in the context of transformational change is that it is fundamental, disruptive and abrupt (Patrickson and Bamber 1995). The dimensions of change across public services are not only dramatic in scope but far-reaching on a global scale.

Welch and Wong (1998) contend that contemporary public service change results primarily from global pressures. Contrary to traditional approaches that maintain public service change emanates from the political, economic and social systems comprising the domestic context, the authors argue that global forces impact on national public services directly and also act upon the internal political, economic and social systems that in turn influence the direction and content of public service change (Welch and Wong 1998).

Claims that the scope of change has resulted in a convergence of trends to enable a notion of a globalized and globalizing public service is the subject of debate (Common 1998; Lynn 2001). Convergence theory posits that global trends are impelling public services across the globe to become similar (Welch and Wong 2001). It has been argued that global forces create common responses to public service reform and thereby similar institutional effects can be discerned across public services on a global scale (Kettl 1997).

Common (1998: 440) identified five possible and interconnected reasons for the spread of universal public service prescriptions for reform and change under NPM:

- The rise of the transnational consultant or management 'guru' transporting a particular public service reform strategy into different countries.
- The adoption of 'new right' politics and policy on an international scale creating a global proliferation of NPM practices and principles.
- The introduction of policy mechanisms to establish market-based approaches to public service policy and service delivery on an international scale, particularly privatization measures of which NPM was perceived as an initial stage.
- The increasing prominence and importance of the role of supranational institutions of governance.
- The growing incidence and receptivity of national governments to policy transfer in terms of an appeal to 'modernizing' government.

While these explanations establish a set of commonalities in relation to change themes and drivers of change in public services and public service organizations and are often reflected as axiomatic in the literature, there is still debate about their explanatory value in terms of the pervasiveness of creating a new model of public service. Lynn (2001: 194) argues that the convergence theory may be 'selective or partial' rather than applying wholesale to all aspects of public services.

The manifest changes in public services have been the object of speculation and contestation about whether or not the character and operation of public services have converged or diverged in the global arena. The object of the discourse is to determine whether change is a part of 'national action' that shapes public services in particular country-specific ways or 'international diffusion' whereby managerial, policy and political trends influence public services creating common and global features of the public service (Lynn 2001). In this way, the concern is to discern whether there are identifiable global trends in public services or whether the outcomes of change are more diverse and that public services are subject to, and consequently shaped by, national or localized contextual influences. Common (1998) claims that convergence is not interchangeable with the notion of globalization as globalization unleashes the supranational forces that transcend geographical boundaries and the authority of national governments but the convergence/divergence thesis leaves intact the ability of nation states to influence public services.

In responding to the debate about forces shaping public services and the subsequent characteristic features of public services, Lynn (2001) sought to bring together a range of academic insights and theoretical perspectives to examine 'administrative and managerial change' in public services. Drawing on the work of systems theorists such as Thompson (1967) and Parsons (1960), Lynn (2001) developed an analytic framework that identifies the different levels of governance in the public service. This model assists in conceptualizing how change at different levels affects and is affected by public service policy, decision making and strategic alignments.

The framework also indicates how broad changes filter through the different sites to shape the character and features of public sector organizations. In this model, governance arrangements are organized into a set of layers that differentiate the macro-level, the meso-level and the micro-level. Lynn (2001) characterizes these layers as belonging to the environmental, institutional, managerial and technical, operational levels of governance and the levels of governance provide a way of ordering and understanding the different contexts in which change occurs. The fifth level establishes a 'loop' in which strategic directions ranging from broad policy to programmatic results are tested against political judgements about the outcomes of change.

The framework serves to illustrate that change creates a dynamic set of relationships that operate not only internally within each level, but also between the different layers. Overall, the framework sought to situate and explain the different elements that comprise a governance system in order to develop a better understanding of the ways in which the application of administrative trends and reform measures on a global or international scale may affect the orientation of national

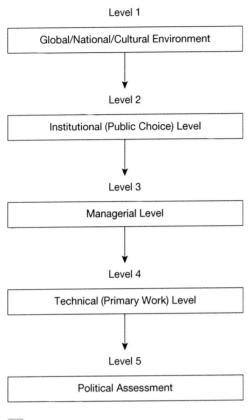

Level 1

| Global/National/Cultural Environment |

Level 2

| Institutional (Public Choice) Level |

Level 3

| Managerial Level |

Level 4

| Technical (Primary Work) Level |

Level 5

| Political Assessment |

Figure 4.1 *Governance levels.*

Source: Lynn (2001: 196).

public service organizations. It also demonstrates how these broad changes then influence the operation and management of public service organizations. Lynn (2001) proposed that national culture and public service institutions mediated the type of change that occurred.

Pollitt (2003) also adopts this framework to examine the role and transition of agencies of the public service and argues that it is crucial to examine public sector organizations according to the different dimensions contained in a multi-layered governance framework, as the cultural, managerial and technical aspects will be different according to particular contexts. Without accounting for differences at the various levels, Pollitt (2003) argues that there will be little understanding of the variables that may affect the performance and operation of agencies and the practicalities of managing complex public service organizations, deriving instead a 'general, abstracted' perception of organizational change devoid of context.

The schematic framework is very useful for delineating the different areas in which public services are influenced by broader trends in governance and those areas in which change results from a dynamic interplay of internal and external factors. The public service and public service organizations, then, are shaped by changes and influences in the cultural environment, in the institutional context and corresponding policy and organizational arrangements of the broader public service, by the managerial actions and responses to the influences in the other levels and by the interaction of context-specific factors within the different levels.

ENVIRONMENT FOR CHANGE AND REFORM

The first level of the framework is the Global/National/Cultural environment (Lynn 2001). This layer establishes the 'background' context to change, and includes nation-specific influences of national culture, but also encompasses broader cross-national and supranational effects of global economic paradigms and international trends in public policy (Pollitt 2003). Common themes in the discourse of broader trends in public service change are the effects of globalization, the pervasiveness of New Public Management (NPM) as the new orthodoxy of public service, a replacement of administrative theoretical constructs with economic ones, the global spread of increasing technological advances and new demands on governments to be more responsive to its citizenry – in order to bridge the disconnection with community (Kamensky 1996; O'Neill 2000).

The globalization of governance is often evidenced by the ubiquity of NPM practices and principles throughout the world. Osborne and Gaebler (1992) claim that the emergence of a new *global* paradigm of public services was evident in the early 1990s. Yeatman (1994) argues that global environmental factors affect the context of public service change and cites the changes in industrial organization to a post-Fordist, flexible specialization model as driving the change to a post-bureaucratic model of the public service. She also suggests that broad social change has driven the public service change agenda particularly as new roles of women have emerged and through the recognition of indigenous rights (Yeatman 1994). Common (1998) contends that supranational institutions such as the International Monetary Fund, the World Bank and the Organization for Economic Co-operation and Development (OECD) initiate and encourage global policy transfer through coercive means by tying development funds, aid and resources to particular, prescriptive policy formulations. Minogue (2001) similarly points to the formulaic policy prescriptions and management reforms that are characteristic of these institutions in their aid strategies.

New Public *Management* sought to transform public services into more efficient and effective managerial, financial and operational principles and practices. Public *administration* framed the operation of the public service as requiring the orderly application of rules, decisions and actions based on consistency and rationality and this approach denoted the traditional model of public service. However, over time the 'old' model of public administration was depicted as monocultural rather than culturally diverse, overly focused on rules and procedures (Dunleavy and Hood 1994; Hood 1998) and non-responsive to the changes wrought by globalization, new economic paradigms, technological advances and more complex community needs (Lynn 2001). Yeatman (1994) proposed that NPM responds to increased social and cultural complexity, greater uncertainty, and heightened expectations of citizenry in relation to their interaction with government, and has the ability to adapt to ongoing and continuous change. However, Stewart and Walsh (1992) contend that rather than implementing a model that achieves demonstrable and improved performance and financial outcomes, NPM has been adopted because of an ideological commitment to the economic, market competition model.

Public service change is argued to be driven by particular 'economic and ideological forces' (Smith *et al.* 1995: 22) in an environment of a fiscal and resource restraint (Zeffane and Macdonald 1993). The intertwining of the constructs of ideology and economy are a recurring theme in the literature examining forces for public service change. Bureaucracies came under pressure to adopt far-reaching changes with the increasing financial limits placed on government and public services (Crawford 1996; Bekker and Zouridis 1999). Economic and 'rational choice' paradigms replaced bureaucratic forms as a means of achieving efficiency. Traditional Weberian notions of bureaucracy relied on rule-driven, consistent decision making and achieving efficient practice based on the narrow specialization of tasks within a framework of the division of labour (Lane 1998). However, Cole (1988) argued that public services under the weight of increasing demand for services became politically insular and governed by 'self interest' rather than public interest, and grew inefficient through being positioned as a monopoly supplier of a range of services. It was posited that exposure to the discipline of the free market would create greater economic efficiencies for delivering public services (Cole 1988).

Continuing advances in information and communication technology also drove an agenda for greater integration of the tasks of a range of government providers in a more cost efficient and timely manner (Crawford 1996; Bekker and Zouridis 1999). Armstrong (1998) argues that information and communication technologies have made knowledge a major source of competitive advantage in the public service and these technologies can provide access to resources on a global scale. These new technologies establish 'new organizational logics' that incorporate virtual and self-organizing modes into more traditional organizational structures (Morgan 1997: 375). Technology is an important driver of public service change in that it realigns work organization, connects groups separated by distance and gives rise to new organizational forms such as boundaryless organizations linked through 'cyberspace'.

55

At the same time, however, governments were faced with greater pressure to respond to citizen demands for more sophisticated, timely and flexible service provision. Yeatman (1998) argued a difficulty arose in reconciling the managerial agenda of creating efficiencies through cost-cutting, downsizing and market prescriptions for service delivery with a requirement for the public sector to be responsive to a range of different stakeholders. Calls for increased attention to address political constituency issues have led to a concerted effort to include citizens in the political process. *Community engagement* concerns a new emphasis on providing framework for interaction and connection between governments and society (Adams and Hess 2001).

As a result of these pressures, 'community' has been included as a crucial stakeholder in calculations about the direction and nature of change in public services. Concomitantly, ways of consolidating community–government relations and codifying formal linkages have been embedded in institutional arrangements as part of the change agenda of public services. Community input through participation in political processes attempts to allow citizens to engage with government and have direct impact on government decision making and policy development (Bishop and Davis 2002). The unresolved tension, then, is to balance competing ideological positions of the withdrawal of public services from a range of service provision and public good delivery with greater demands on government by citizens to co-produce service and policy prescriptions for attending to social, economic and political needs.

Hede (1992: 23) considers that the managerial reforms of NPM are 'virtually universal'. However, NPM has contested antecedents (Hood 1991). Hood (1996: 151) suggests that the principles of NPM are far from universal and so should be more appropriately conceived of as a 'plural future'. In this way, competing agendas and differential and partial applications of NPM can be explained. Hood (1996) argues that public service change agendas are quite different due to different policy and programme emphases although he sees these differences as forming a consistent national reform response. Other authors have suggested that different sectors within a national system will also experience quite different approaches to implementing public service change agendas (Caiden 1999).

Harrinvirta (2000) observes the scale of change at a national level in public services has not been consistent as evidence indicates that changes have been transformational in some cases and incremental in other instances. While some nations implemented sweeping transformational changes throughout the public service as in the case of New Zealand (O'Neill 2000; Boston *et al.* 1996), other nations such as Norway responded with a more incremental approach, focusing on management and efficiency rather than 'rolling back the state' (Christensen and Laegreid 2003). Common (1998: 448) argues that NPM is not part of a globalized phenomena of public services policy transfer but NPM has only experienced piecemeal adoption across the globe and this indicates evidence of a 'global policy community that disperses NPM to receptive political and administrative elites in individual countries' rather than a coherent global strategy.

PUBLIC SERVICE CHANGE CONTEXT AND INSTITUTIONAL CHANGE

It was argued that the period from the mid-1800s until the latter part of the twentieth century was a time in which the operating principles of the public service remained fairly static (Peachment 1991). However, since that time change has been a prominent and consistent feature of public service operation and organization (O'Neill 2000). The changes to the public sector have been in response to the increasing pace and sequencing of the processes of change (Gersick 1991; Kessler and Chakrabarti 1996; Weick and Quinn 1999).

Hede (1992) suggested that the public sector over time has been characterized by three separate periods of reform. The three reform movements influencing the character of the contemporary public sector are identified as the merit reforms, equity reforms and the managerial reforms. Since the introduction of managerial reforms, it is argued that two other reform themes can be added and these are the market reforms (Hood 2001; Rhodes 2000) and reforms that brought the community back in to processes of government, or state–civil society mixes (Vigoda 2002; Wettenhall 2003). Keast and Brown (2003) suggest that the *managerial* reforms focused attention on reorienting and restructuring the internal operation of public service organizations and the latter *market* and *community* reforms related to externalizing aspects of public services. 'First wave' managerial reforms attempted to transfer private sector management practices and techniques into establishing a more efficiently operating public service, however, the 'second wave' reforms transferred public service operations to the private and community sector, incorporating entrepreneurial and market based approaches to solve the 'crisis' of inefficient and ineffective public administration.

Hede (1992) argued that the first set of reforms began in the mid-eighteenth century and involved a focus on abolishing political patronage. The problem of patronage was addressed through measures that created tighter centralized control over recruitment and selection processes (Parker 1942). The second major area of reform was the equity reforms that were contended to have begun in the 1950s and gained impetus in the 1970s (Hede 1992: 23). The equity reforms sought to eliminate discrimination and promote equality of opportunity in public sector employment and encourage a more diverse and representative workforce (Brown 1997). Equity reforms were formulated on the basis of removing barriers to employment opportunities, career progression, and the full range of job categories without regard to a person's race, gender, marital status, disability or ethnic origin. The aim was to secure greater representation in all employment categories for traditionally disadvantaged groups of employees. These reforms were achieved within the prevailing paradigm of public administration.

Hede (1992) contends the third area of reform; the managerial reforms moved public service activity away from a traditional emphasis on administration to management. Changes to the public service throughout most liberal democracies were premised on corporate management principles and the shift in public service operation and orientation has been substantial and consistent across most Western nations (Weller 1996: 1). Since the introduction and adoption of corporate management practices, marketization of public services and increasing reliance on other sectors to provide services has challenged traditional concepts of public service operation and service delivery (Wettenhall 2003; Brown and Keast 2003). Government failure was attributed to the general malaise of administration, bureaucracy and organization in public services.

A cause of widespread dissatisfaction with public administration as a means of organizing the activities of the state was the inability to respond quickly and flexibly to changes in the economic and social context and an inability to deliver policy and programmes appropriate to the changed circumstances. Minogue (2001) contends that bureaucratic inefficiency and discontent with the notion of an 'activist' state were the drivers of change. The outcomes of the welfare state and a highly planned bureaucratic system focused attention on the overarching paradigm that produced the negative conceptualization of the 'heavy hand' of the state.

Minogue (2001: 5) suggested that the criticisms of the development of welfare state were:

- the state was unresponsive but all-pervasive and fostered citizen dependency rather than self-sufficiency (invasive state);
- the role of the state had become all encompassing over time and was unable to carry out functions and responsibilities effectively (over-extended state); and
- the state had become captured by elite groups that used the state to serve their own interests rather than the public interest (private interest state).

The cumulative effect of this discord was an appeal for better governance, a conversion from public service provision to market provision to gain efficiencies and the transformation of bureaucratic processes to managerial principles.

Public services in all OECD countries came under pressure to change in the 1980s and it is argued they responded to the reform agenda in broadly similar ways (Harrinvirta 2000). Market and deregulationist prescriptions for the operation of the public service resulted in tighter budgetary regimes, a shift from an emphasis on market failure to government failure (Harrinvirta 2000) and a concomitant move from using the resources of government to achieve social equality to a focus on mutual obligation between citizens and government (Giddens 1999). An ongoing and continuous construct of change rather than a one-off and episodic change agenda was a prominent feature of academic discussion about the public service and public service organizations during the late twentieth and early twenty-first century.

The shift from public administration to public management in the 1980s signalled the emergence of the large public service change agenda that has gained momentum from that time. The relative stability of the public service for the most part of the nineteenth century may have led to the image of a public service with an inability to proactively anticipate and make strategic calculations about change. Issues and challenges to public services centre on the rapid pace of change in policy, governance and practice, meeting demands for governments to engage with citizens in new and more deliberative ways and operating within an environment in which cost-cutting and limited authority and reach of government affects the capacity and capability of government to react to calls for greater accountability and responsiveness.

INSTITUTIONAL LEVEL CHANGE

The framework outlined by Lynn (2001) identified the institutional level of governance as a significant arena in which the mode of public sector organization was pertinent to understanding change. Accordingly, at this level, issues of governance and the formal and legislatively driven relations between government and public service organizations take on greater prominence (Lynn 2001; Pollitt 2003). Lynn (2001: 195) suggests that the institutional level comprises elements of both formal authority through legislative mandate and influence through 'broad strategic alignments' with an array of stakeholders, or 'publics'. The institutional level of the public service includes the infrastructure of government and bureaucracy (Christensen *et al.* 2002), political systems of government including rule-making apparatus and routines of political behaviour (March and Olsen 1989). Lynn *et al.* (2001) contend that institutional level comprises hierarchical executive structures including bureaux, agencies, departments and commissions, together with the set of authorities that come from applying rules and resources to activities of government. Geva-May (2002) includes in the institutions of governance those constitutional political arrangements such as cameral/bicameral legislature, unitary/federal systems and executive government.

At an institutional level, Lindquist (2000: 150) suggests that the shape of public service reform and change is contingent on 'government ideology, intergovernmental relations and negotiations, trade regimes and deficit reduction strategies'.

Institutional level change occurs through altering legislation developed to define the prevailing governance arrangements and through shifting strategic preferences by aligning with different combinations of stakeholders. Legislation in

of autonomous agencies as well as the adoption of community-centred approaches to governance and, policy and service delivery. These distinct areas have been conceptualized as the state, the market and civil society.

The introduction of the community into the mix indicated a shift away from government-centric approaches to policy and services delivery. As Brown and Keast (2003) observe:

> Increasingly governments are looking to move beyond the utilisation of the community as a 'gap filler' to capitalise on the networks of social capital located in communities as a way of both enhancing policy development and implementation and, connection.

The shift to community and networks then, signalled a move from relying on 'traditional integration mechanisms of the hierarchy and market' to a system that relies on networks of relationships built on common values and trust (Brown and Keast 2003). Denhardt and Denhardt (2000) reconceptualize the role of the public service in this more community-centric and relational approach as 'serving' rather than 'steering'.

A further elaboration of the incorporation of new forms of public services is the focus on integration at a whole of government level. The concern in this area translates into calls for more coordinated activity and 'joined up' or holistic government (6, *et al.* 2002). Waterfield (1997) suggests that government is responding to institutional change by forming alliances and being involved in partnering arrangements with other levels of government, business and the community. These new forms of public service activity and organization are based on relationships built between different organizational members and other stakeholders rather than enacted through formalized authority of position and location within organizational hierarchy or legally mandated through contractual arrangements. The shift to networks of relationships and integrated governance structures in order to deliver services, policy and decision making were driven by systems change, demographic change and changing paradigms of what constitutes public interest and public good.

DRIVERS OF INSTITUTIONAL CHANGE

Contemporary public services comprise complex interrelationships between a large array of stakeholders consisting of actors from government, business and community sectors, making easy identification of the origin and influence of a set of change drivers elusive. Christensen *et al.* (2002) suggest that historic national influences affect the outcomes of institutional change, such that the political and social machinery already in place shape the kinds of response to the reform agenda at an institutional level in different countries.

O'Neill (2000) contends that significant drivers of institutional change include the broad influences of globalization, a 'disaffected citizenry', blurring of the boundaries between private, public and community sector organizations and advances in technology. Waterfield (1997) also puts forward a similar set of drivers of change and suggests that financial cutbacks, restructuring on a global scale, increasing technological advances and changing labour demographics and higher expectations for services on the part of citizens have fuelled the agenda for change. Demographic changes wrought by the increasing proportion of older workers, greater longevity and increased cultural diversity also drove change (O'Neill 2000).

Since the 1980s there have been declining numbers employed in the public service as a result of reform and restructuring of public services. A study by the OECD indicates that there is an ageing of the public service workforce and that public services are not employing younger workers, as there is an absence of 16–24-year-old workers and a decline in the numbers of those in 25–34 year age group (OECD 2000b). These demographics show that there are global trends in recruitment and employment in public services. Implications for managing public services are significant. The profile and pool of prospective senior managers may be constrained, training and development will need to be reconfigured and the traditional career pattern of promotion from within through an internal labour market will be disrupted.

Davis (1996) argues that changes in the public service have been driven by proponents of the public choice theory who posit that the efficient operation of the public sector should be characterized by the separation of management and policy from the delivery of public goods and services. According to the public choice model, the traditional public sector model is argued to operate on a principle of self-interest at the expense of efficient and effective public services (Davis 1996: 307). Public choice proponents drove the agenda for marketization and contracting out public provision of services ostensibly in order to insulate the state from fiscal burdens and overreliance on public provision of services. However, the recent shift to community-centred approaches to public service organization indicates that the reach of economic models may have limits in public service contexts.

Schwartz (1997), in comparing New Zealand and North American models of public service change, found that broad changes in the institutional arena were driven by an agenda to change individual's behaviour at a public service organizational level. O'Neill (2000) argues that institutions respond to disruptive change by either 'circling the wagons' and resisting change or using the opportunity to transform public service structures and systems.

The trajectory of reform from less bureaucratic structures to more flexible, entrepreneurial structures, is not a straight line, nor is there a clear-cut delineation between deregulated and regulated models. The rhetoric of deregulation and choice masks the inherent contradictions of the new mode of governance. Christensen and Laegreid (2003) argue that the model of NPM is a hybrid that 'prescribes centralization, regulation, and control as well as decentralization, flexibility and autonomy' and the forces will play out in different ways across time, country location and policy context. Thus the national setting and policy environment as well as temporal location establishes important variations in the way that broad public service trends and reforms are taken up at an institutional level.

The shift, then, in institutions of public service may be to a position of re-regulation rather than deregulation. Deregulation under NPM is manifest in exhortations to looser controls, letting managers manage and adopting market mechanisms rather than bureaucratic controls to allocate public goods and services and may simply be about different forms of regulation with new types of control over competition, pricing, monopoly supply and service (Hood and Scott 1996: 341). With the rise of the market approach to governance, greater prominence was accorded to an economic model. However, the tension between markets and economically rational behaviour rather than administratively rational behaviour and working to a 'public purpose' creates competing models rather than a 'seamless' approach to managing under principles of NPM. Hybrid forms are argued to arise when public services are confronted with competing demands to be efficient yet accountable to a wide range of stakeholders, financially focused on the bottom line yet quality driven, consultative with community and egalitarian yet required to meet narrow economic interests (Waterhouse et al. 2003).

The managerialist agenda of New Public Management was more than a set of techniques to provide greater system efficiencies, but a results-oriented strategy relying on the achievement of cultural and ideological changes. Marketization approaches consolidated this trend. However, as public service organizations shed bureaucratic and vertical structures for more horizontal and relationship-oriented approaches, there arose a need for new types of governance arrangements in place to respond to change. Cross-cutting initiatives in public services were introduced to resolve problems of fragmentation and poor or inappropriate service delivery (Flynn 1999). Common (1998: 448) argues that the pace of institutional change has been 'gradual' rather than 'radical' as evidenced by the *ad hoc* adoption of NPM practices and the resilience of bureaucratized processes and ways of operating.

However, the reduction in the role and reach of central government and the retreat from government service delivery (Wettenhall 2003) indicates a fundamental shift in government that has played out in changes to the institutions of government, in public service organizations and their day-to-day management, operation and service delivery.

ORGANIZATIONAL LEVEL CHANGE

Shifts in broader public service policy, programmes and service provision have resulted in a discourse of continuous and continual change as a backdrop of organizational life. The third and fourth governance levels outlined by Lynn (2001) encapsulate change within public service organizations and comprise the managerial and technical levels. Managerial level governance involves the interaction of organizational actors and organization structure to attain strategic alignment (Lynn 2001). Pollitt (2003) contends that the managerial level considers responses to the reform strategies in intra-organizational and inter-organizational arenas. A crucial aspect is the management of relations between the different organizational actors. According to Lynn (2001) organizational change is translated from the broad trends adopted in the institutional level for implementation in this managerial level. The pace and character of change is reliant on how managers broker relationships and balance competing interests in the organization, management, administration and core business of each public service organization.

The primary work level is concerned with the operational aspects of governance. This level is concerned with work 'on the ground' or at the practitioner level and comprises the nexus of programme and delivery. It involves the strategic positioning of public service organizational members and service clients or recipients (Lynn 2001).

PUBLIC SECTOR CHANGE CONTEXT AND ORGANIZATIONAL CHANGE

Patrickson and Bamber (1995) argue for multi-dimensional model of organizational change incorporating managerial, technical and cultural aspects in order to understand the different organizational dimensions in which change occurs. This conceptualization accords with the managerial and primary work level outlined in Lynn's (2001) governance levels, but adds a cultural dimension. Concepts pertaining to organizational change include cultural pluralism, involvement, participation, cooperation, motivation and leadership. These thematic areas are discussed in the following chapter.

The scope and reach of organizational change is not bounded by organizational borders but also link to influences in the broader political and economic context. Change in public service organizations is mirrored by the volatility experienced in all industry sectors. The business environment has also undergone significant changes. A study of organizational change indicated that downsizing, rationalization/restructuring were the most prevalent responses to change as 66 per cent of organizations had undertaken change in these areas in the three-year period covered by the study (Smith *et al.* 1995).

Despite the use of terms such as paradigm shift and transformational change to describe the 'state of play' in public services, there is less collective enthusiasm to suggest that public service organizations themselves have undergone concomitant sweeping changes. There is concern that public services may be resistant to change

65

or only be capable of small-scale incremental changes (Harrinvirta 2000; Waterfield 1997). This seeming contradiction may be partially explained by the fact that broad changes and trends may not filter down to the lower levels of the governance framework, particularly the technical, primary work level. It may be that lower levels of public service organizations remain by-and-large untouched by large-scale change, especially in the lowest level of the governance framework where the day-to-day work of organizational members may remain unaffected by broader change. It may be the case also that incremental change adjusts organizational members' perceptions such that they do not perceive that significant changes have occurred and in order to understand the scope and degree of change there is a need to examine shifts over time.

Terms such as resistance to change, traditional public service culture and bureaucratic culture (Harrinvirta 2000; Waterfield 1997) are used in relation to describing public service organizations to infer that dramatic or far-reaching change has not occurred or to convey that the 'modernizing' project has failed. This research also alerts to the importance of culture in calculations about implementing and managing successful change initiatives.

POLITICAL ASSESSMENT

The fifth and final governance layer is political assessment. This level is concerned with establishing the context for assessing decisions and actions in public services on a political level (Lynn 2001). At this level, judgements about the effectivity of programmes are made (Pollitt 2003). Political assessment is not simply about performance measurement, however; it includes criteria that articulate performance measurement with judgements about the political efficacy of programmes and organizations.

Aucoin (1990) suggests that governments are continually required to balance financial considerations, particularly those emanating from constrictions in international monetary movements and 'unrelenting demands' for government provision and delivery of public goods and services. These tensions have been resolved in contemporary public services by establishing an overarching framework coupling public choice and managerialist prescriptions for public service operating principles and action (Aucoin 1990). In this way, the type of political assessment pursued will be driven by the prevailing political context. Contemporary public choice and NPM models seek to rein-in bureaucratic power and replace bureaucratic systems with managerial systems that allow more flexible organizational arrangements and thus require formulation of specific change agendas that align with and reinforce those frameworks and principles.

Change agendas and programmes may require more than rational planning and purposeful action. March and Olsen (1989: 31) caution that 'There are social costs when competent expert advice is ignored because it is given at a bad time, or in an incomprehensible way, or so that it offends a key political actor or belief'. In this way, political context is also a very important component of developing a change agenda and concomitantly, political assessment is crucial for calculating and evaluating the receptivity and purchase of change programmes and recommendations for reform.

CONCLUSIONS

The nature of change in public services and PSOs has been characterized as transformational and resulting in the emergence of a new public service paradigm. This chapter has examined from an historical perspective the processes of change that have brought about these circumstances. The environment for change at macro-meso- and micro-levels, ranging from the broad global arena to internal micro-organizational operations, has been explored. Contextual factors that shape change in the public sector are increasingly wide-scale and global. Greater economic integration and internationalization of policy and management prescriptions for public services have played a significant part in large-scale adoption of change along with increasing technology. However, the influence of more localized factors is also at work. Organizational and managerial context are also significant levels, however, as these deliver the day-to-day policy, programmes and services. Public service change crucially affects communities and ultimately, affects the quality of life of the citizenry and as such requires careful integration of contextual factors with internal organizational requirements for change.

The convergence thesis, while having wide appeal as an explanation for the widespread adoption of New Public Management principles, has not demonstrated that local factors are less relevant to calculations about the shape of public services following change efforts. For example, the universalizing tendencies of NPM are thwarted when market prescriptions are applied to public service provision in developing countries that have no local economy in which privatization may occur.

A governance framework was utilized to establish a way of ordering the multiplex and often overwhelming plethora of changes occurring and to clarify the conceptualization of change by separating out the different levels at which public service change takes place. Isolating the different levels within the governance framework allows explanation of the situation that while change may be pervasive within particular contexts, other levels may experience little change. Moreover, understanding the political level alerts to the situation that there may be ideological rather than rational calculations in response to the change context. Implementation is not just about choosing and implementing a programme of change that reflects 'best practice' but understanding political contingencies that may affect the successful implementation of a change programme.

67

The external context of globalization, trends in public sector governance, and perceptions of the import and impact of changes to the ways the public service operates are important considerations in change initiatives.

DISCUSSION QUESTIONS

1   How compelling is the evidence for the convergence thesis? Use examples to illustrate your arguments.
2   Choose a change initiative in a public service or public sector organization with which you are familiar. Use the governance levels framework to identify the context(s) of change, the drivers of change and the different levels of change.
3   Is there evidence of a new paradigm emerging within public services or public service organization?

REFERENCES

6, P., D. Leat, K. Selzer, and G. Stoker (2002) *Toward Holistic Government. A New Reform Agenda*. London: Palgrave.

Adams, D. and M. Hess (2001) Community in public policy: Fad or foundation? *Australian Journal of Public Administration* 60: 13–23.

Armstrong, A. (1998) A comparative analysis: New public management, *Australian Journal of Public Administration* 57(2): 12–24.

Aucoin, P. (1990) Administrative reform in public management: Paradigms, principles, paradoxes and pendulums, *Governance* 3(3): 115–37.

Bekker, V. and S. Zouridis (1999) Electronic service delivery in public administration, *International Review of Administrative Sciences* 65: 13–195.

Bishop, P. and G. Davis (2002) Mapping public participation in policy choices, *Australian Journal of Public Administration* 6(1): 14–29.

Boston, J., J. Martin, J. Pallot. and P. Walsh (1996) *Public Management, The New Zealand Model*. Auckland: Oxford University Press.

Brown, K. (1997) Evaluating equity outcomes in state public sectors: a comparison of three housing agencies, *Australian Journal of Public Administration* 56(4): 57–66.

Brown, K. and R. Keast (2003) Citizen-government engagement: community connection through networked arrangements, *Asian Journal of Public Administration* 25(1): 107–32.

Caiden, G. E. (1999) Administrative reform: proceed with caution, *International Journal of Public Administration* 15: 85–102.

Christensen, T. and P. Laegreid (2003) Governmental Autonomization and Control – the Norwegian way. Paper presented to the *7th International Research Symposium on Public Management*, Hong Kong, 2–4 October.

Christensen, T., P. Laegreid and L. Wise (2002) Transforming administrative policy, *Public Administration* 80(1): 153–78.

Cole, R. (1988) The public sector: The conflict between accountability and efficiency, *Australian Journal of Public Administration*, XLVII, 223–32.

Common, R. K. (1998) Convergence and transfer: A review of the globalisation of public management, *International Journal of Public Sector Management* 11(6): 440–50.

Crawford, P. (1996) *The Serious Business of Governing*. Marrickville, NSW: Hale and Iremonger.

Davis, G. (1996) Making sense of difference? Public choice, politicians and bureaucratic change in America and Australia. In G. Davis and P. Weller (eds) *New Ideas, Better Government*. St Leonards: Allen & Unwin.

Denhardt, R. and J. Denhardt (2000) The new public service: Serving rather than steering, *Public Administration Review* 60(6): 549–59.

Dunleavy, P. and C. Hood (1994) From Old Public Administration to New Public Management, *Public Management and Money*, July–September: 9–16.

Flynn, N. (1999) Modernising British Government, *Parliamentary Affairs* 52(4): 582–97.

Gersick, C. J. G. (1991) Revolutionary change theories: A multilevel exploration of the punctuated equilibrium paradigm, *Academy of Management Review* 16: 10–36.

Geva-May, I. (2002) From theory to practice: Policy analysis, cultural bias and organizational arrangements, *Public Management Review* 4(4): 581–91.

Giddens, A. (1999) *The Third Way: The Renewal of Social Democracy*. Malden, MA: Polity Press.

Harrinvirta, M. O. (2000) *Strategies of Public Sector Reform in the OECD Countries: A Companion*. The Finnish Society of Sciences and Letters and the Finnish Academy of Science and Letters.

Hede, A. (1992) Equity reform in public administration: A longitudinal study of executive attitudes, *International Journal of Public Sector Management* 5(1): 23–9.

Hood, C. (1991) Public management for all seasons, *Public Management* 69: 3–19.

Hood, C. (1996) Beyond progressivism: A new 'global paradigm' in public management, *International Journal of Public Administration* 19(2): 151–77.

Hood, C. (1998) *The Art of the State: Culture, Rhetoric, and Public Management*. Oxford: Oxford University Press.

Hood, C. (2001) Public service managerialism: Onwards and upwards, or 'Trobriand cricket' again? *The Political Quarterly* 72(3): 300–9.

Hood, C. and C. Scott (1996) Bureaucratic regulation and new public management in the United Kingdom: mirror-image developments? *Journal of Law and Society* 23(3): 321–45.

Kamensky, J. (1996) Role of the 'reinventing government' movement in federal management reform, *Public Administration Review* 56(3): 247–55.

Keast, R. and K. Brown (2003) Experiments in social diversity. In E. Anderson, E. Smith and J. Teicher (eds), *Toward Public Value? Management & Employment for Outcomes Conference*. Melbourne, 24–5 November.

Kessler, E. H. and A. K. Chakrabarti (1996) Innovation speed: A conceptual model of contents, antecedents, and outcomes, *Academy of Management Review* 21(4): 1143–91.

Kettl, D. (1997) The global revolution in public management: Driving themes, missing links, *Journal of Policy Analysis and Development* 16(3): 446–62.

Kettl, D. (2000) *The Global Public Management Revolution*. Washington, DC: The Brookings Institute.

Lane, J. (1998) *The Public Sector: Concepts, Models and Approaches*. London: Sage.

Lindquist, E. (2000) Reconceiving the center: Leadership, strategic review and coherence in public sector reform. In *Government of the Future*. Paris: OECD.

Lynn, L. E., Jr (2001) Globalization and administrative reform: What is happening in theory? *Public Management Review* 3(2): 191–208.

Lynn, L., C. Heinrich and C. Hill (2001) *Improving Governance: A New logic for Empirical Research*. Washington, DC: Georgetown University Press.

March, J. G. and J. P. Olsen (1989) *Rediscovering Institutions: The Organizational Basis of Politics*. New York: Free Press.

Minogue, M. (2001) The internationalization of new public management. In W. McCourt and M. Minogue (eds), *The Internationalization of Public Management*. Cheltenham, UK: Edward Elgar.

Morgan, G. (1997) *Images of Organization* (2nd edn). Thousand Oaks, CA: Sage.

OECD (2000) *Recent Developments and Future Challenges in Human Resource Management in OECD Member Countries*. Background Paper by the Secretariat, Paris: OECD.

O'Neill, R. J., Jr (2000) Forces of change in the public sector, *The Public Manager* 29(3): 4–5.

Osborne, D. and T. Gaebler (1992) *Reinventing Government: How the Entrepreneurial Spirit is Transforming the Public Sector*. Reading, MA: Addison-Wesley.

Parker, R. (1942) *Public Service Recruitment in Australia*. Melbourne: Melbourne University Press.

Parsons, T. (1960) *Structure and Process in Modern Societies*. New York: The Free Press of Glencoe.

70

Patrickson, M. and G. Bamber (1995) Introduction. In M. Patrickson, V. Bamber and G. Bamber (eds), *Organisational Change Strategies, Case Studies of Human Resource and Industrial Relations Issues*. Melbourne: Longman.

Peachment, A. (1991) Reforming the public sector: Global trends, local action. In A. Peachment (ed.), *The Business of Government Western Australia 1983–1990*. Sydney: Federation Press.

Pollitt, C. (2003) Agencies, Apples and Pears: Mapping the Agency Debate. Paper presented to the *7th International Research Symposium on Public Management*, Hong Kong, 2–4 October.

Pollitt, C. and C. Talbot (eds) (2003) *Unbundled Government – A Critical Analysis of the Global Trend to Agencies, Quangos and Contractualisation*. London: Routledge.

Rhodes, R. (2000) New Labour's civil service: Summing up joining-up, *The Political Quarterly* 71: 151–66.

Schwartz, H. M. (1994) Public choice theory and public choices: Bureaucrats and state reorganization in Australia, Denmark, New Zealand and Sweden in the 1980s, *Administration & Society* 26(1): 48–77.

Schwartz, H. M. (1997) Reinventing and retrenchment: Lessons from the application of the New Zealand model to Alberta, Canada, *Journal of Policy and Analysis and Management* 16(3): 405–22.

Smith, V. C., A. S. Sohal and S. D'Netto (1995) Successful strategies for managing change, *International Journal of Manpower* 16(5/6): 22–33.

Stewart, J. and K. Walsh (1992) Change in the management of public services, *Public Administration* 70: 499–518.

Thompson, J. D. (1967) *Organizations in Action: Social Science Bases and Administrative Theory*. New York: McGraw-Hill.

Vigoda, E. (2002) From responsiveness to collaboration: Governance, citizens, and the next generation of public administration, *Public Administration Review* 62(5): 527–40.

Waterfield, S. (1997) The challenges facing provincial public services, *Canadian Public Administration* 40(2): 204–17.

Waterhouse, J., K. Brown and C. Flynn (2003) Change management practices: Is a hybrid model a better alternative for public sector agencies? *International Journal of Public Sector Management* 16(3): 230–41.

Weick, K. and R. E. Quinn (2000) Organizational change and development, *Annual Review Psychology* 50: 361–86.

Welch, E. and W. Wong (1998) Public administration in a global context: bridging the gaps of theory and practice between Western and non-Western nations, *Public Administration Review* 58(1): 40–9.

Welch, E. and W. Wong (2001) Effects of global pressures on public bureaucracy: modelling a new theoretical framework, *Administration & Society* 33(4): 371–402.

Weller, P. (1996) The university of public sector reform: Ideas, meanings, strategies. In G. Davis and P. Weller (eds), *New Ideas, Better Government*. St Leonards: Allen & Unwin.

Wettenhall, R. (2003) Three-way categorisations, hybrids and intersectoral mixes in the governance equation, *Asian Journal of Public Administration* 25(1): 57–86.

Worrall, L., C. L. Cooper and F. Campbell-Jamison, (2000) The impact of organizational change on the work experiences and perceptions of public sector managers, *Personnel Review* 29(5): 613–36.

Yeatman, A. (1994) The reform of public management: An overview, *Australian Journal of Public Administration* 53(3): 287–95.

Yeatman, A. (1998) Trends and opportunities in the public sector: A critical assessment, *Australian Journal of Public Administration* 57(4): 138–48.

Young, D. (2000) Alternative models of government-nonprofit sector relations: Theoretical and international perspectives, *Nonprofit and Voluntary Sector Quarterly* 29(1): 149–72.

Zeffane, R. and D. Macdonald (1993) Uncertainty, participation and alienation: Lessons for workplace restructuring, *International Journal of Sociology and Social Policy* 13(5/6): 22–52.

FURTHER READING

Governance and public policy

Lynn, L., C. Heinrich and C. Hill (2001) *Improving Governance: A New Logic for Empirical Research*. Washington, DC: Georgetown University Press.

The book outlines and analyses a framework for examining governance at the different cultural, institutional and organizational levels. It examines and explains interactions between different stakeholders and political activities between these different levels.

Pollitt, C. and C. Talbot (eds) (2003) *Unbundled Government – A Critical Analysis of the Global Trend to Agencies, Quangos and Contractualisation*. London: Routledge.

Edited book that explores the movement to shift service and programme delivery from within public service to external organizations. Contributions examine aspects of the process of divesting the state of responsibility for service and policy delivery from the bureaucracy.

Public management models

Boston, J., J. Martin, J. Pallot and P. Walsh (1996) *Public Management, The New Zealand Model*. Auckland: Oxford University Press.

This book examines the distinctive 'New Zealand model' of public service reform and traces the transformation of public services and public service organizations under the auspices of New Public Management.

Kettl, D. (2000) *The Global Public Management Revolution*. Washington, DC: The Brookings Institute.

This book examines the transformation of public services as a global and globalizing phenomenon. It traces the antecedents of this paradigm shift and suggests that globalization and devolution have combined to create a new model of public service.

Chapter 5

Organizational culture and managing change in public service organizations

LEARNING OBJECTIVES

By the end of the chapter you should be able to:

- classify and evaluate different ways of identifying organizational culture;
- understand how organizational culture affects change management; and
- identify elements and features of the culture of public service organizations.

KEY POINTS OF THIS CHAPTER

- Organizational culture is neither easily defined nor determined.
- Organizational culture is recognized as an important component of change but there is debate about how to understand the impact of culture.
- A three-perspective approach to understanding cultural change is introduced to provide a framework that allows a single organization to be viewed in multiple ways.
- There are four central features of culture that recur throughout the breadth of literature about organizational culture, namely culture is stable; it is an unconscious process; members give it meaning; and it is based on shared understandings.
- The culture of public service organizations is different from that of business organizations but there are commonalities in working with culture in terms of general principles of change management.

KEY TERMS

- **Organizational culture** – the shared ideas, customs, assumptions, expectations, traditions, values and understandings that determine the way employees will behave.
- **Integration, differentiation and fragmentation perspectives** – these outline and identify respectively cultural similarities in organizations, oppositional cultural groups and multiple and conflicting cultural views.

This chapter sets out to define and explore the concept of organizational culture and determine the different ways of understanding organizational culture in order to better comprehend the management of change. It situates the discussion about organizational culture within the broader debate relating to the management of change in public services and public service organizations as culture is recognized as an important component of any change initiative. Identification of organizational culture allows insight into the type of organizational response to change, the receptivity of organizational members to change and the ways in which successful organizational change initiatives may be shaped and implemented.

Change agendas involve typically structural and strategic adjustments to organizations, but it is the 'intangible' components of those organizations that may yield the greatest threat to or facilitation of organizational change. The dimensions of change require consideration of these intangible aspects in order to understand more comprehensively those factors that promote or influence successful change initiatives. Research about change and the management of change is investigated to determine whether the character, values and dimensions of public services and public service organizations that make up culture affect organizational change initiatives in particular ways. Prior research is also examined to establish whether the public sector, because of its location apart from the private and third or community sectors, has a specific cultural orientation that requires different treatment in implementing change. The role of organizational culture is explored and models and definitions of organizational culture are put forward to assemble and categorize the competing perspectives about culture, change and performance. The cultural factors that may promote successful change are examined.

THE ROLE OF ORGANIZATIONAL CULTURE

Organizational culture is a crucial aspect of change management initiatives, but it does not comprise the entire change problematic. Cultural values, while important indicators of the meaning and principles ascribed to public endeavour, also vie with the institutional, governance and political-administrative arrangements comprising structures, systems and means-ends objectives to describe and bound the characteristics of the domain of public activity (Veenswijk and Hakvoort 2002).

However, the critical role of culture may be evidenced when cultural elements are ignored in the introduction of change programmes. Lawson and Ventriss (1992) argue that change initiatives become 'stuck' if the culture of an organization is not well understood, while Patrickson and Bamber (1995) suggest that organizational change will have little impact or effect if the existing culture of the organization is not altered as part of the change strategy. Accordingly, any organizational change initiative should be cognizant of the impact of organizational culture in relation to the propensity and ability for an organization to change. The existing cultural dimensions of the organization need to be identified. In order to achieve a successful change effort there is a requirement to work systematically with the set of values, beliefs and behaviours that 'embody' organizational culture to enable change to occur. Distinguishing elements of organizational culture and understanding the impact of culture are important aspects of implementing organizational change initiatives.

However, while organizational culture is an important consideration in developing a programme of change, there appears to be little consensus about how culture should be understood and the ways in which culture might interact and influence a particular change programme. Organization theory and theoretical constructs within political science offer differing insights into the dimensions of culture.

In organizational development literature, organizational culture is conceptualized as the key to unlocking the potential to reap substantial organizational benefits. Among the claims highlighting the importance of organizational culture in organizational development research, it is conceived as a powerful tool to assist in achieving greater organizational productivity (Kopelman et al. 1990), improving organizational performance (Schwartz and Davis 1981; Wilkins and Ouchi 1983) and promoting organizational effectiveness (Weiner 1988). Langan-Fox and Tan (1997) contend that organizational culture improves economic performance, enhances employee commitment and establishes a competitive advantage for organizations. In this context, understanding organizational culture is considered a crucial element in improving organizational performance. By understanding and working with the culture of organizations, the prospect is that benefits will accrue in terms of financial and business rewards.

Political science approaches suggest that an understanding of culture allows greater insight into the political and power dimensions of public activity. Inclusion of these contextual and environmental factors permit incorporation of an organizational analysis with broader social considerations and, at the same time connects organizational processes and structures with organizational members' principles and belief systems (Hood 1995). The latter aspect is a significant departure from organizational theory where the link is between internal individual beliefs and values that are translated into external group actions and behaviour. According to

Hood (1995) structure and process are implicated in change in addition to cultural aspects. Identifying and working with public culture in this conceptualization is concerned with explaining divergence from outcomes anticipated by change agendas and pointing to sites of possible instability to allow programme corrections so as to avoid change implementation failure.

The project of identifying the existing culture of an organization, making calculations about whether the culture will assist or hinder a change agenda and then changing that culture to one that might achieve greater productivity, economic efficiency or support a change initiative is extremely complex. There is enormous difficulty in translating the promise of organizational culture to the reality of organizational life. Organizational culture is a problematic concept to define, identify, and understand. How to identify what an organization's culture is, how to work with culture, what needs to be altered to change an organizational culture and what the outcomes should be is a complicated area to interrogate. Moreover, there is a lack of consensus in relation to whether the culture of an organization can be intervened upon to achieve programmatic change (Ogbonna and Harris 1998). However, the literature acknowledges that organizational change and culture change are both potential vehicles to enhance organizational performance and effectivity (Lawson and Ventriss 1992; Schein 1985). Pollitt (2003) argues that culture is an important aspect of providing a means for uncovering localized norms, principles and common understandings to construct and reconstruct analytical categories of public service change.

Different ways of analysing corporate culture are manifest in the variety of approaches to understanding: how an organization is viewed, what the values of an organization are, and what an organization is. The proliferation of models gives an indication of the diversity of frameworks available to analyse corporate change. The following discussion provides some insight into the array of models available to understand the elements of corporate culture and how change strategies might impact on the organizational climate and performance. Understanding the existing culture of an organization also allows some insight into how organizations might transform or be changed through change programmes.

MODELS OF ORGANIZATIONAL CULTURE

The appearance of corporate culture in the 1980s and early 1990s brought greater consideration of underlying precepts to the study of organizations. O'Toole's (1985: 275) definition suggests that the culture of an organization is constituted by the behaviour of organizational members when he states:

> Culture is the unique whole – comprising shared ideas, customs, assumptions, expectations, philosophy, traditions, mores, values and

understandings — that determines how a group of people will behave. When one talks of a corporation's culture, one means that complex interrelated whole of standardized, institutionalized habitual behavior that characterizes that firm.

It is clear from this definition that homogeneity of action forms the basis of corporate culture and establishes a common set of activities from which a particular type of culture of an organization may be outlined.

Other authors (Green 1988; Peters and Waterman 1982; Deal and Kennedy 1982) suggested that organizational culture resides in the intangible aspects of an organization. Peters and Waterman (1982) and Deal and Kennedy (1982) contended that a single culture could be identified through discovering core values and beliefs particular to each organization. Green (1988: 6) defined corporate culture as:

> The amalgam of shared beliefs, values, assumptions, significant meanings, myths, rituals and symbols that are held to be distinctive for each and every organization.

In these definitions, behavioural traits are subsumed under a notion that culture resides in non-material aspects of the organization and specifically relates to principles and mores embedded within organizations. Moreover, this definition signals that the notion that behaviour is a critical component of culture is not universal in definitions of organizational culture.

Schein (1985) argued that organizational culture is the basic underlying assumptions of people within organizations that are manifested in espoused values, behaviour and organizational artefacts. The definition put forward by Schein (1985) encompasses all aspects of organizational life, from material objects, actions and moral precepts. It presupposes that all aspects of organizational life are involved in the production of culture.

In all these conceptualizations, the premise underpinning these works is that high performing firms possess a corporate culture that is critical in accomplishing business success. As Deal and Kennedy (1982: 19) proposed, the articulation of corporate culture to organizational activities creates '. . . a new law of business life: In Culture there is Strength'. The corollary to this is that poor performing or under-performing companies needed to change their culture in order to achieve better performance. Change management strategies in this context were premised on the notion that organizational culture should be altered and, in order to achieve this, employees' beliefs and behaviours needed to be reoriented.

While not united on the characteristics and features of organizational culture, early work on organizational culture posited that a distinct organizational culture for each organization could be identified. The notion of a singular, unifying culture that can be discerned and therefore manipulated to change the way an organization performed was a key construct in the conceptualization of organizational culture. The early accounts of corporate culture assumed an orderly distribution of shared behaviours, beliefs and values held by employees within an organization which can then be identified and manipulated in order to achieve improved corporate performance. However, later work acknowledged that organizational culture operated in diverse and complex ways with often unpredictable outcomes and effects (Martin 1992; Bate 1994). There still remains little agreement whether an organization will have a single, strong culture or multiple and diverse cultures. A common thread throughout the early work was that corporate culture was an important tool to manage corporate change and this theme continues throughout more contemporary writing on organizational culture.

CULTURE AND ORGANIZATIONAL LIFE

Schein (1985) suggested that culture forms from collective meaning assumed by organizational members about organizational life and resides in different organizational layers, from material objects within an organization to the more abstract levels of concepts, ideals and assumptions. Schein (1985) proposed that culture could be analysed on three different levels. First, the visible artefacts such as manner of dress, public documents and office layout indicate the culture of an organization. The second level of analysis is the values that cause organizational members to act as they do. Schein (1985) contended that the third level is where culture may be more accurately understood as the underlying assumptions are learned responses that originate in espoused values.

   Through the consideration of Schein's (1985) third level of culture, the underlying assumptions of organizational members, the potential for difficulties to emerge when changing organizational cultures becomes most apparent. Where the espoused assumptions have proved to be successful in dealing with problems in the past, it would be anticipated that efforts to change them would be met with, at the least, apprehension, if not resistance. The change effort in many organizations does not address this deeper level of analysis. Moreover, many change efforts simply address the surface level of change and rely simply on changing the visible representations of the 'old' organization to effect change without addressing other deeper aspects. In order to develop a more advanced approach to organizational change, there needs to be a shift from simply changing artefacts of uniform, documents and décor to also changing espoused values *and* basic assumptions. Bate (1994) contends that Schein's three-level framework for describing the different levels of meaning and process of culture has been taken up as the standard for determining the culture of an organization. However, in invoking the entire range of actions, values and assumptions, Bate (1994) contends that Schein's work is so

79

all-encompassing that all aspects of the organization may be included in the notion of organizational culture, thereby conflating the notion of organization and culture. In this way, Bate (1994) argues that changing the culture of an organization cannot be achieved in isolation; cultural change also affects structure, strategy and organization. While organizational structures, culture and the organization itself may have been previously thought of as different and independent notions, Bate (1994) contends they are *interdependent* rather than *independent* concepts and that strategies for change must include involving a range of organizational roles such as organization development professionals, strategists and designers to work in an integrated manner to achieve successful change. The integration of cultural change then is an important aspect of understanding how culture change is intertwined with organizational change and strategic direction setting. Bate (1994) also argues that cultural dimensions exist at both the organizational and sub-organizational level, particularly involving subgroups of profession, workgroup or occupation. Schein (1985) argues that organizational culture is manifest at both the individual and group levels and affects how the organization adapts to change.

Martin (1992) suggests a three-perspective approach to examining cultural change arguing that a single organization can be viewed in multiple ways. The three categorizations of cultural change are the Integration, Differentiation and Fragmentation perspectives. Differing perspectives highlight the different ways in which organizational principles, values, symbols, rituals and events may be interpreted and understood by employees. Integration looks to find cultural similarities in organizations, Differentiation distinguishes oppositional cultural groups and Fragmentation identifies multiple and conflicting cultural views. In this way, a variety of cultural identities and ways of understanding cultural phenomena may be discerned and moves away from a simplistic focus on organizations possessing a single identifiable culture.

The Integration perspective acknowledges that some aspects of the culture of an organization will be coherent and shared by the majority of employees within that particular organization. The Differentiation perspective establishes a lens by which different subgroups with an organization can be viewed and contextualized. In this sense, the Differentiation approach offers insights into and determines the ways in which subcultures within the organization may react. The Fragmentation perspective suggests that a culture is unable to be definitively identified within an organization. This perspective is based on the assumption that ambiguity and transience is the basis of organizational life. Insights into how an organization assumes a multiplicity of often-conflicting viewpoints are examined in this approach.

Martin (1992: 160) argues that in conceptualizing the different approaches to planned change, both the Integration and Differentiation perspectives focus on 'conscious, goal-directed decision making and ideological solidarity . . .' as a major tenet of the change process. A Fragmentation perspective, on the other hand, views change as emanating from multiple and conflicting sources. This perspective offers insights into the ways that employees interact within organizations, especially those employees who have not traditionally been given a 'voice' in organizational research. Martin (1992) suggests the Fragmentation perspective may provide a rationale for advising that managers should not try to seek homogeneity but identify variation and value diversity. An Integration perspective (Martin 1992) draws together the main elements of the common culture of an organization.

Taking a Differentiation perspective sheds light on the ways in which different groups within organizations perceive culture and change. In this way, differences between the different subcultures including between differing functional groupings, between professional groups and other administrative, technical and para-professional occupations may be identified.

A Fragmentation perspective acknowledges the difficulty in attributing a single culture to diverse organizations. Changing culture then is fraught with problems in targeting a particular manifestation of culture such as values and beliefs as these are continually shifting and defy easy identification and thus simple change. However, despite difficulties in identifying a single culture, or even multiple cultures, the Fragmentation perspective is useful to recognize the multiple and conflicting cultures and understanding how these multiple cultures can co-exist. Diverse interests underlying the common espoused beliefs can then be articulated to the change process. The Fragmentation perspective (Martin 1992) suggests that difference is an acceptable starting point for change processes and managing change.

The contribution of authors such as Bate (1994), Martin (1992) and Schein (1985) to the discussion and debate about corporate culture is to begin to differentiate types of organizational culture and allow for calculations about the effect of organizational subgroups having different cultures. The debate has not been resolved but easy assumptions about the pre-eminence of a single overarching culture of an organization without recognition of different underlying cultural constructs and values may derail organizational change programmes.

CULTURE AND CHANGE

Langan-Fox and Tan (1997) suggest that there are four central features of culture that recur throughout the breadth of literature about organizational culture. First, is that the notion of culture is considered to be stable and resistant to change. Second, organizational culture is taken for granted by organizational members rather than being part of a conscious process of developing cultural constructs. Third, organizational members give meaning to what culture is and finally, the type of organizational culture rests on the shared understandings of organizational members. These common strands in the literature give some insight into the ways in which culture might be identified and operationalized and calculations about organizational change might be made. Characteristics of culture, such as stability and opposition to change, have important implications for the conduct of organizational change programmes. Formulaic approaches to change that do not recognize employees' deeply embedded and diverse understandings of organizational life and the resultant complexity of their responses to change (including resistance and hostility) will fail to deliver the desired change outcomes.

Patrickson and Bamber (1995: 3) suggest that a successful change model that incorporates a focus on organizational culture should contain the following features:

- a clear strategic vision;
- the commitment of senior managers;
- symbolic leadership;
- support systems that provide a good 'fit' with the new strategy;
- good leaders committed to change appointed;
- key disrupters removed; and
- constant communication with key stakeholders (internal and external).

The model proposed by Patrickson and Bamber (1995) to enable successful change in the culture of an organization focuses on developing identifiable future goals and direction. There is also a strong emphasis on the role of leadership to provide direction for the change process and the role of managers to support the change. Communication is recognized as an important element of successful change and it is acknowledged that change needs to incorporate the alignment of strategy with systems. However, the culture change model does not give guidance about how to change an organizational culture.

Beer and Walton (1990) found that change initiatives failed in part because leaders did not clearly articulate the objectives of the change with the appropriate organizational strategies and interventions. Public service organizations, in particular, have come in for specific attention in the failure to achieve change objectives due to existing cultural norms and values that are not conducive to adaptation and alteration (Brooks and Bate 1994).

Programmes of culture change include total quality management and customer service as mechanisms for strategic advantage (Langan-Fox and Tan 1997). Cultural aspects needed to be considered particularly in circumstances in which two or more organizations intended coming together, changes in the size and shape of organizations, and changes in direction and strategy. Langan-Fox and Tan (1997: 274) argue that the organizational culture of organizations needs to be considered during periods of change especially in relation to 'mergers and acquisitions, growth or downsizing phases, in an organization's life cycle, and periods of conflict or diversification'.

Gilmore et al. (1997: 174) argue that the 'unintended side effects of cultural agendas, can undermine — even defeat — the intended change process'. They identify four main side effects of cultural change efforts that work against the successful implementation of change programmes:

- Ambivalent authority: for example, ordering employees to become empowered.
- Polarized images: rhetoric that casts all that is new as progressive and all that is old as regressive.
- Disappointment and blame: finger-pointing up and down the management hierarchy for the inevitable setbacks that accompany change.
- Behavioural inversion: for example, empowerment assertions that mask a reassertion of hierarchy.

There is a need to identify the objectives of the culture change in order for the change effort to be successful (Langan-Fox and Tan 1997).

ORGANIZATIONAL CULTURE DIMENSIONS

Langan-Fox and Tan (1997) differentiate between qualitative and quantitative methods of understanding and examining culture, arguing that qualitative methods tend to be contextually driven and require a high degree of interpretive work and quantitative methods rely on already established categories of investigation that do not necessarily link to environmental or organizational contexts.

In a study of the extant literature on organizational culture, Detert *et al.* (2000) suggest that organizational culture can be mapped over eight dimensions. Specifically, these authors use the Total Quality Management approach to understand culture dimensions. Organizational change then needs to take into consideration the effect of these dimensions when implementing organizational change initiatives. The propensity for organizational change efforts to fail signifies the importance of accounting for a range of variables in the 'change equation'. There remains a problem of organizations reaching a stage of stasis in a change agenda if managers and leaders do not first understand the type of organizational culture (Lawson and Ventriss 1992). Detert *et al.*'s (2000) identification and conceptualization of the different dimensions of culture assists in addressing the concern of Patrickson and Bamber (1995) that change programmes will not achieve their aims unless the existing culture of the organization is modified and that this should occur as an integral element of the change strategy. Detert *et al.* (2000) identify eight dimensions of the relationship between organizational culture and change:

1 *The basis of truth and rationality in the organization.* Organizational members may require evidence of data in order to accept the need for change.

2 *The nature of time and the time horizon*. Is a long-term organizational time horizon or short-term horizon required? How is time measured in relation to the change? This has implications for planning and change management strategies.

3 *Motivation*. Are people motivated from within or from an external source? Should people be rewarded for achievement or punished for failing to achieve?

4 *Stability versus change/innovation/personal growth*. Some organizational members may be very open to change and others work best in a stable environment or may have a fear of change. Continuous improvement or continuous change programmes can be threatening to those who value stability.

5 *Orientation to work, task and co-workers*. For some within PSOs, there is an attention to task and the sense of achievement that comes with completing tasks. For others, however, the social context of work and the relationships with co-workers are more highly valued.

6 *Isolation versus collaboration/cooperation*. Some workplaces and workers are organized according to exceedingly autonomous work practices to encourage efficiency; whilst other workplaces foster teamworking and highly collaborative arrangements in order to achieve better decision making and outcomes.

7 *Ideas about control, coordination, and responsibility*. Tight control is exhibited by formalized rules and procedures and centralized decision making. In loosely controlled organizations, decision making is the product of negotiation and power sharing and flexibility is valued. The degree of control is a cultural artefact that impacts on the way work is organized, and coordinated and the way in which groups/individuals are allocated and work assignments are undertaken.

8 *Ideas about orientation and focus – internal and/or external*. In this dimension, whether an organization is controlled by or is in control of its environment is an important consideration. In addition, the focus of the organization may be internal to a workforce of engineers, scientists, professionals or staff, or it may look to external consultants, outside expertise, customers or competitors.

The Detert *et al.* (2000) framework suggests that there are different cultural expectations for different organizational members. In this way, identifying a single strong culture may be elusive. Morgan (1997) warns that a strong organizational culture may be antithetical to growth and adaptation to changing environments and cites the example of companies identified as 'excellent' in Peters and Waterman's influential book, *In Search of Excellence* in the 1980s were struggling for survival in the 1990s. Morgan (1997: 217) goes on to suggest that, 'Their particular style of excellence had become a trap that prevented them from thinking in new ways and from transforming themselves to meet new challenges'. For Morgan (1997), the role of the manager is crucial to the organizational change effort and the task is one of organizational transformation achieved by interrogating the ways different metaphors shape and construct organizational life.

Detert *et al.* (2000) are cognizant of the possibility that a single culture will not be easily generalized to a particular organization. The possibility of cultural conflict will affect change processes and there is a need to understand subcultures and counter-cultures within organizations (Detert *et al.* 2000). The notion of 'fit' is an important consideration in culture studies. Nadler and Tushman's (1980) work on fit between various elements of organizational life such as individual and task fit, fit between the formal and informal organization, and fit between task and organization are crucial determinants of organizational outcomes. The conceptualization of 'fit' is useful for the public service context especially in relation to understanding the fit between public service culture and propensity for change.

THE CULTURE OF PSOs AND CHANGE

Scholars have spent some time debating whether a business model would 'fit' with the unique character of the public service (see Yeatman 1994, 1998). It is argued that debates on what made the public service 'different' focus on the different sets of accountabilities. However, at the same time, the extension of the government into the business and non-profit sector has created different relationships for business. There is a need, however, to adapt to a 'political' model of engagement for business in order that the business models of culture change can operate in the public service environment. The political level of the governance framework comes into play to allow for the particular orientation of the public service.

Waterfield (1997: 207) argues that the pressures experienced by public services in terms of financial restrictions, reducing service provision, greater demands by citizens and new obligations from international agencies combine to require in public services a culture of 'continuous change'. The concept of continuous change is new to public service organizations as change has traditionally been conceived of as a one-off event or episodic.

Geva-May (2002: 587) identified several different levels and manifestations of public service culture, including socio-political culture, bureaucratic culture, civil service organizational culture and the culture of local accountability that operate to determine the different orientations to policy and programme outcomes. At the institutional level, socio-political culture affects broad government decision and action, and results in either a consensual or adversarial mode of policymaking and a conceptualization of government as either benign or intrusive. In relation to the culture of bureaucratic orientation, cultural considerations will shape orientations to bureaucracy as either neutral or partisan and employment as either career service or performance and outcome driven. Civil service organizational culture influences the mode of delivery of service and the vehicles of policy such that third party service delivery or in-house, internal models will prevail. The local accountability culture affects the extent of openness, transparency and accountability.

85

The culture of public service organizations is argued to require a different conceptualization of change. The 'difficulty' in implementing change in public services is argued to stem from the culture or specifically, an identifiable 'public service' culture and the related imperviousness of this culture to change. Claver *et al.* (1999: 458) argue that the negative aspects of a bureaucratic culture includes 'excessive conformism' and 'higher authority appropriation', and results in 'passiveness, mechanicism and lack of new ideas'. The cultural components of change in public services signify that change needs to take account of the specific culture of public services but at the same time, understand that diversity and subcultures will be present.

DISCUSSION QUESTIONS

1   Use Martin's three-perspective approach of Integration, Differentiation and Fragmentation to characterize the culture of a public service organization with which you are familiar. Compare and contrast the findings from your examination of the different perspectives.
2   Choose a change initiative in a public service or public sector organization with which you are familiar. Use the notion of culture to determine the issues that would be pertinent to understanding the propensity of the organization to undertake change.

REFERENCES

Bate, P. (1994) *Strategies for Cultural Change*. Oxford: Butterworth-Heinemann.

Beer, M. and E. Walton (1990) Developing the competitive organization: Interventions and Strategies, *American Psychologist* 45: 154–61.

Brooks, I. and P. Bate (1994) The problems of effecting change within the British civil service: a cultural perspective, *British Journal of Management* 5: 177–90.

Claver, E., J. Llopis, J. L. Gasco, H. Molina and F. J. Conca (1999) Public Administration: from bureaucratic culture to citizen-oriented culture, *International Journal of Public Sector Management* 12(5): 455–64.

Deal, T. and A. Kennedy (1982) *Corporate Cultures. The Rites and Rituals of Corporate Life*. Reading, MA: Addison-Wesley.

Detert, J. R., R. G. Schroeder and J. J. Mauriel (2000) A framework for linking culture and important initiatives in organizations, *Academy of Management Review* 25(4): 850–63.

Geva-May, I. (2002) From theory to practice: Policy analysis, cultural bias and organizational arrangements, *Public Management Review* 4(4): 581–91.

Gilmore, T. N., G. P. Shea and M. Unseem (1997) Side effects of corporate cultural transformations, *Journal of Applied Behavioral Sciences* 33(2): 174–89.

Green, S. (1988) Understanding corporate culture and its relation to strategy, *International Studies of Management and Organization* XVII (2): 6–28.

Hood, C. (1995) Control over bureaucracy: Cultural theory and institutional variety, *Journal of Public Policy* 15(3): 207–30.

Kopelman, R., A. Brief, and R. Guzzo (1990) The role of climate and culture in productivity. In B. Schneider (ed.), *Organizational Culture and Climate*. San Francisco, CA: Jossey-Bass.

Langan-Fox, J. and P. Tan (1997) Images of a culture in transition: Personal contracts of organizational stability and change, *Journal of Occupational and Organizational Psychology* 70: 273–93.

Lawson, R. B. and C. L. Ventriss (1992) Organizational change: The role of organizational culture and organizational learning, *Psychological Record* 42(2): 205–19.

Martin, J. (1992) *Cultures in Organizations: Three perspectives*. New York: Oxford University Press.

Morgan, G. (1997) *Images of Organization* (2nd edn). Thousand Oaks, CA: Sage.

Nadler, D. and M. Tushman (1980) A model for diagnosing organizational behaviour, *Organizational Dynamics* 9(2): 35–51.

Ogbonna, E. and L. C. Harris (1998) Managing organizational culture: Compliance or genuine change? *British Journal of Management* 9: 273–88.

O'Toole, J. (1985) *Vanguard Management. Redesigning the Corporate Future*. New York: Doubleday.

Patrickson, M. and G. Bamber (1995) Introduction. In M. Patrickson, V. Bamber and G. Bamber (eds), *Organisational Change Strategies, Case Studies of Human Resource and Industrial Relations Issues*. Melbourne: Longman.

Peters, T. and R. Waterman (1982) *In Search of Excellence*. New York: Harper & Row.

Pollitt, C. (2003) Agencies, apples and pears: Mapping the agency debate. Paper presented to the *7th International Research Symposium on Public Management*, Hong Kong, 2–4 October.

Schein, E. H. (1985) *Organizational Culture and Leadership: A Dynamic View*. CA: Jossey-Bass.

Schwartz, H. and S. Davis (1981) Matching corporate culture and business strategy, *Organizational Dynamics* 10: 30–48.

Veenswijk, M. B. and J. L. M. Hakvoort (2002) Public–private transformations. Institutional shifts, cultural changes and altering identities: Two case studies, *Public Administration* 80(3): 543–55.

Waterfield, S. (1997) The challenges facing provincial public services, *Canadian Public Administration* 40(2): 204–17.

Weiner, Y. (1988) Forms of value systems: A focus on organizational effectiveness and cultural change maintenance, *Academy of Management Review* 13: 534–45.

Wilkins A. and W. Ouchi (1983) Efficient cultures: Exploring the relationship between culture and organizational performance, *Administrative Science Quarterly* 28: 468–81.

Yeatman, A. (1994) The reform of public management: An overview, *Australian Journal of Public Administration* 53(3): 287–95.

Yeatman, A. (1998) Trends and opportunities in the public sector: A critical assessment, *Australian Journal of Public Administration* 57(4): 138–48.

FURTHER READING

Corporate culture

Deal, T. and A. Kennedy (1982) *Corporate Cultures. The Rites and Rituals of Corporate Life*. Reading, MA: Addison-Wesley.

This book examines the corporate culture and performance of organizations. It suggests that culture is the basis of an organization and the organizational members need to be aligned with the identified culture of the organization.

Peters, T. and R. Waterman (1982) *In Search of Excellence*. New York: Harper and Row.

This book is one of the early works on the 'new' focus on corporate culture that linked culture with organizational performance. The premise was that 'excellent' companies were based on a strong, identifiable corporate culture.

Chapter 6

Implementing change in public service organizations

LEARNING OBJECTIVES

By the end of this chapter you should be able to:

■ understand the orientation to change in the public service and public service organizations;

■ develop an in-depth knowledge of the possible ways of managing change within public service organizations;

■ differentiate between planned change and emergent change programmes; and

■ evaluate different methods of change management within public service organizations.

KEY POINTS OF THIS CHAPTER

■ Models of planned and emergent change are identified and their use in change efforts is explored.

■ Change communication is an important element of the change process.

■ The fundamentals of successful change programmes are identified and examined.

KEY TERMS

- **Monologic communication** is linear, one-way communication that treats communication as an instrument for conveying and receiving organizational messages.
- **Dialogic communication** is two-way communication that creates meanings through interaction and relationship-building between participants.

Undertaking and implementing successful organizational change initiatives in complex organizational forms is a challenging task. Beer and Nohria (2000) found that the majority of all corporate change initiatives and programmes tend to fail, reporting research findings that around 70 per cent of change programmes are not successful. These results give an indication of the complexity and difficulty of implementing and sustaining organizational change initiatives. While the management of change has common elements across all organizations, implementation of change initiatives in public service organizations, in particular, may pose specific dilemmas and difficulties due to the different orientation, values and objectives of the sector from the private, for profit sector. Public services and public service organizations may also react and respond to different types of incentives, mandates and policy prescriptions.

In this chapter the different approaches to implementing public sector change are identified and analysed and the implications for practice are outlined. Despite the existence of an array of various types of change programmes and different models of change, common themes in change agendas may be distinguished. The evaluation of change efforts is explored to determine whether in the context of implementing a change programme, the efforts can be understood to have achieved desired outcomes. The chapter identifies shared elements of organizational change agendas, and investigates the utility of these to identify a universal prescription for successful change efforts. However, it is also acknowledged that the type of change strategy adopted affects the scope of change and the features of a change programme. Service-wide change is examined to identify the ways that institutional level approaches to change are conceptualized and implemented. Organizational level approaches to implementing change are also identified and discussed. The organizational response may be reactive to externally imposed change or to proactively anticipate the future agenda for change and develop a coherent range of responses to facilitate the transition to new organizational forms.

ORGANIZATIONAL CHANGE MODELS AND CHANGE STRATEGIES

The scale and scope of change programmes in public services and public service organizations are important aspects of the different change models. The scale of change may be conceptualized as wide-ranging, 'frame-breaking' *transformational* change or small-scale and slow-shifting differences embodied in *incremental* change models.

Transformational change

Kleiner and Corrigan (1989) suggest that transformational change can be described as radical, groundbreaking alterations that exhibit a profound break with accepted patterns of organizational behaviour and operation. It is contended (Nutt and Backoff 1997) that the scale and scope of change in organizations result in a requirement for large-scale change that fundamentally shifts an organization. This 'fundamental shift' is at the base of transformational change.

Nutt and Backoff (1997) argue that organizational transformation is often implemented as a response to contextual volatility and may be achieved by enacting leadership-led radical change. Patrickson and Bamber (1995: 4) argue that successful organizational transformation can only be achieved with 'appropriate' leadership and suggest that leadership qualities include being strong, competent, hard-driving and lateral thinking. It is contended (Nutt and Backoff 1997) that large-scale change is effected by a leader identifying an inspiring vision for the organization and bringing together a diverse range of stakeholders to implement the vision and, at the same time, identifying organizational blockages to achieving that vision.

Incremental change

Incremental models of change suggest that change should be implemented in a gradual manner (Patrickson and Bamber 1995). While large-scale transformational change is a common goal of organizational change management efforts, research findings indicate that incremental change is the usual outcome of change initiatives (Pettigrew *et al.* 2001). This finding suggests that change efforts concentrating on transformational change models may underestimate the enormity of the task or fail to achieve the large-scale change required. However, Waterfield (1997: 216) argues that an incremental approach to change 'will not work' and the focus on re-engineering and restructuring as ways of implementing change, did not deliver the required scale of change, citing only small-scale improvements as a result.

At an organizational level, two broad types of organizational change strategies are outlined, namely *planned* change strategies and *emergent* change strategies. Planned change programmes are deliberate, linear and driven from the senior ranks of an organization (Thornhill *et al.* 2000). Planned change typically involves utilizing a set of organizational diagnostic tools that enable mapping of the different

91

Doyle *et al.* (2000) argue that public service organizations experience greater difficulty than the private sector in implementing change due to the unique nature of the public service operating without recourse to the profit motive and requiring impartial, consistent outcomes. In this way, an underlying premise is that 'bottom line' imperatives, the reliance on financial considerations and the market transactions of private sector organizations provide a better guide to establish the impetus and direction of change required for organizational restructuring and improved organizational outcomes. It is argued (Robertson and Seneviratne 1995) that the public sector is different from the private sector in that the multiple and conflicting constituencies, institutional culture, longer chains of implementation, different types of accountabilities and highly formalized processes create different operating conditions and organizational environment.

In comparing leadership and leadership styles in implementing and managing successful change initiatives, a study by Brosnahan (2000) found that both private and public sector leaders exhibited the same types of leadership qualities and characteristics, although there were differences in operationalizing these different leadership traits. It was found that activities such as developing a vision and strategies to achieve that vision, establishing a network of human, financial and capital resources to undertake the strategies and gathering a team of people with high levels of enthusiasm and drive to succeed in working towards the identified vision were common to leaders in both sectors (Brosnahan 2000). However, findings also demonstrated that public sector leaders operationalize organizational visions quite differently as the vision and missions of public sector organizations were more extensive and less well defined and incorporated a complex array of stakeholders often with competing interests. Du Gay (2003) suggests that the discourse of change should be more appropriately considered within a specific political and value context and argues the public service context would not appear conducive to universalizing principles of reform and change.

Caiden (1999: 827) likens implementing public service change and reform initiatives to trying to control a 'boat in a storm' and suggests that change programmes will always be altered from the original course and have a great likelihood of being 'sunk without a trace' or 'shipwrecked with no hope of rescue'.

Lewis and Thompson (2003) identify key drivers and facilitators of public service change programmes and suggest that these elements need to be considered as part of developing a coherent approach to change on a whole of department basis:

- current theory and practice in change management at organizational, management and individual levels;
- CEO and Senior Management commitment;
- application of the Balanced Scorecard;
- development of a macro-planning framework;
- development of a strategic policy function;

- focus on whole of government outcomes and priorities;
- identification of future resource and capability requirements;
- community engagement – consultation, research; and
- industry expectations.

Lewis and Thompson (2003) argue that the challenge for implementing a successful organizational change programme is the 'co-ordinated application' of these key elements along with the allied activities of ensuring change readiness and fostering the change management ability of management and employees. It is important to gain employee acceptance of strategic drivers of change through processes such as organizational learning, engaging employees as well as other stakeholders in the change process, and the practical application of the drivers (Lewis and Thompson 2003). Thornhill et al. (2000) contend that the perceptions of change will affect organizational members' reactions to change initiatives; thus if the change is perceived negatively, there is a greater propensity to resist change efforts.

Pettigrew et al. (2001: 697) identified six key areas that should be considered in order to gain a better understanding of organizational level change. First, they identified a need to shift from one-off, single focus studies of change to incorporating multiple contexts and levels of analysis. Second, research that included changes over time, history, processes of change and action were required to extend knowledge about change over a longer period. Third, the link between change processes and organizational performance needed to be better understood in terms of change outcomes. It was also argued that international perspectives on organizational change should be utilized to determine global patterns of change. Issues of change receptivity, customization and pace of change needed to be investigated as well as differences between episodic and continuous change. Finally, forging a partnership between academics and practitioners in researching change was argued to establish an enhanced understanding of change.

Pettigrew et al.'s (2001) identification of six change areas requiring further exploration points to the perceived inadequacies of contemporary organizational change research in providing insights into the dynamism of complex systems over time and across geographical boundaries. These areas constitute identifiable gaps in understanding the processes, principles and outcomes of change in organizations. However, there are insights about organizational change and change within public service organizations that can inform change processes and the management of change in crucial ways.

IMPLEMENTATION OF CHANGE

The implementation stage of a change programme is a critical step in a change agenda. Since Pressman and Wildavsky's (1973) seminal work on understanding the reasons for failure of employment schemes in Oakland, there has been acknowledgement that implementation is a crucial part in any change agenda. Prior to incorporating analysis of policy and programme implementation, studies concentrated on improving the bureaucratic machinery to administer programmes. This process involved a concentration on creating 'more rational, scientific, efficient, hierarchically controlled' administrative systems (Mazmanian and Sabatier 1989: 4). The introduction of implementation as a separate phase of a change process allows greater understanding of the range of influences on policy and programme outcomes rather than focusing narrowly on the operation of bureaucratic systems and also gives a prominent place to the role of context in affecting change.

A series of general implementation hazards have been identified and these provide decision makers and policy makers with a set of factors that need to be considered prior to embarking on a change initiative. Implementation is affected by problems of external constraints, insufficient time and resources, multiple implementing agencies, an absence of consensus regarding objectives, and a lack of communication, coordination, and commitment (Davis *et al.* 1988: 126–7). In this way, implementation strategies for change programmes need to account for the particular environment in which the change is being undertaken and address the identified problems by allocating appropriate time and resources, allowing multiple and competing objectives to be consolidated and build consensus and commitment.

Thornhill *et al.* (2000) argue that the method of implementing change will crucially affect whether organizational members accept or resist the change initiative and suggest that change can be implemented through a top-down or bottom-up approach. Top-down approaches to change may be unsuccessful in implementing and establishing change initiatives as these approaches fail to incorporate employees' contributions into the change process (Stace 1996). There are a range of issues that need to be considered in terms of employees' contributions to change efforts, particularly in relation to representation and 'voice' issues; however, there seems to be agreement that successful change requires input from a range of organizational members.

EMPLOYEE PARTICIPATION AND 'AGENTS OF CHANGE'

McHugh *et al.*'s (1999) study of a change programme in a public service organization found that change programmes were more likely to succeed when change is initiated by 'front line' staff at the boundaries of the organization rather than by senior manager fiat.

Bruhn *et al.*'s (2001) study of the effects and implications of employee participation in the implementation of planned change found that differential levels of participation are required during the different phases of the planned change initiative. Employees may gain little from being consulted after the major decisions about scope and extent of change have already been taken. Employee inclusion in planned change initiatives while considered an important aspect of the change process, may not routinely deliver better outcomes in terms of organizational productivity and performance. Inclusion also requires upskilling of both employees and managers in negotiation, complex decision making and building consensus, and thus success may be elusive due to time constraints, limited resources, and political considerations that require bringing competing perspectives to reach an agreement. (See Table 6.1.)

Bruhn *et al.*'s (2001) study highlights the importance of ensuring employee acceptance and commitment to the change process. Deciding at what level and to what extent employees should be involved in change management initiatives, however, is a complex question to resolve. Without employee participation, there may be little ownership of the change initiative and poor outcomes, but involvement is a time intensive process that may unduly raise expectations about the extent to which organizational members' contributions can be accommodated in change initiatives. While the involvement of organizational members is considered to be a crucial component of change management, less is known about what kind of participation (authority, representation, decision making, policy formulation) leads to successful organizational change management.

An important influence in the success of change initiatives is communication. Often communication has been considered unproblematic and its utility has been to inform organizational members of the change programme. However, understandings about the role of communication in change initiatives have shifted to conceiving of communication as intimately linked in the change problematic. Different ways of communicating and different purposes of change communication have been discerned.

CHANGE COMMUNICATION

The selection of appropriate communication strategies is an important element of successful change initiatives. Change programmes have tended to appropriate monologic communication strategies for planned change programmes but the approach has not shifted to accommodate different types of change including the more prevalent continuous change context. Doyle *et al.* (2000) argue that traditional monologic forms of change communication such as directed, top-down communication styles are problematic, as these do not guide change communication in contemporary environments that encompass continuous change. Table 6.2 illustrates the key differences between monologic and dialogic communication.

Dialogic change communication strategies are argued to be helpful in relation to supporting innovation and organizational change (Bokeno and Gantt 2000).

Table 6.1 *Respondents' perceptions of benefits and problems resulting from employee participation in planned change*

Benefit	Problem
Ensures 'buy in'	Time intensive
Employees have greater commitment to and cooperation with change	Union agenda and choice of representatives limit diversity of views
Change more likely to succeed	Not all suggestions can be accepted
Employee ownership of change	Raises false expectations
Staff accepts change better	Those not involved feel disenfranchised
Employees feel part of the team	Participation by employees may be biased by how change will affect their jobs
Sense of partnership with management	Employees limit focus to their job level
Increased morale	Employees too close to problems
Motivation	Take time from client service
Trust	Can cause dissension and fragmentation
Enthusiasm	Unwillingness of employees to accept critique of their participation
Job satisfaction	Cynicism when change does not happen
Creates ideas	Pressure for quick fixes
Encourages practical view of change	Management does not listen
Reveals problems not seen by management	Management involved employees but use only their own ideas (cosmetic participation)
Employees know nuts and bolts of programme	Employees may not be risk takers
Employee understanding of client needs	Employees may not see 'big picture'
More client-focused outcomes	Employees may lack sufficient knowledge and experience
Employees see 'whole picture'	Process can become bogged down in the detail
Promotes job development	
Develops employee skills	
Employees become problem solvers	
Increases accountability	
Hold policy makers and administration accountable for understanding the impact of change	
Increases employee creativity	
Empowers employees	

Items are listed in hierarchical order of response.

Source: Bruhn *et al.* (2001: 220).

Table 6.2 *Differences between monologic and dialogic communication*

Differences	Monologic communication	Dialogic communication
Process	Seeking to instrumentalize receivers of information by engaging in goal directed, feedback orientations.	Both parties have genuine concern for each other, rather than seeking to fulfil their own needs. Creating meanings by means of interaction and dialogue
Purpose	Achieving a relationship characterized by power and authority over people to achieve specific ends Views employees as means to make profit	Move a discussion up or down between levels of abstraction
Style	Command, coerce, manipulate, exploit, directive	Authenticity, inclusion, confirmation, supportive climate, a spirit of mutual equality
Focus	Communicators' message	Relationships and attitudes that participants have toward each other

Source: Botan 1997; Kent and Taylor 2002; Pearson 1989, cited in Frahm and Brown 2003.

However, Frahm and Brown (2003) contend that dialogic communications involves a complex mix of skills and attributes:

> Dialogic communication requires sophisticated communicators, that is, people who are comfortable relinquishing their power bases, suspending their beliefs and committing to alternate interpretations in order to build a relationship.

In this way, while dialogic communication offers the possibility of achieving innovation and successful change programmes, it is certainly more difficult to undertake.

Frahm and Brown (2003) in examining the utility of change communication strategies in different organizational change contexts suggest that if stability and control is required in the change effort to achieve, for example, organizational outcomes such as downsizing and embedding change initiatives, then monologic, directed communication is necessary. However, if more complex change is required, such as culture change, responding to financial crisis or large-scale organizational restructuring, dialogic communication through problem-solving groups or discussion boards is needed to progress change (Frahm and Brown 2003).

Strategies for implementing successful change initiatives

DiMaggio and Powell (1983) argue that organizational change is characterized by isomorphic behaviour whereby organizations tend to become similar to each other by mimicking innovations and programmes. Organizations undergoing change then, may play out change agendas that do not necessarily suit their particular circumstances and may impose new regimes of change that are borrowed from other contexts and for perhaps quite different purposes.

Doyle *et al.* (2000: S72) suggest the following strategies for successfully implementing organizational change initiatives:

1 Establish corporate control over the time, pacing and scheduling of change initiatives, taking a controlling overview of multiple initiatives, avoiding initiative overload and allowing those affected time to adjust.
2 Establish systematic and visible preplanning, monitoring and assessment mechanisms.
3 Develop effective stress management procedures.
4 Adopt an innovative, focused approach to organizational communication, particularly targeting employee involvement, management–employee relations, cross-functional communications and also communication between senior and middle managerial ranks.
5 Develop systematic mechanisms for capturing effectively the personal and organizational learning from change.
6 Introduce effectively resourced 'damage control' strategies, where change has increased work intensification, fatigue, burnout, self interest and cynicism, and reduced loyalty, commitment and trust.
7 Introduce pan-organizational programmes for the development of change management expertise.

These suggestions indicate that the successful implementation of change crucially relies on communication across levels and layers of the organization and establishing a systematic framework for developing, monitoring and evaluating the change strategy. These frameworks, however, do not suggest *what* should be addressed within organizations to achieve the desired change.

Morgan (1997) argues that the type of change agenda adopted crucially depends on how an organization is viewed and suggests that this perception constitutes the 'metaphor' of the organization. Morgan (1997) offers a set of alternate lenses for discerning the underlying framework of meaning within the organization which is subsequently utilized to guide the change agenda and suggests that images of the organization will differ according to whether the organization is viewed as a machine, an organism, as culture, a brain, a political system or a 'psychic prison'.

For example, if an organization is viewed as a machine, change will be viewed as a 'process' that would contribute to a well-functioning set of operations; or alternatively, if the organization were viewed as an organism, attention will be given to ways that employees' needs might be satisfied to consequently increase employee motivation and commitment to the change process.

Smith *et al.* (1995) argue that change agendas should be devised according to the responses to a series of key questions that then shape and guide the organizational change programme:

> Which business should they be in? Which activities should be discarded? Which activities could be contracted out? Which activities are not performed currently but should be performed? What are the business goals including market share expansion to be gained each year? How will the goals be achieved? What is the time frame for achievement? Who is accountable for the change process?

In their research on developing successful strategies for managing change in public sector organizations, Smith *et al.* (1995: 33) found that one of the most important aspects of successfully implementing change was that 'change should be powered by a strong vision'. In addition, however, it was suggested that line managers need to be included in the process of change as these managers form an integral part of the implementation chain. Patrickson and Bamber (1995) suggest that gaining middle management support for change is a vital part of a successful change strategy, and warn that many change initiatives founder through middle management antagonism or simply through inertia and lack of co-operation.

Organizational members' involvement is critical as employees need to work with the changed systems and processes but also need to understand and support the change initiative objectives and the organizational goals. Streamlining of operations, systems change to achieve productivity (coordination and control) are often utilized to achieve change. Evaluation of the change initiative was found to be crucial (Bruhn *et al.* 2001).

The extent to which a corporate change agenda can be applied more widely depends on a range of key issues such as:

- extent of CEO and senior management commitment;
- identification of the nature of the existing corporate culture;
- strength of organizational change drivers;
- recognition of the need to change by internal and external stakeholders;
- skills to engender change – present or developing;
- support from stakeholders to change; and
- recognition of successful change effort.

101

Stace (1996) argues that strategic intent of the organization, change strategy and the human resource system are highly interconnected in calculations about an overall programme of organizational change. Dunphy and Stace (1990) developed a 'situational model of change' that considered the scale and scope of change, the type of change management and the leadership style of change. They found that, contrary to expectations about the type of change model required to achieve successful organizational change, the charismatic transformation model of change advocated by change theorists and practitioners was rarely utilized. The authors (Dunphy and Stace 1990) also found that maintaining a minimal level of change did not lead to higher performance. The results of their research indicated that the most successful change initiatives implemented were either a 'consultative' or 'directive' management style, and organizational leaders and managers needed to be adept enough to shift between the two styles as situations and external environments change (Dunphy and Stace 1990).

Stace (1996) suggests that 'best practice' in organizational change may be achieved by adopting an eclectic, pragmatic, culturally sensitive and situational approach to change. This approach relates to a contingency model whereby change efforts are 'tailored' according to particular identified organizational features.

Achieving successful change processes

Studies of successful change programmes found that delivering system-wide change necessitates the adoption of multiple change levers that involve adjusting structural arrangements and changing organizational boundaries as well as altering organizational processes (Pettigrew et al. 2001). The success of the change effort is, partially at least, linked to accurate and positive perceptions of the direction of corporate change (Hill and Jones 1998). Those organizational change programmes that focused on structure and boundaries without changing organizational processes were not able to deliver improved organizational performance (Pettigrew et al. 2001).

Lewin's (1952) work in relation to the force-field theory that established behaviour as a product of an individual operating within their contextual location alerted organization theorists to the problems of narrowly focusing on individuals within an organizational setting and ignoring the role of the environment in shaping behaviour. Krackhardt and Porter (1985) argue that the broader social context highlighted by Lewin in his force-field theory has often been ignored in organizational change studies. Sturdy and Grey (2003) suggest that organizational change management typically evacuates notions of the political context and power from understandings of managing change within organizations. The governance framework outlined by Lynn (2001) acknowledges the political dimension of change and so provides a more comprehensive approach to understanding change.

Sturdy and Grey (2003) cite the research by Van de Ven and Poole in 1995 that discovered over one million references to change and development across the disciplines. The success of change initiatives may be contingent on working through and deliberating a plethora of advice, research outcomes, and theory that is overwhelming. However, Hill and Jones (1998: 449) contend that specific, identifiable elements are present in all change processes and these form a coherent set of steps in the process of managing change. The steps comprise determination of the need for change; identification of impediments and barriers to change, and implementation and evaluation of the change process.

CONCLUSIONS

Understanding whether or not change programmes have been implemented successfully in many case studies is derived from posing two questions – the first focuses on what was the intent of the change programme and the second is to ask to what degree the organization has changed. Change programmes and initiatives, however, are not usually interrogated to determine whether the correct strategy was utilized in the first place.

Moreover, Sturdy and Grey (2003) argue against accounts of organizational change management that universalize the notion of change as a constant, position change programmes and agendas as management-led and offer simplistic 'how to' prescriptions about change. Within the logic of change programmes it is often assumed that there is embedded a rational and strategic response to the changing environment. However, political and contextual factors often play a significant part in the adoption of particular types of change agendas and the ability to adapt to changing circumstances is an important feature of public service organizations.

A range of studies suggest that a critical component of the successful implementation of change is the articulation of a vision for the organization. Strategic leaders create a vision that encompasses a view of the future state of the organization. The organizational vision is then linked to the broader issue of positioning the organization in such a way that organizational members have a clear focus of their decisions and actions and are motivated to advance the change agenda. In addition, communication is an important conduit of change and an area that is often overlooked in implementing change agendas.

There is no clear-cut formula for achieving successful organizational change. Managers and those implementing programmes of change within organizations need to be cognizant of the importance of balancing the tension between maintaining enough organizational stability to retain functionality and developing a momentum of change in order for implementation of the change to occur. Measuring outcomes and charting the 'success' of change initiatives implemented in public services and public service organizations is confounded by the absence of clear sets of indicators such as increased profits or improved outputs that may be found in the private sector, but the multiplex and diverse interests and stakeholders relating to public purpose also point to the greater complexity and nuances demanded of managers and organizational members in implementing public service change initiatives.

CASE STUDY

Managing change in the electricity industry: a tale of change in two countries

Australia: the Electricity Trust (South Australia)
The electricity supply authority in the state of South Australia was a highly technically oriented organization that was virtually a monopoly supplier of electricity. In 1980, it was confident that the organization was well positioned to move into the next decade. The trust operated on a ten year planning cycle, had built a reputation for technical excellence, was a low cost producer of electricity, and perceived as 'an advanced technological organisation offering secure life-long employment to high-quality engineering graduates . . .' (Patrickson 1995: 76).

However, the environment altered during the mid-1980s due to changes in the 'financial, political, social and ecological' context (p.76); demand for electricity did not increase as predicted, the relative cost advantage of production was eroded, consumer complaints became more strident and there was increasing government demands to improve efficiency. Poor public perceptions of the Trust arose from two areas, first the community felt that the Trust was culpable in the devastation caused by a series of bushfires and second, structural change in the industry causing gas prices to rise increased the cost of power to the consumer. Downturn in manufacturing as a result of structural adjustment meant that the industry sector could not continue to increase production and generation capability. Greater scrutiny of the operation of public sector entities resulted in tighter accountability measures in relation to expenditure and operation of public service organizations.

The Trust needed a response to these pressures for change. The change agenda initially suffered from lack of support and organizational inertia, as any changes implemented were marginal and focused on internal modification of procedures and processes. Greater change effort came with a new CEO who was appointed in 1988 from a private sector rather than a public service background and he chose to restructure in two areas – the operations function and the commercial function. As part of the agenda for change, he developed a vision for the company future, took a strategic rather than a technical planning focus and initiated culture change as well as organizational restructuring. Consultants were engaged to facilitate change and these consultants ran workshops and seminars aimed at 'enculturating' the workforce into a new commercial and customer oriented culture.

Other elements of the change strategy were culture and structure change, development of skills and leadership capabilities, introduction of improved systems, strategic planning initiatives and reduction of staff numbers. Some senior personnel were demoted and a new senior management team drawn together that was smaller, younger and with a more balanced skill set.

The change was geared to enable the organization to 'shed its former public sector image' to transform 'the culture of the organization' to incorporate a more strategic, adaptable, commercial and environmentally aware perspective into operation and policy. The emphasis was on shifting the culture from technical management and planning to greater managerial diversity and strategic planning.

Source: Patrickson (1995).

New Zealand: Electricity Corporation of New Zealand

In 1987, the New Zealand Electricity Division was converted to a commercialized entity, the Electricity Corporation of New Zealand (ECNZ) that operated under the State Owned Enterprises Act. The case of change in ECNZ was described as radical political reform (p. 63). The legislation that created and governed State Owned Enterprises (SOE) ensured that the ECNZ operated in a deregulated environment and was required to pay dividends and taxes. The shift was achieved by adopting a market-based model that espoused a culture of commercialization and profit seeking.

Two principles elaborated by the change team drove the change process. The first was that devolution of authority should be central to the new model in order to ensure smaller organizational units operating on performance based management and responsible for commercial outcomes; and the second was that both internal and external contestability should be built into the new system to ensure delineation between purchaser and provider and a competitive environment to create organizational efficiencies. An external consultant and a young, reform-oriented team who were given a 'clean slate' on which to design and manage the change carried out the translation to the new entity. The process was one-way and directive as wide consultation was argued to result in the process of reform being 'sidetracked'.

Separate 'business units' were created for production and retailing of electricity and the new organization incorporated a new focus on marketing and customer service. A new management team was sourced from outside the organization as a way of promoting a business culture and this move was considered to be a powerful mechanism in 'changing the dominant engineering and production culture of the old organisation' (Spicer *et al.* 1995: 68). A board of directors was appointed and the new board comprised members who possessed skills and expertise in the business sector.

A four-part strategy was developed to transition to the new organization. First, managers were given the freedom to manage autonomously. The second arm of the strategy was the creation of an internal market to drive competition based on contracting out, internal user pays systems and purchaser–provider arrangements. Third, a profit-oriented culture was developed through decentralizing authority and responsibility by establishing cost and profit centres for organizational sub-units, and finally, performance management initiatives were introduced.

Managerial discretion and autonomy increased significantly with restructuring to remove organizational layers within the organization and move from a divisional to a functional structure. It was considered that the creation of internal markets and competition was implemented successfully with the shift to contracting and user pays systems. A profit focus and commercial orientation were created with the establishment of business units and culture change to support these initiatives. However, performance incentives and bonus pay for senior managers could not be implemented satisfactorily. Performance measures appeared to be out of alignment with the operating environment of flexible and autonomous organizational structures and managerial strategies. Bonus payments were set to achieving 100 per cent of targets and if targets were exceeded, there was no further bonus. There were also complaints by managers of performance targets being set too high.

In the NZ case, the legislative requirements of the SOE Act drove a significant change agenda with a focus on profit, competition and managerial autonomy. There was considerable emphasis on changing the engineering, production culture to a commercial, results-oriented culture.

Source: Spicer *et al.* (1995).

Utilities across the globe have come under increasing pressure to privatize, or create agencies that disestablish structures of government monopoly provision. While both these organizations were described as undergoing *transformational* change, the ECNZ example was considered a case study of *radical* organizational change. Initially, the Electricity Trust in Australia focused on achieving *incremental* change as a preferred response to pressures for change but lost control of the change agenda when these more moderate alterations were not seen to be adequate to the environmental, political or community demands. The change agenda shifted to a *strategic* organizational change programme following the appointment of a CEO who proactively drove the change programme.

In November 2003, the *Weekend Australian* newspaper reported that power costs in South Australia had risen 25 per cent since the deregulation of the electricity industry in January 2003.

Source: *Weekend Australian*, 8–9 November (2003).

DISCUSSION QUESTIONS

1   What were the main drivers of change in each of these cases?
2   What are the elements of commonality and difference in these two cases?
3   Can an international dimension of the responses to change management be discerned?
4   In what ways does the framework of governance levels (Lynn 2001) apply to the case studies? How useful is the framework for understanding the different levels of change?
5   What are the relevant issues in successfully managing change in each of the cases?
6   To what extent does this case of change within the electricity generation and supply industry demonstrate that public service organizations are similar/dissimilar to firms within the private sector?

REFERENCES

Beer, M. and N. Nohria (2000) *Breaking the Code of Change*. Boston, MA: HBS Press.

Bokeno, R. M. and V. W. Gantt (2000) Dialogic mentoring, *Management Communication Quarterly* 14: 237.

Botan, C. (1997) Ethics in strategic communication campaigns: the case for a new approach to public relations, *The Journal of Business Communication* 34(2): 188–202.

Brosnahan, J. (2000) Public sector reform requires leadership, *Government of the Future*. Paris: OECD.

Bruhn, J. G., G. Zajac and A. A. Al-Kazemi (2001) Ethical perspectives on employee participation in planned organizational change: A survey of two state public welfare agencies, *Public Performance & Management Review* 25(2): 208–28.

Caiden, G. E. (1999) Administrative reform: Proceed with caution, *International Journal of Public Administration* 22(6): 815–32.

Davis, G., J. Wanna, J. Warhurst and P. Weller (1988) *Public Policy in Australia*. Sydney: Allen and Unwin.

DiMaggio, P. J. and W. W. Powell (1983) Institutional isomorphism. In D. S. Pugh (ed.) *Organization Theory*. London: Penguin Books.

Doyle, M., T. Claydon and D. Buchanan (2000) Mixed results, lousy process: The management experience of organizational change, *British Journal of Management* 11 (Special Issue): S59–S80.

Du Gay, P. (2003) The tyranny of the epochal change: Epochalism and organizational reform, *Interdisciplinary Journal of Organization* 10(4): 663–84.

Dunphy, D. (1996) Organizational change in corporate settings, *Human Relations* 48(5): 541–52.

Dunphy, D. and D. Stace (1990) *Under New Management: Australian Organisations in Transition*. Sydney: McGraw-Hill.

Frahm, J. and K. Brown (2003) Organisational change communication: Lessons from public relations communication strategies, *Australia and New Zealand Communication Association Conference*, 11 July, QUT, Brisbane.

Hill, C. and G. Jones (1998) *Strategic Management: An Integrated Approach*. Boston: Houghton Miffin.

Kent, M. L. and M. Taylor (2002) Toward a dialogic theory of public relations, *Public Relations Review* 28, 21–37.

Kettl, D. F. (2000) The transformation of governance: Globalization, devolution, and the role of government, *Public Administration Review* 60(6): 488–97.

Kleiner, B. and W. Corrigan (1989) Understanding organisational change, *Leadership & Organization Development Journal* 10(3): 25–31.

Krackhardt, D. and L. Porter (1985) When friends leave: A structural analysis of the relationship between turnover and stayers' attitudes, *Administrative Science Quarterly* 30: 242–61.

Lewin, K. (1952) *Field Theory in Social Science*. London: Tavistock Publications.

Lewis, D. and R. Thompson (2003) You've changed the culture: Now, how do you sustain it? *Human Resources and Employment Review* 1(1): 37–64.

Lindblom, C. (1959) Science of muddling through, *Public Administration Review* 19: 79–88.

Lynn, L. E. Jr (2001) Globalization and administrative reform: What is happening in theory? *Public Management Review* 3(2): 191–208.

McHugh, M., G. O'Brien and J. Ramondt (1999) Organizational metamorphosis led by front line staff, *Employee Relations* 21(6): 556–76.

Mazmanian, D. and P. Sabatier (1989) *Implementation and Public Policy*. Lanham: University Press of America (originally published 1983, Scott Foresman).

Morgan, G. (1997) *Images of Organization* (2nd edn). Thousand Oaks, CA: Sage.

Nutt, P. C. and R. W. Backoff (1997) Facilitating transformational change, *Journal of Applied Behavioral Science* 33(4): 490–508.

Orlikowski, W. J. (1996) Improvising organizational transformation over time: A situated change perspective, *Information Systems Research* 7(1): 63–92.

Patrickson, M. (1995) The Electricity Trust. In M. Patrickson, V. Bamber and G. Bamber (eds), *Organisational Change Strategies, Case Studies of Human Resource and Industrial Relations Issues*. Melbourne: Longman.

Patrickson, M. and G. Bamber (1995) Introduction. In M. Patrickson, V. Bamber and G. Bamber (eds), *Organisational Change Strategies, Case Studies of Human Resource and Industrial Relations Issues*. Melbourne: Longman.

Pearson, R. (1989) A theory of public relations ethics, unpublished PhD. Ohio: Ohio University.

Pettigrew, A. M., R. W. Woodman and K. S. Cameron (2001) Studying organizational change and development challenges for future research, *Academy of Management Journal* 44(4): 697–713.

Pressman, J. and A. Wildavsky (1973) *Implementation*. Berkeley: University of California Press.

Robertson, P. J. and S. J. Seneviratne (1995) Outcomes of planned organizational change in the public sector: A meta-analytic comparison to the private sector, *Public Administration Review* 55(6): 547–58.

Senge, P. M. (1990) *The Fifth Discipline: The Art and Practice of the Learning Organization*. New York: Doubleday Currency.

Shapiro, P. (1996) *Fad Surfing in the Board Room*. Oxford: Capstone.

Smith, V. C., A. S. Sohal and B. D'Netto (1995) Successful strategies for managing change, *International Journal of Manpower* 16(5/6): 22–33.

Spicer, B., M. Powell, D. Emanuel and R. Bowman (1995) Managing radical organizational change in New Zealand's largest state-owned enterprise. In M. Patrickson, V. Bamber and G. Bamber (eds), *Organisational Change Strategies, Case Studies of Human Resource and Industrial Relations Issues*. Melbourne: Longman.

Stace, D. (1996) Transitions and transformations. Four case studies in business-focused change. In J. Storey (ed.), *Blackwell Cases in Human Resource and Change Management*. Cambridge, MA: Blackwell Business.

Sturdy, A. and C. Grey (2003) Beneath and beyond organizational change management: Exploring alternatives, *Interdisciplinary Journal of Organization* 10(4): 651–62.

Thornhill, A., P. Lewis, M. Millmore and M. Saunders (2000) *Managing Change: A Human Resource Strategy Approach*. Harlow: Pearson Education.

Valle, M. (1999) Crisis, culture and charisma: The new leader's work in public organizations, *Public Personnel Management* 28(2): 245–57.

Van den Ven, A. and M. Poole (1995) Explaining development and change in organizations, *Academy of Management Review* 20(3): 510–40.

Waterfield, S. (1997) The challenges facing provincial public services, *Canadian Public Administration* 40(2): 204–17.

Wheatley, M. (1994) *Leadership and the New Science: Learning about Organizations from an Orderly Universe*. San Francisco: Berret-Koehler.

Worrall, L., C. L. Cooper and F. Campbell-Jamison (2000) The impact of organizational change on the work experiences and perceptions of public sector managers, *Personnel Review* 29(5): 613–36.

FURTHER READING

Planned change

Lewin, K. (1952) *Field Theory in Social Science*. London: Tavistock.

The mechanisms and enabling factors of *planned change* are examined. It is found there is greater success and less resistance to be encountered in instilling change in a group than it is to change any one individual. Organizational change proceeds in three steps: 'unfreezing, moving and freezing'.

Nutt, P. (1992) *Managing Planned Change*. New York: Macmillan.

The focus of the book is improving organizational performance using *planned change*. The processes, implementation and management of planned change initiatives within organizations are examined. Case studies of different types of change initiatives outlining the pitfalls and success factors of undertaking planned organizational change are included. Strategies for initiating and implementing change are identified and a typology of change is outlined according to the internal drivers of change, the underlying assumptions about change and processes of change. The roles of those who 'sponsor' the change by identifying the need for change and starting the process and those who carry out the change, 'planners' are examined.

Morgan, G. (1997) *Images of Organization* (2nd edn). Thousand Oaks, CA: Sage.

The central premise of this book is that metaphors are powerful tools to understand organizations. 'Images' of organizations are drawn from a review of organizational development, politics, science and philosophy research and literature. *Metaphors of organizations* conceptualize firms as machines, brains, organisms, politics, or 'psychic prisons' and identifying the prevailing metaphor assists in shaping appropriate responses to change. Metaphors that construct organizations as machines, for example, focus on the different elements of organizational life as constituent parts that work together with precision to achieve predetermined goals, and efficiency is achieved by specialization and routinized tasks.

Emergent change

Quinn, R. (1996) *Deep Change: Discovering the Leader Within*. San Francisco: Jossey-Bass.

The book suggests that large-scale change can result from an individual's efforts to influence an organization. The role of the *change agent* is explored and the potential for altering the organization by an internal leader is examined. Deep change is conceptualized as transformational change that creates new knowledge and ways of acting and interacting and is contrasted with incremental change which is characterized as processual, easily reversed change that does not afford lasting or immutable change. The precepts of deep change centre on the ways that individuals within organizations can achieve change by changing their values and beliefs about themselves and their place in the organization. The principles rely on eschewing traditional control mechanisms and adopting persuasion, leading by example and lateral thinking techniques.

Senge, P. (1990) *The Fifth Discipline: The Art and Practice of the Learning Organization*. Boston, MA: Doubleday Currency.

Understanding the ways that organizations adapt and change is a critical component of this work. Organizational learning as a competitive advantage and creating the conditions through which organizational learning can take place is a major theme, illustrated by examples from business practice. A '*learning organization*' is represented as an organic model comprising three interconnected levels: individual, group and organization. It relies on identifying and working with five 'disciplines' comprising values, shared insights and vision together with a systems and team approach to understanding organizational life. The five interrelated disciplines form the basis of the organizational learning model: a systems approach, individual learning, understanding and developing mental models of organizational life, developing a shared vision and finally, adopting a team learning mode.

Wheatley, M. (1996) *Leadership and the New Science: Learning about organization from an orderly universe*. San Francisco: Berrett-Kohler.

Organizations and organizational life are characterized as organic, self-organizing systems. Core organizational competencies for dealing with complex situations centre on relationship building, networking and teamworking in order to build trust and quality relationships. The skills for change in a chaotic environment are planning for an unknown future, establishing conversation and story telling capabilities and developing meaningful intra-organizational relationships.

Part III

Managing innovation in public service organizations

Chapter 7

Understanding and managing innovation in public services

LEARNING OBJECTIVES

By the end of this chapter you should:

■ be clear about the nature of innovation and be able to summarize the key issues in its management;

■ have developed an understanding of the role and place of innovation in public management; and

■ be able to identify the key issues for its management by a PSO.

KEY POINTS OF THIS CHAPTER

■ Innovation is a different process to invention and involves the implementation and/or adaptation of new knowledge. There are three elements involved – the actors (innovators), the process (innovating) and the outcome (innovations). The core element that differentiates innovation from incremental change is the impact of discontinuity in the change process.

■ A number of approaches to the classification of innovation have been developed. The most effective one for public services is a relational typology that maps changes in the needs addressed against changes in the service delivery system. This allows innovation to be differentiated from incremental change and for three different modes of innovation to be identified.

■ Previous research has identified a cluster of design factors that are related to successful innovation. These are its *relative advantage* over previous modes of services, its *compatibility* with the existing service system and/or skills mix, its *ease of comprehension* by its end users, the extent to which it is possible to undertake trials prior to full adoption of the innovation ('*trialability*') and the *observability* of its impact(s) within a realistic timescale.

KEY TERMS

■ **Innovation** – the introduction of newness into a system usually, but not always, in relative terms and by the application (and occasionally invention) of a new idea. This produces a process of transformation that brings about a discontinuity in terms of the subject itself (such as a product or service) and/or its environment (such as an organization, market or a community).

■ **Discontinuous change** – change that represents a sharp break with organizational structures, processes and/or skills from the past.

■ **Incremental change** – the modification or improvement of an existing service configuration that builds upon the existing organizational structures, processes and/or skills rather than replacing them.

■ **Competitive advantage** – an advantage that a firm gains in a market as a result of being a 'first mover' in introducing a specific innovation.

INTRODUCTION

This chapter is intended to review the key literature about innovation. Its starting point will be a review of the organization studies literature upon the nature of innovation. This will be followed by a discussion of some other key conceptual developments in this field, which will be of use in the subsequent analysis. It will continue with an exploration of the public management and social policy literatures about innovation. In particular it will focus upon innovation in the personal social services as an exemplar of work in this area.

A particular task here is to try to integrate this literature together. This task is an essential one for understanding innovation in public services, for the literature is very differentiated. For example, in the field of voluntary and non-profit activity, more than twenty years ago Knokke and Prensky (1984) noted the lack of attention that organization theory had given, and continued to give, to this field. Taking a UK focus, in an excellent review of the field, Paton (1993) has also lamented the dearth of such material, which applied organization theory to the study of the innovative activity of voluntary and non-profit organizations (VNPOs) in particular:

> [A]lthough the amount of [such] work has increased noticeably in recent years, this is not a substantial body of work, and the amount of 'proper research' in particular is very limited. To some extent, this simply reflects the absence in the UK of an indigenous management research tradition . . . But another reason for the limited amount of work is the fact that few mature researchers have given much attention to this field . . .'
>
> (Paton 1993: 21–2)

This is not to say that such work is not being done. In the UK, for example, both Wilson (Butler and Wilson 1990; Wilson 1992) and Huxham (1993; Huxham and Vangen 1996) have produced important work upon VNPOs from the perspective of organization theory. Moreover, in the US such important scholars as DiMaggio and Powell (1988) and Singh *et al.* (1991) continue to make significant contributions.

This present volume is very much part both of the growing recognition of the relevance of management and organization theory to the study of public management, and of the contribution that the study of PSOs can make to this generic management theory. It will look in particular at the application of the 'innovation studies' sub-literature to the study of the innovative capacity of PSOs. As will be demonstrated below, this has been (almost) wholly neglected in the discussion of this capacity. Yet not only has this literature an important contribution to make to this discussion but this dialogue itself has the potential to contribute back to the further development of organization theory.

The chapter is accordingly split into four sections:

- the innovation studies literature;
- the existing literature on innovation in public services;
- a consideration of the insights into the innovative capacity of PSOs to be gained by combining these literatures; and
- a concluding section considering the implications for managing the innovative capacity of PSOs.

THE ORGANIZATION AND MANAGEMENT STUDIES LITERATURES

Structure of this section

The innovation studies literature is complex. It is addressed here in a number of interrelated sub-sections:

- the **nature of innovation**, including its *theoretical background* and *approaches to defining and classifying innovation*;
- the **characteristics of innovation**, including the *design attributes of innovations* and the *innovation process*;
- the **attributes of innovative organizations**, including their *structure*, their *internal culture and management/leadership*, and their *relationship to their external environment*; and
- a **review section**, which considers whether it is possible, on the basis of this material, to construct *a unified theory of innovation*.

117

The nature of innovation

The general topic of innovation has inspired vast amounts of research, theorizing, speculation, and wishful thinking. The extensiveness of the research and theorizing has been well documented . . . the extensiveness of the speculation and wishful thinking is less easily documented, but nonetheless real. Innovation is advocated . . . by sundry philosophers, journalists, politicians, industrialists, and social reformers.

(Kimberly 1981: 84)

Theoretical background

The study of innovation has formed an important part of the social sciences since their inception. The early studies were economic ones concentrating on the role of innovation in macro-economic change, and were developed by the founding fathers of both market and Marxist economics – Adam Smith (1910), Marshall (1966) and Marx (1974).

In the early twentieth century this macro-economic conception was developed further in the work of Schumpeter and Kondratiev. Schumpeter (1939) drew links between the development of 'the market' and of innovation, and emphasized the role of the entrepreneur. Kondratiev (1978) linked innovation into the cyclical pattern of macro-economic growth and development, with each cycle linked to a key invention and its subsequent innovation. Scholars in this tradition maintain that the Western economies are now in the fifth Kondratiev cycle, based upon the new information technology (for example, Barras 1989).

Whereas these studies of the nineteenth century and early part of the twentieth century concentrated upon this macro-economic concept of innovation, the latter half of the twentieth century saw a greater emphasis upon its micro-economic implications, together with a widening of its study to include sociological, political and psychological perspectives. A particular concern has been to explore the impact of the macro-economic framework upon the micro-level behaviour of individual firms and organizations. Key studies here have been those concerning the links between the competitive environment and the urge for firms to innovate in order to gain a *competitive advantage* (Porter 1985; Gomulka 1990), and those concentrating upon the role of innovation in the organizational lifecycle (Bessant and Grunt 1985).

This approach has been an important component of the organization and management studies literature that has developed subsequently. Indeed innovation is seen as such a fundamental managerial issue in this literature that it has focused the attention of the four great management 'gurus' of this period – Kanter (1985), Drucker (1985), Peters (1988), and Adair (1990).

118

This section will review this substantial literature about innovation from the organization studies and management fields. It will commence by reviewing attempts to define innovation and to differentiate it from invention. It will then go on to examine the nature of innovation. In particular it will discuss the need for a conceptual typology of innovation and link this to the perceived attributes both of innovation and of innovative organizations. It will also highlight the three most significant hypotheses about the causal factors that produce innovative capacity (that it is a function of their structural characteristics, their internal culture or their external environment). These will be linked to a fourth hypothesis (that it is a function of their institutional framework) that has arisen out of dedicated work on innovation public services. The section will end by looking at attempts to develop models of the process of innovation and its management.

Defining innovation

One of the difficulties in reaching a consensus upon a definition is the sheer heterogeneity of studies of innovation. Within the purely academic sphere the extent of discussion of innovation is enormous – the present author encountered twenty-three different definitions of innovation in preparing this chapter. One example of this heterogeneity will suffice to make the point. Within the confines of the business management literature, innovation has one range of definitions that portray it quite specifically as the key tool used by entrepreneurs to change the profit-yield of resources and to produce an advantage over their competitors:

> Entrepreneurs innovate. Innovation is the specific instrument of entrepreneurship. It is the art that endows resources with a new capacity to create wealth. Innovation indeed creates a resource.
>
> (Drucker 1985: 27; see also Heap 1989)

Contrast this with the more wide-ranging definition developed by Rogers and Shoemaker (1971), though still within the broader management literature, and which echoes the earlier seminal work of Barnett (1953):

> An innovation is an idea, practice, or object perceived as new by an individual. It matters little . . . whether or not an idea is 'objectively' new as measured by the lapse of time since its first use or discovery . . . If an idea seems new to the individual, it is an innovation.
>
> (Rogers and Shoemaker 1971: 19)

Despite this diversity it is nonetheless possible to suggest four features that form the core of a definition of innovation. The first of these is that an innovation

119

represents *newness*, Beck and Whistler (1967) argue for an absolute definition of such newness, as literally 'first use' of a piece of new knowledge. However, most studies have preferred to use a relative definition of it, as relating to something new to a specific person, organization, society, or situation, irrespective of whether it represents a genuine 'first use' (Knight 1967; Mohr 1969; Pettigrew 1973; and Zaltman *et al.* 1973).

Ultimately it is wrong to see these views as alternatives. Rather they represent different forms of innovation. Kimberly (1981) brings them together by suggesting the twin concepts of *objective* and *subjective* innovation. The former is something that is significantly different from what has gone before – it is, quite literally, a 'first use'. The latter is something that is seen as new to those involved in its adoption, but is not necessarily its first use – it represents the diffusion of an idea/process developed elsewhere to a new situation (and may also involve its modification/ adaptation in this process). A related differentiation has also been made by Downs and Mohr (1976), between *intrinsic* and *extrinsic* innovation.

The second feature of innovation is its *relationship to invention*. Whilst there is a consensus that invention is the actual generation of new ideas, there is none as to whether this is an intrinsic part of innovation. Urabe (1988: 3) asserts that innovation:

> consists of *the generation of a new idea* and its implementation into a new product, process, or service . . . Innovation is never a one-time phenomenon, but a long and cumulative process of a great number of organizational decision making processes, ranging from *the phase of generation of a new idea* to its implementation phase.
>
> [my emphases]

Although this view is supported by a number of authors (Thompson 1965 and Adair 1990, for example), it is not a unanimously held one. Other studies differentiate innovation from invention. Whilst the latter process is the actual generation of new ideas, innovation is seen as the *process of adoption or implementation of a new idea*, whereby new ideas are converted into an actual product or service (Knight 1967; Aiken and Hage 1971; and Twiss 1987). Linked to the previous point this might be either the first use of such new knowledge, or its diffusion to a new situation.

Again it seems foolish to create an unnecessary counter-position here. What is clear is that innovation always involves the adoption and implementation of new ideas, and may sometimes coalesce indistinguishably with their actual invention or discovery.

The third facet of innovation is that it is *both a process and an outcome*. Whilst many studies concentrate upon its processual nature, as a process of transformation (Thompson 1965; Pettigrew 1973; Urabe 1988), it is also possible to talk of 'an innovation' as the actual product of this process (Kimberly 1981). However, the foci of these two approaches are different, and it is important to be clear which is being addressed in any particular study.

The final feature is perhaps the most significant one – and this is that innovation must involve *change or discontinuity*, both in terms of the transformation of an idea into actual reality, and also in terms of its impact upon its host organization (Wilson 1966; Nystrom 1979; and Robert and Weiss 1988). The key here is to differentiate *organizational development* from *innovation*. Both are forms of organizational change and both, over time, can lead to significant changes in the configuration of an organization, its product/service, and/or its market. However, organizational development occurs within the existing product-service-market paradigm. This paradigm is not challenged or changed, but one or more of its elements may be modified and developed over time. With innovation, by contrast, there is change in this paradigm. Innovation leads to change occurring in the configuration of the product-market paradigm and leads to the creation of a new one. This 'paradigmatic shift' changes the nature of the product/service and/or the market for it in a way that is discontinuous from what has gone before.

This issue of discontinuity is an essential distinction to make in the understanding of innovation (Tushman and Anderson 1985). Whilst, in the long term, incremental change can lead to significant changes in the production process and/or in the nature of a good or service, these changes occur within the existing paradigm (the improvement in the efficiency of canals as a transport system in the late eighteenth century, for example). Innovation, however, changes the prevailing paradigm (as with the replacement of canals by railways in the nineteenth century).

Pulling the threads of our four features together, it is possible to propose a general definition of innovation as:

> the introduction of newness into a system usually, but not always, in relative terms and by the application (and occasionally invention) of a new idea. This produces a process of transformation that brings about a discontinuity in terms of the subject itself (such as a product or service) and/or its environment (such as an organization, market or a community).

Classifying innovation

As with definitions of innovation, the management literature is not short of typologies for classifying innovation. The focus here will be upon the five most common classifications. Whilst this might not be entirely exhaustive, it does cover the most important approaches.

The simplest typology classifies innovation according to its original impetus. Thus innovation is classified as resulting from either *research push* (that is, from the development of an innovation on the basis of research) or *market pull* (that is, from

BOX 7.1 THE DISTINCTIVE ELEMENTS OF INNOVATION

Innovation is characterized by:

- *newness* (either objective or subjective);
- *its relationship to invention;*
- being both *a process* ('innovating') and *an outcome* of that process ('an innovation'); and
- *discontinuity* with the prevailing organizational, product/service or market paradigm.

the development of an innovation on the basis of marketing analysis). Although useful in explicating the origins of innovation, this typology is limited in its usefulness. As Freeman (1982) has noted, push and pull factors are often both involved in the origin of an innovation. Consequently, it is important not to differentiate them but rather to understand the relationship between them (Burgelman and Sayles 1986). Moreover, this classification has an implicit assumption in it that invention is an integral part of the innovation process. As we have seen above, this is not always the case.

A second typology also focuses on the origins of innovation, though this time at an organizational level. This approach derives from the early work of Cyert and March (1963). They argued that innovation can be classified as either *distress innovation* (arising because an unsuccessful organization needs to change to avoid extinction) or *slack innovation* (arising because an organization is successful, and so has sufficient surplus resources to carry the risks of innovation).

This approach is useful because it does focus attention upon the resource issues involved in innovation and relates them to their organizational context. However, its environmental analysis lacks sophistication – for example, it takes no account of other possible environmental factors which might stimulate innovation, such as a shift in the prevailing public-policy paradigm (Rothwell and Zegveld 1981). At the organizational level it also, once again, presents a dichotomous typology. It fails to allow for the analysis of innovation by organizations that are not in either of the stated extreme situations.

The third approach to a typology is based upon *the perceptions of the beneficiaries or users of an innovation.* In one of the smaller number of studies of innovation in public organizations, Daft and Becker (1978) make the important point that innovations are not a homogeneous or objectively perceived group of entities but can have a range of different attributes. Which of these will be emphasized will depend upon the perceptions of the most significant stakeholders. Different groups will emphasize different points of these attributes. Thus, in analysing the development of a new teaching programme, they show how its innovative content could differ dependent upon which group (students, teachers, administrators) was most influential in its development.

This approach is developed further by Von Hippel (1978, 1982). He adopts a *cui bono* ('who benefits') approach, similar to that of Blau and Scott (1963) in their seminal analysis of formal organizations. In particular he looks at the differing level of benefit to be achieved by the user and the manufacturer of an innovation. He argues that ultimately it is the perceptions of the beneficiaries that are most telling in defining the nature of an innovation. Atuahene-Gima (1996) has also used this perspective to differentiate between the success factors for innovation in the manufacturing and the service sectors.

It is perhaps unfair to describe this approach as a true typology. It has not been developed so formally. Nevertheless it is an important contribution to understanding the different types and perceptions of innovation, by concentrating attention upon the producer-user/beneficiary relationship.

The fourth approach is probably the one adopted most commonly. This classifies innovation by its outcome(s). The usual framework is to look at whether the innovation is one that is a genuinely new *product or service* for the end-user, or if it is a new *process* for producing existing products and services (Bessant and Grunt 1985). Some studies have specified a wider range of outcomes. Knight (1967) adds organizational structure and personnel innovation to product and process, Starkey and McKinlay (1988) add work organization and management innovation to them, and Zaltman *et al.* (1973) are most ambitious, creating five types of innovation: product, process, organizational, personnel and policy.

At its simplest, this product-process way of classifying innovation has the benefit of simplicity, and additionally draws attention to one of the core characteristics of innovation identified in the previous section (that is, whether it is a process or an outcome). A more radical development of this kind of typology, though, is where classification upon the basis of product and process innovation is employed as the starting point for a larger model of the process of innovation as a whole.

In this model, product innovation is seen as *radical innovation*, which represents true discontinuity with the past and which redefines the organizational environment. Abernathy and Clark (1988) call this 'creative destruction', because it allows a qualitative jump forward in product/service definition that can render all existing organizational competencies obsolete. Process innovation, by contrast, is seen as *incremental*, providing continuity with the past by refining existing organizational competencies for more efficient production. In this sense, this classification is a way of differentiating between true innovation and organizational change.

A final version of this approach links these two processes together with the life-cycle of organizational development. Radical product/service innovation is thus linked to new industries and firms, where technological jumps are being made. By contrast, incremental process innovation is linked to established industries and firms, where refining the existing product processes can develop efficiency and profitability (Holloman 1980; Urabe 1988). This approach to classification is found in its most developed form in the work of Bessant and Grunt (1985).

As with the typologies discussed previously, this approach has its strengths. It focuses attention upon the links between innovation, its organizational environment, and its impact upon that environment. However, whilst the product–process dichotomy can be useful, when used in isolation, it does have drawbacks. It forces one to focus on one or the other, when in fact both might be of interest. As noted above, an inherent characteristic of innovation is that it has both a processual and an outcome content. This typology obscures this important point by making them alternatives. It obscures the fact that an innovation may be a product for one organization, which develops a new work process, for example, and a process for another organization, which uses this process to produce some other product or service (Abernathy and Utterbach 1988). This does not mean that the distinction is unimportant. On the contrary, it can be extremely important to explore the differing impacts of an innovation upon its producers and end-users. However, as a means of classifying innovations in a mutually exclusive way, it has clear limitations. Moreover, even advocates of this approach in the manufacturing sector (Bhoovaraghaven *et al.* 1996) acknowledge that it has its limitations in the service sector, where production and consumption occur contemporaneously (Normann 1991).

Finally, the lifecycle model is also often too static and linear in its presentation. At one level it confuses the discontinuity of innovation with the incremental development of organizational change. As Herbig (1991) has noted: no matter how incremental an innovation might be across an industry or sector as a whole, for the individual firm its impact can often be to produce discontinuity, marking a break from its practices of the past. Abernathy *et al.* (1983) have also made the important point that this lifecycle is not a one-way process: it is possible for industries and firms to *de-mature* and to revert to an earlier stage of the lifecycle.

The final approach to the classification of innovation is in many ways the most satisfying one. This derives from the influential work of Abernathy. Initially, Abernathy (1978) also adopted a linear lifecycle model, though he took this a stage further by integrating concepts, from Burns and Stalker (1961), of organic and mechanistic organizations (which concepts will be discussed further below), the former being linked to radical innovation and the latter to incremental innovation.

However, in Abernathy *et al.* (1983), he moves away from this linear and positivist view of industrial development, and argues that it is possible for organizations to *de-mature*, to move away from the standardized mass production of a mature company, with an emphasis upon process innovation, and once more embrace diversity of product production, with a reasserted emphasis upon radical innovation. This de-maturity, he argues, could frequently be brought about by a major change in the environment of an organization.

Developing from this more dynamic, and satisfying, analysis of the organizational lifecycle, Abernathy *et al.* go on to develop a two-dimensional typology of innovation, based upon its impact both upon the production processes of an organization and upon the existing markets and users of a product or service (Figure 7.1). Thus, *architectural innovation* changes both the markets for a product or service and its production (the classical radical innovation). *Regular innovation*, by contrast, refines existing production processes and markets (incremental innovation). *Niche-creation innovation* is one that preserves existing production competencies, but creates new markets and users for a product or service, usually by re-packaging or re-marketing it. Finally, *revolutionary innovation* applies new technology to the production process for existing products and markets, creating an efficiency gain. This approach is important because it does not treat product and process innovation as separate entities but rather explores the relationship between the two, as it does between the producers and end-users of a service or product. It disaggregates the concepts of *product* and of *process innovation* to explore their relationships with the user group of an innovation, as well as with each other. Nor does it necessarily link one type of innovation to a specific point in the lifecycle of an organization. Instead it allows for this cycle to, quite literally, be cyclical, and encounter the same conditions again, if in a different plane. Further, it allows the issue of discontinuity and continuity to be explored, in terms of the impact of a new process or product/service, thus allowing true innovation to be differentiated from organizational development. For these reasons, this classification is a qualitative move forward, away from the traditional linear ones described previously.

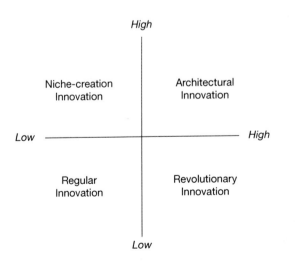

'x' axis – the impact of an innovation on the production system.

'y' axis – the impact of an innovation on the market.

Figure 7.1   A typology of innovation.

Source: Based on Abernathy *et al.* (1983).

Table 7.1   *Approaches to classifying innovation*

Nature of classification	Key writers
Classification as research-push or market-pull	Burns and Stalker (1961)
Classification as produced by organizational distress or organizational slack	Cyert and March (1963)
Classification by 'cui bono' – who benefits and how	Daft and Becker (1978), Von Hippel (1978, 1982), Atuahene-Gima (1996)
Classification as a product or a process innovation (and its variants)	Zaltman *et al.* (1973), Bessant and Grunt (1985), Starkey and McKinlay (1988), Urabe (1988)
Classification by the relationship between the impact of an innovation on its organizational context and upon the wider market	Abernathy *et al.* (1983)

In summary, then, this section has reviewed a number of approaches to classifying innovations (Table 7.1), based upon their source (in both processual and organizational terms), their users and beneficiaries, and their outcomes. These all illuminate important aspects of innovation but, it is argued, none by itself supplies a satisfactory classification of innovation. For this it is important to examine some of the relational issues, rather than relying solely upon one-dimensional typologies. In this context, the typology developed by Abernathy *et al.* is felt to be the most satisfying. This highlights the different relationships possible between the impact of an innovation upon the production of goods or services of an organization, and upon its impact upon its actual and potential users and beneficiaries.

The characteristics of innovation

There are whole ranges of studies that seek to pinpoint the distinctive characteristics of innovations. However, as Mohr (1987) has highlighted, they do not necessarily amount to a unified and validated body of theory about innovation:

> The reason why innovation theory does not easily tell us what we want to know . . . is that there is a failure to pin-point precisely what our questions are. It turns out that one cannot simply wonder about innovation and have all of one's curiosity resolved by a compact, unified, parsimonious collection of theoretical statements. Social scientists have tried to

develop many of these statements, but they tend to answer different questions, if any at all, and do not easily connect with one another.

(Mohr 1987: 13)

Zaltman *et al.* (1973) make a vital distinction in differentiating the attributes of *innovations* (the services or products produced by the process of innovation) from those of *innovators* (the organizations/individuals responsible for the innovation process). This sub-section therefore will review the literature with regard to the *characteristics of innovations*, followed by the *process of innovation and its management*. The following sub-section will then move on to examine the key issues in relation to *the innovators* themselves.

The design attributes of innovations

These are explored in most detail in the influential study of Rogers and Shoemaker (1971). This study details five optimal attributes that it argues that users of an innovation require, in order for it to be successfully adopted (Box 7.2). This list has been used, incorrectly, by some, as a 'checklist' of factors to be built into successful innovations. Rather, though, it is more of an 'aide memoir' for issues that need to be confronted in designing innovations. All five attributes do not have to be present for an innovation to be successful – but if one is missing then this suggests where the weight of effort needs to be placed, in terms of managing the process.

Other, more limited studies have been undertaken since this early work. Cooper and Kleinschmidt (1993), for example, argued for *product differentiation* as being the sole major factor in identifying successful innovations. Such one-dimensional approaches do not convince, however, when compared to the earlier study. Zaltman *et al.* (1978) develop this argument by taking a contingent approach to these dimensions and stress that it is important in any given situation to differentiate between

BOX 7.2 THE FIVE ATTRIBUTES OF SUCCESSFUL INNOVATIONS

- *relative advantage* over what preceded it;
- *compatibility* with existing technologies/skills;
- *ease of comprehension* by end-users;
- *trialability*; and
- *the observability of its results* and achievements.

Based on Rogers and Shoemaker (1971)

which of these are the necessary attributes of a successful innovation and which are of secondary importance. Finally, Daft and Becker (1978) combine this latter approach with a typology of innovation outcomes, to develop a matrix for the analysis of successful innovation.

Like many of the approaches to classifying innovation discussed in the previous section, these approaches to defining the attributes of successful innovation have been criticized for their over-rationality. Clark (1987) has argued that these existing studies have been dominated by economics and have also concentrated upon *isolating variables* rather than upon highlighting *their relationships to each other.* Clark and Stanton (1989) have further argued that the process of *the transformation of knowledge* has been neglected by concentrating upon the intrinsic attributes of innovations in isolation. They also contend that such an attributional approach to innovations assumes that they are a homogeneous group of entities. In fact, they argue, they are heterogeneous 'bundles of elements', which need a dynamic and relational rather than a static and discrete analysis.

Another significant criticism of the study of the attributes of innovations is the inherent assumption that innovations must be normatively good. Indeed, the role attributed to innovation in market economies is almost that of such a normative good. As will be seen below, innovation is often assumed to be a key linkage between a competitive environment and the behaviour of individual firms (Drucker 1985; Porter 1985). This is especially true of the influential work of the 1980s of Tom Peters (Peters and Waterman 1982; Peters and Austin 1985; Peters 1988).

Other critics have taken issue with this assumption, however. Knight (1967), Rosner (1967) and Kimberly (1981) had all previously argued that it is quite possible for innovations to have negative effects both upon their adopters and upon society in general. For firms, innovations can be expensive to develop and they risk being prey to imitators who copy (and improve) their innovations, whilst not risking the development costs. Similarly, for society an innovation can have immense social costs (in terms of pollution, for example), despite any economic benefits. This latter point has led Mole and Elliot (1987) to argue for the importance of public control of innovations, to limit their social costs. Atuahene-Gima (1996) has also pointed to the need to distinguish between the characteristics of successful innovations in the manufacturing and the service sectors.

Finally, Van de Ven (1988: 105) has also argued against the positivism implicit in many studies of the attributes of innovations, which assume an implied link between goodness and usefulness:

> Innovation is often viewed as a good thing because the new idea must be useful-profitable, constructive, or solve a problem. New ideas that are not perceived as useful are not normally called innovations: they are usually called mistakes.

To conclude, the studies of the attributes of innovations do have some insights to offer. They do, for example, draw attention to the dimensions involved in their successful adoption. However, it is not possible to use these dimensions in a mechanistic predictive way – Zaltman *et al.* (1973) were right to point out the contingent nature of these attributes. Moreover, this review has uncovered that there is an assumption of an inherent benefit in innovation in many such studies that belies its potential risks and costs. These include lost opportunities to develop in other directions and the costs to firms of the actual process of innovation, as well as their possible social costs. These more negative aspects of innovation also need to be taken into account in developing a more rounded view of it.

The process of innovation

The study of the process of innovation is one with a great lineage, stretching back to the sixteenth-century political philosophy of Machiavelli! Traditionally, innovation has been viewed as a linear process. This view is well characterized by Mole and Elliot (1987: 14):

> The innovation process typically involves a series of stages ranging from the idea of invention, through the product design, development, production, and adoption or use.

Other studies have challenged this linear model. As early as 1966, Wilson argued that the process was not linear but cyclical, with key feedback points within it. Subsequently Pelz (1985) and Clark (1987) also argued against a linear model as being too static and one-dimensional. Rather they argue that it is multi-dimensional and multi-directional.

However one models the entire process, though, it is agreed generally that three dimensions are involved in it: an optional one of invention, and two essential ones of implementation, and diffusion. The *invention stage* is, as the earlier discussion suggested, an optional stage. Innovation can often mean solely the application of new knowledge rather than its 'invention' or discovery. Invention is an important activity in its own right, nonetheless.

As discussed earlier, one of the key arguments in the literature is whether the generation of new ideas is pulled by 'pure' research (Burns and Stalker 1961), or 'pushed' by market and consumer demand (Von Hippel 1978, 1982). Inevitably, perhaps, the most sophisticated studies have synthesized both the above perspectives, arguing that both have a role. In particular, Abernathy *et al.* (1983) have argued for an understanding of the source and impact of inventions in relation to both the creation of new knowledge and the needs of the market.

Implementation is often seen as the core of innovation, involving the introduction and adaptation of a new idea within a new environment. Four interlinked factors are identified in the literature as important to an understanding of this stage. The first is the organization itself. Research has suggested that different organizational characteristics are appropriate to different stages of the innovation process: whilst an open decentralized organization is required for the generation of ideas, a hierarchical and centralized one is more effective for their implementation (Normann 1971; Aiken and Hage 1971; Rowe and Boise 1974). The issue here is the relationship between the open communication required in the invention stage (Tidd 1995) and the managerial direction needed in the implementation stage, which often involves negotiating opposition to change. A separate but linked analysis concerns the relationship between efficiency and innovation within organizations and the extent to which it is possible to achieve both these organizational states simultaneously (Heap 1989).

The second factor is the importance of the existence of an organizational environment committed to innovative change. The key factor here is the development of organizational values and an organizational culture that encourages and stimulates innovation (Starkey and McKinlay 1988).

This links into the third identified characteristic, which is the role of individuals in the process of implementation. The influence of individuals is significant at several different organizational levels. Schon (1963) and Knight (1987) both point to the role of the product champion in managing the implementation of a new product or service. By contrast Hage and Aiken (1967), Hage and Dewar (1973) and Hage (1980) all emphasize the role of senior management as providing leadership and innovative values for the innovative organization. These issues will be discussed further below, in the section on the characteristics of innovating organizations.

The final factor in the implementation stage is that of its micro-process within the organization. Here the debate centres on whether this is predominantly a rational or a political (i.e. interpersonal) process. Carson (1989) and Adair (1990) make a case for a wholly rational approach, in which the implementation of innovation is rigorously planned. However, this is strongly challenged by a number of empirical and theoretical studies (notably Kimberly 1987, Golden 1990, and Frost and Egri 1991). The case is most strongly made, though, in the seminal work of Pettigrew (1973: 20–1):

> Political behaviour is likely to be a special feature of large-scale innovative decisions. These decisions are likely to threaten existing patterns of resource sharing. New responses may be created and appear to fall within the jurisdiction of a department or individual who has not previously been a claimant in a particular area. This department, or its principal representative, may see this as an opportunity to increase its, or his, status and rewards in the organization. Those who see their interests threatened by

the change may invoke resistance in the joint decision making process. In all these ways new political action is released and ultimately the existing distribution of power is endangered.

In the late 1980s, efforts were made to bring these schools together in a 'contingency' model (Beer and Walton 1987; Nadler 1988). These emphasize the importance of bringing rational and political processes together, dependent upon the specific environmental configuration of an organizational innovation. Whichever approach is preferred, and the preference here is towards the contingency model with its emphasis upon environmental analysis, all analysts are clear upon the need for a positive management role in the innovation process. This is discussed further below, in the section on the innovators.

Diffusion is the final stage of the innovation process. This is the means by which a specific innovation is transmitted from one user on to others, be they individuals or organizations. The key work in the study of diffusion is undoubtedly that of Rogers and Shoemaker (1971), discussed above. They specify a process by which *awareness of new knowledge* is followed by *persuasion by its proponents* and its subsequent *testing*, to *final decision making*. Basing their work both on an extensive review of diffusion studies and on communication theory, they argue that the pattern of diffusion of an innovation will follow a 'normal curve', moving from the 'innovators' through to the 'laggards'. Moreover, if this distribution is viewed cumulatively, rather than discretely, it forms the 'S-curve' that is the basis of much analysis of individual innovation diffusion. This detailed study has been criticized for its over-emphasis upon the role of the individual, rather than of the organization. However, some important modifications have been suggested. Three are especially important.

First, Mohr (1987) has argued that the traditional model of diffusion has excluded the importance of evaluation in the process. This makes it a cyclical process, rather than the traditional linear one. Second, Mort (1991) has argued against the use of *diffusion* as a metaphor for the process and instead favours *percolation*. This is because it concentrates attention upon the environment in which innovation takes place, rather than seeing it as a self-contained process.

Finally, Herbig (1991) has argued also against the 'S curve' as helping in understanding the impact of innovation upon an organization. He contends that this model implies an incremental continuity to the process that might well describe the diffusion process for an industry or market as a whole. However, as was noted earlier, the impact upon individual organizations within this environment is to produce discontinuity. In these circumstances, he argues that catastrophe, rather than diffusion, theory is more appropriate for aiding understanding of the process of innovation for an individual firm.

The attributes of innovators

In reviewing this sub-body of literature, three distinct foci can be drawn out, to explain the innovative capacity of an organization. These are its formal structure, its internal environment, and its external environment and its relationship to this. Each of these will be examined in turn.

Organizational structure

The starting point for any discussion of this factor has to be a clear conception of what formally constitutes an organization. Zaltman *et al.* (1973: 106) give a clear definition of the formal aspects of an organization:

> [It is] a social system created for attaining some specific goals through the collective efforts of its members. Its most salient characteristic is its structure that specifies its operation.

Early work on the relationship between organizational structure and innovation emphasized the importance of the overall configuration of an organization. This is best epitomized by Burns and Stalker (1961) and Thompson (1965). The former, highly influential, study counter-posed the mechanistic organization to the organic one. The former relied upon highly specified and distinct organizational specialisms among its staff, with a strong vertical line management. The latter, by contrast, had a high degree of task complexity and sharing, and a more horizontal organizational structure with a greater degree of lateral connection. Burns and Stalker hypothesized that the mechanistic organization was most suited to stable conditions whilst the organic one was more adaptable in unstable conditions, and by implication, more innovative. This model was supported by Thompson, who contrasted the bureaucratic organization (as centralized and formalized) with the innovative organization, which possessed more participative management and freedom of communication:

> The bureaucratic orientation is conservative. Novel solutions, using resources in a new way, are likely to appear threatening. Those having a bureaucratic orientation are more concerned with the internal distribution of power and status than with the organizational goal accomplishment.
>
> (Thompson 1965: 5)

Following on from these studies, later ones were concerned to break down these 'ideal' types into their constituent parts, in order to examine their impact. In particular, the issues of centralization of power, formalization of roles, and organizational complexity were explored. Some of these studies confirmed the model of Burns and Stalker. Thus, for example, Hage and Aiken (1967) contended that centralized decision making did indeed inhibit the ability of an organization to innovate, whilst organizational complexity encouraged openness and the exchange of ideas.

Other studies took a more paradoxical view in their analyses, however. As discussed previously, Wilson (1966) argued that there was a contradiction between the types of organizational structures required for the generation (or invention) of innovative ideas and for their implementation. The former process did indeed require open non-hierarchical structures. The latter, however, benefited from a centralized structure that could be forceful in implementation. This position was similarly argued by Sapolsky (1967) and Zaltman *et al.* (1973). Even Aiken and Hage (1974) subsequently modified their earlier position to suggest that the ability of organizations to be innovative could vary over time, dependent upon their needs and their environment.

The earlier static model of Burns and Stalker thus has subsequently been replaced by a more contingent one. This acknowledges that organizational structure is a significant predictor of innovative capacity, but that innovation may well require different organizational structures at different stages of the process, or that a specific organization will need to be able to cycle between different modes of structure, dependent upon its needs in relation to innovation.

The internal organizational culture and the role of organizational management/leadership

The second group of studies which have attempted to explain the innovative capacity of the innovative organizations are those concerned with their internal culture. These studies have tended to concentrate upon three issues – the size of an organization, the nature of organizational leadership, and the nature of organizational life (such as the communication channels and processes within an organization and the complexity of organizational tasks).

With regard to *organizational size*, a whole range of early studies found a clear relationship between the greater size of an organization and its ability to innovate (Mansfield 1963; Becker and Stafford 1967; Mohr 1969; Langrish *et al.* 1972). However, later studies have taken a different view, starting with the seminal SAPPHO study at the University of Sussex, which associated small organizational size with innovativeness (Freeman 1973; Stroetman 1979; Ahlbrandt and Blair 1986). This debate has continued, with Pavitt (1991) and Haveman (1993) advocating the significance of small size and Azzone and Maccarrone (1993) that of large size.

Da Rocha *et al.* (1990), summarizing the arguments, suggest that the proponents of size as a predictor of innovation are actually using this as a proxy for resource availability (in terms of capital, personnel and expertise), whilst those supporting smallness are similarly using it as a proxy for a less bureaucratic organizational structure and for greater freedom for individual action. Damanpour (1996) has also argued for a contingent model that relates the significance of organizational size to environmental uncertainty.

Overall, the decision on the relationship of size to innovation is one still to be proven. Certainly there is no one clear conclusion relating it to innovation as a whole. It remains to be seen whether more specific studies can locate size in a more contingent way, in terms of different stages, or types, of innovation.

Moving on to *organizational leadership*, there is little dispute in the literature that senior management commitment to innovation is a key factor in innovative organizations. However, three distinct roles can be delineated in this unanimity.

The first is the role of the general manager to direct their organization, and to enable/make things happen (Kamm 1987; Baden-Fuller 1995). As was noted earlier, the implementation of innovation can require a 'hands-on' and directive managerial approach at a senior level, if innovative ideas are to be turned into reality. Boeker (1997) has also argued that the positive performance of 'top teams' is a key determinant of successful organizational transformation. A more normative version of this argument is the emphasis upon entrepreneurship as a key trait in senior management for innovative organizations, where the emphasis is upon resource acquisition and its transformation into products or services. Drucker (1985), quoted previously, is a good example of this approach, as are Robert and Weiss (1988: 8):

> Innovation is the tool of entrepreneurs . . . This simply requires a willingness to see change as opportunity instead of as threat and to employ some process for the orderly examination of change. Innovation is the entrepreneur's method of moving extra resources and assets from low yield and profitability to areas of high yield and productivity.

A further modification of this approach, though, is that of the 'intrapreneur' (Pinchot 1985; Knight 1987), who is:

> . . . a corporate employee who introduces and manages an innovative project within the corporate environment, as if he or she were an independent entrepreneur.
>
> (Knight 1987: 285)

A second role envisaged for management in innovation is the creation and management of an organizational culture. This was first suggested by Burns and Stalker (1961) and has been given considerable prominence in the work of Hage (Hage and Aiken 1967; Hage and Dewar 1973; Hage 1980). Here the role is not so much the proactive development of innovation as the creation and support of a climate that supports innovation throughout the organization. Innovation and change hence become basic values of the organization. This view was subsequently expressed more succinctly by Jelinek and Schoonhoven (1990: 203):

> A strategy for innovation is contained not in 'plans', but in the pattern of commitments, decisions, approaches, and persistent behaviours that facilitate doing new things . . . [Managers] behave, make decisions, and commit in ways that persistently foster innovation.

It is important to emphasize that this requires a distinctive managerial approach to be taken. Nystrom (1979) and Heap (1989) have pointed out that there is an irreconcilable tension between the needs of an organization to be efficient and to be innovative. They maintain that a choice needs to be made between the mass production of standardized products/services, with limited risks, but often small profit margins, and innovation of new products/services, with greater risks but also potentially greater profits. The two choices require different leadership styles, it is argued. Despres (1991) has argued that the failure to understand this dichotomy, and the limitations of the rational model of management in general, has been one of the major constraints on the innovative capacity of organizations. Further, Colville and Packman (1996) have argued that, even where the nature and significance of cultural management is understood, it can be notoriously difficult to achieve.

The final leadership role is somewhat different from the above two. It is not necessarily located at a senior management level, and indeed may often be represented by a lower-level figure in the organization. This is the role of the 'product champion' or 'hero innovator' who supports an innovation at its early stage of development, even when it does not seem to accord with the strategic direction of the organization. Both Schon (1963) and Fischer *et al.* (1986) argue that this role is required because of the inability of formal organizations to respond to change. Thus a mediator is needed to balance the present needs of the organization for stability against its future need for change.

Moving on to the final aspect of the internal environment of an organization, *its organizational life or routine*, three factors have been emphasized here. These are the nature of the staff group of an organization, the complexity of the tasks that they undertake, and the nature of organizational communication.

All three of these factors were integrated in the early model of Burns and Stalker (1961), of the organic organization. Subsequent studies have sought to separate out these factors rather more. Both Aiken and Hage (1971) and Iwamura and Jog (1991) have argued for the educational and professional level of the staff group of an organization as being a key factor in promoting innovation by that organization. Doudeyns and Hayman (1993) have also argued for this as

135

a key statistical indicator of the innovative potential of organizations. In contrast, Zaltman *et al.* (1973) and Abernathy and Utterbach (1988) have emphasized the importance of task complexity as promoting innovative activity within organizations.

Attention has been turned to the role of communication channels and patterns within organizations as a key factor in their innovative potential. Poole (1981, 1983a, 1983b; Poole and Roth 1989) has been a most influential scholar in developing this perspective and Van de Ven *et al.* (1989) subsequently integrated this factor into their holistic model of innovative organizations. Albrecht and Hall (1991) have also maintained that internal communication is *the* key factor in organizational capacity to innovate.

Given the complexity of organizational life Rickards (1985) recommends, once again, a *contingent* approach (Lawrence and Lorsch 1967), which examines the interplay of these, and other internal factors. Importantly this approach also places these internal environmental factors in the context of their interrelationship with the external environment of an organization. The wider role of this external environment as a potential factor in the innovative capacity of organizations must now be examined.

The relationship of an organization to its external organizational environment

The central flaw in some of the organization studies literature is that it tends to treat organizations as if they exist in a vacuum. Further, whilst a number of studies, from as far back as 1969, have recognized the importance of the external environment in innovation, they have had little of substance to say about the nature and extent of its influence (for example: Mohr 1969, 1987; Abernathy and Utterbach 1988). This has led some to dismiss the utility of the innovation studies literature, as being unable to predict innovative capacity and trends, precisely because of its neglect of environmental issues (Mensch 1985). However, this is an area whose contribution is growing. As will be seen below, though, this contribution has its own problems.

Those studies that have addressed the external environment have usually stemmed from one of two sources. *The first source* is those studies which have their roots in the economics literature and which have been concerned almost wholly with the activities of for-profit organizations in the marketplace.

The focus here is the issue and impact of the competitive environment. A core component of this approach is the link between this competitive environment, innovation, and a competitive advantage for one firm over other firms within this market. Thus, it is the spur of inter-firm competition that defines the direction and nature of any innovation. This in turn gives the successful innovator a competitive advantage through which to gain a price and/or market-share advantage over its competitors (see Kamien and Schwartz 1982; Nelson and Winter 1982; Gomulka 1990; Nelson 1993a; and Morris and Westbrook 1996).

In the words of one of the major advocates of this view, innovation:

> is one of the principal drives of competition. It plays a major role in industry structural change, as well as in creating new industries of all the things that can change the rules of competition, [innovation] is among the most prominent.
>
> (Porter 1985: 164)

The argument is most concisely summarized by Nelson (1993b: 364):

> For-profit business firms in rivalrous competition with each other are the featured actors [in innovation]. Firms innovate in order to gain competitive advantage over their rivals or to catch up with them. A firm that successfully innovates can profit handsomely. On the other hand, in an industry where competitors innovate, a firm is virtually forced to do so, or fall further behind.

> In most industries a company gains profit from its innovation by getting it out into the market ahead of its competitors, moving rapidly down the learning curve, and supporting the product and improvements to it through sales and service efforts.
>
> (Nelson 1993b: 367)

A second rather different perspective upon the inter-organizational environment is provided by the network theory perspective (Powell *et al.* 1996; Robertson *et al.* 1996). Camagni (1991a: 3) focuses upon the *innovation milieu*, which is defined as 'the set . . . of mainly informal social relationships [within] a limited geographic area'. From this perspective, innovation is seen to arise not out of the competition between organizations, but from their interaction. Alter and Hage (1993: 2) argue that there is now a move away from competitive relationships with other organizations within a particular market and toward collaboration:

> Until recently, US corporations adopted organizational structures that were large and centralized . . . Corporate strategy was to eliminate competitors to gain control over their buyers or suppliers, and the methods were merger, price war, and large advertising budgets . . . Profit making organizations' primary objective, of course, was to gain maximum leverage over needed resources by besting rivals by whatever means were at hand . . .

> Today, however, many companies are developing structures that are smaller, decentralized, and based on strategies of cooperation and horizontal relationships . . . [This] has led to a variety of obligational networks, bound together by sub-contracts and comparative contracts among small firms, and strategic alliances and joint ventures among large and small firms.
>
> (see also Tidd 1995)

This has happened, they say, because of the increasing complexity and open-endedness of many organizational goals, and because of the desire to share risks in an uncertain market. Nohria (1992) agrees, arguing that organizational networks are now an essential component of *the new competition*, where expertise and knowledge are so widely dispersed that collaboration with some organizations in your market sector is essential to gaining a competitive advantage over other organizations (see also Burt 1982, 1992; and Best 1990). In this model, thus, innovation can only occur through collaboration, which brings together the knowledge, capital and personnel necessary for its achievement (Kreiner and Schultz 1993). An important issue here is that networks are seen, not as an alternative to competition, but as a different and currently more effective way through which to achieve a competitive advantage.

The second source of studies about the external environment is those studies which have developed out of an explicitly contingent approach to the study of organizations, emphasizing the interrelationship between the structure and internal environment of an organization and with its external environment as being the key trigger to innovative activity (Astley and Van de Ven 1983; Rickards 1985). From this literature it is possible to discern two interrelated views about the impact of this interrelationship. These are concerned with the relationship of an organization to its end-users, and its overall strategic orientation to the market (Berry 1994).

The role of end-users in shaping the innovative capacity of organizations has been a consistent theme in much of the organization studies literature (Von Hippel 1978, 1982; Freeman 1982; Twiss 1987; Robert and Weiss 1988), as discussed above, and views marketing as one of the prime motivators of innovation. Probably one of the most forceful proponents of this view, though was Tom Peters:

> The excellent companies are better listeners. They get a benefit from . . . closeness that for us was truly unexpected. Most of the real innovation comes from the market.
>
> (Peters and Waterman 1982: 193)

An alternative view of this factor places the relationship to end-users within the overall strategic orientation of an organization. At one level this concerns the direct commitment to innovation as a goal (or *the* goal) of an organization, highlighted

138

in relation to organizational leadership previously (Nystrom 1979; Heap 1989). More fundamentally, however, it concerns also its wider strategic orientation to its environment.

The decisive work here is certainly that of Miles and Snow (1978) and Pfeffer and Salancik (1978), though other formulations of this approach can be found in Astley and Van de Ven (1983) and in Cho *et al.* (1996), while in Beekum and Ginn (1993) is a rare application to the public sector. Zahria and Pearce (1990) also provide an excellent critique of this model. The core argument of this approach is that organizations have a choice in the way in which they relate to their external environment. This environment is a complex multi-faceted reality, and managers can choose what they focus on within it, and how they choose to interpret what they see there. Miles and Snow developed four managerial *gestalts*, or mind-sets, through which to analyse these strategic approaches. These are displayed in Box 7.3. In these gestalts, it is the prospector and the analyser who are likely to unlock the innovative potential of an organization, through their dynamic approach to the environment.

The environmental approach to innovative capacity thus includes two views as to its causality. The first concerns the impact of that environment itself. This has invariably been posed in terms of the market environment, and the argument has been developed in terms of whether the search for increased profits in this market has promoted innovation through either competition or collaboration. The second approach has concerned the strategic response of organizations to their environment and the extent to which this has seen innovation or stability as the best means through which to achieve organizational survival and growth.

Yet if these approaches identify different routes for the release of the innovative capacity of organizations, they converge nonetheless upon the acceptance of the prevailing environmental paradigm as being one of the market. They are alternatives only in that they identify different perspectives upon this paradigm.

BOX 7.3 THE MILES AND SNOW STRATEGIC *GESTALTS*

- *the defender*, who seeks stability and offers a limited product line, with an emphasis upon efficiency;
- *the prospector*, who seeks a dynamic environment and offers a broad or changing product line to respond to this;
- *the analyser*, who seeks a balance between stable and dynamic markets, and who offers a mix of efficient and flexible products; and
- *the reactor*, who reacts on the spur of the moment, with no consistent strategy.

Review: towards a unified theory of innovation?

> Innovation is not a homogeneous category. All innovations share the characteristic of newness, but beyond newness the array of innovations adopted by any organization may be a mixture of types each having different attributes . . . some types of innovation ideas percolate up the organization, some are imposed from above, and other types of ideas move in both directions. The consequence of this heterogeneity is that the adoption of ideas from different innovation sub-categories will be related to different organizational and environmental factors and will follow different processes. Studying one innovation category will produce markedly different findings from the study of another category.
>
> (Daft and Becker 1978: 120–1)

This chapter has thus far taken in a 'grand tour' (or perhaps 'package trip'?) of innovation, from the perspective of the managerial and organization studies literature. It began by defining innovation and by developing a typology of it. It then moved on to look at the characteristics of innovations before concluding by discussing the actual process of innovation.

Such a broad review is unlikely to produce closely linked conclusions. Nonetheless, a number of important points do rise to the surface. First, innovation is about the introduction and adoption of new ideas that produce a change in the existing relationships between an organization and its internal and external environments. Second, any typology of innovation needs to take account of its impact on both these environments. An example of just such a typology is that of Abernathy *et al.* (1983). Third, the process of innovation involves an optional stage (invention) and two compulsory ones (implementation and diffusion/evaluation). Fourth, it is vital to emphasize the issue of *discontinuity* in discussing innovation, and in differentiating it from other, more incremental, forms of organizational change. Finally, the management of the changes inherent in innovation involves both rational and political components. The precise balance between these needs has to be analysed for any particular innovation.

The key question in concluding this review is to ask whether this literature offers a single unifying theory of innovation. The answer to this is a resounding 'no'. As should have become clear in this review, the act of innovation is a nexus of a number of heterogeneous elements. To try to bring all of these within the realms of one theory stretches the credibility of our bounded rationality. Such a conclusion is not original, and has been well argued before (Downs and Mohr 1976; Daft and Becker 1978; Clark 1987; Mohr 1987).

However, if it is not possible to construct a single theory of innovation, it is possible to develop some guidelines for its understanding. First, there is a need for more focused research within clearly defined fields of innovation. These fields should be homogeneous enough to be able to produce generalizable results (within that field) and be developed with a view to comparison with data from other fields. Again, this is no new insight. The SAPPHO team made a similar call in the early 1970s (Achilladelis *et al.* 1972; Rothwell 1975). The importance of defining the field of analysis to organizations with a shared environment, or niche, has also been demonstrated by the 'organizational ecology' studies of more recent years (Hannan and Freeman 1989).

Second, any theory needs to be developed within a model of contingency that acknowledges the situational specifics of innovation. Thus the emphasis should not be upon defining static configurations of characteristics that might identify innovative organizations. Rather it should be upon developing an understanding of the relationships involved in the event and process of innovation. This is a complex task. At the very least it requires two-dimensional analyses, such as those of Nystrom (1979) and Daft and Becker (1978). It could also make use of three-dimensional models, such as catastrophe theory (Herbig 1991), rather than the more one-dimensional models, such as diffusion theory (Rogers and Shoemaker 1971).

Finally, the development of a contingency model of innovation theory requires a greater understanding of, and weighting given to, the effects both of the characteristics of innovative organizations and of the external environment upon innovation. This is discussed in greater detail in the next section. In sum, this section has argued against the development of overblown and over-ambitious innovation theory. In its place it calls for a series of smaller-scale innovation models, within specific contexts. These need to be based upon the contingency paradigm and in particular need to acknowledge the influence of the external environment as a key variable in the process of innovation.

THE PUBLIC MANAGEMENT LITERATURE ON INNOVATION

This section explores the literature on innovation in public services. It is split into five sub-sections:

- an **overview of research** about innovation in public services;
- innovation and **public policy**;
- innovation and the **management/organization of PSOs**;
- innovation in the specific field of **community care services**;
- and a discussion of our **understanding of the nature of innovation in public services, and its implications for management practice in PSOs,** on the basis of this research and literature.

141

Research about innovation in public services

The emphasis in the management of PSOs has changed over the last thirty years. In the 1960s, with the rationing of the war and post-war years not long gone, the emphasis was upon establishing a minimum basic entitlement for everyone, within the context of an expanding welfare state. The 1970s and early 1980s, however, saw a period of retrenchment of mainstream services, as the resource base of the state contracted, compared to invariably expanding populations and changing demography, as well as developments in perceptions of need.

The period since the mid-1980s has seen a third phase develop, with 'innovation' as its watchword, and especially in the field of the personal social services (PSS). This has encompassed both innovation for reasons of efficiency, because of the growing population of adults and children recognized as having special needs, but with no commensurate increase in the resource base, and innovation for reasons of effectiveness, because of the pressure on services to meet increasingly individual definitions of social need. Whilst this trend has been especially marked in the UK and the US, similar trends are also current across the world (see for example Pinto (1998) on the developing world and Eshima *et al.* (2001) on Japanese experience).

The literature about the PSS, in particular, has produced a large number of studies of innovation. It is argued here, however, that the majority of these have been either descriptive, or evangelical, and often written within the framework of the professional social work paradigm. There is nothing wrong with this in itself; indeed it is an important contribution to the development of efficient and effective social work services. However, these studies have failed to address the equally important organizational and managerial issues which innovation raises, and have frequently been written (once again) in isolation from the organization studies literature, which could have contributed much to an understanding of these issues.

Accordingly, this section will commence by reviewing the existing studies of innovation in PSOs and draw some conclusions from these. In particular, it will pay attention to those studies that have attempted to develop a model of innovation in public services. It will argue that there is a lack both of good empirical evidence about innovation by PSOs and of a solid framework by which to analyse it. A final section will draw these two literatures together with that of managerial literature discussed earlier, and explore what potential contribution the latter can make to the former.

As indicated previously, there have been numerous studies of innovation by PSOs. This review will concentrate primarily, though not exclusively, on the field of the PSS, for that is where the majority of studies have been located. It will focus upon research in three areas: the prevailing public policy/PSS paradigm, the management and organization of the PSS, child-care services, and community services.

Innovation and public policy

One of the key developments of the late 1980s and early 1990s was the promotion of innovation to the status of a policy goal in its own right. On the one hand, this sprang from the overriding concern of national governments at that time to introduce a more business-oriented and competitive paradigm into the provision of public services. The intention here, combining a mixture of Schumpeterian and neo-classical models of economics, was both to introduce the winds of 'creative destruction' into these services through competition and to encourage cost efficiencies through the expansion of the market model into the provision of public services. These intentions have been the subject of critical analysis by, among others, Le Grand (1991).

On the other hand, there was also pressure from advocates of professional groups, particularly in the PSS, to raise innovation to the status of a policy goal. The King's Fund Institute (1987) in the UK certainly argued for the centrality of innovation in the community-care reforms, though without ever really defining what this meant. In a more polemical vein, Smale and Tuson (1990) at the National Institute of Social Work argued for innovation to be elevated to the status of a method of social-work intervention. The UK Department of Health also explored the model of *outcome funding* as a way of allocating scarce governmental funding for the PSS, with an emphasis upon innovation as an indicator of success (Williams and Webb 1992).

A third approach has also been advocated by Kinder (2002) who has argued for the use of rigorous case study analysis as a means by which to advance public policy practice. In doing so he emphasizes the importance of knowledge transfer and management to the innovation process.

Yet if innovation has become a policy goal at this time, even if a rather indeterminate one, there have been few studies of the rationale for, or impact of, it. Those that have addressed this issue have primarily been American, rather than British. Feller (1981), for example, has suggested that this concentration upon innovation was an example of 'conspicuous production' – that is, that it was a way of managers proving their effectiveness in an arena where few, if any, objective measures of success existed. A similar argument has also been advanced from the standpoint of the institutional analysis of organizations by Singh *et al.* (1991).

Innovation in the management and organization of PSOs

There is little doubt that the work of the Personal Social Services Research Unit (PSSRU) at the University of Kent in the UK has been highly influential in focusing attention upon the need for a managerial approach to innovation by PSOs (see, for

143

example, Davies and Challis 1986; Davies *et al.* 1990; Knapp *et al.* 1990). It is undoubtedly more rigorous than much of such work, deriving from the lucid theoretical framework provided by the *production of welfare* model of the PSS and pioneered again by the PSSRU (Knapp 1984). However, despite its rigour at this level, if still lacks any analysis of the nature and process of innovation itself.

This is also true of the other studies of management innovation in the PSS:

- Goldberg and Warburton (1979) reviewed the management of workloads in SSDs and developed an alternative *case review* model.
- Healy (1989) produced a major review of management innovation practices in SSDs.
- Hardy *et al.* (1989) reviewed innovative management arrangements for joint working in the PSS.
- Dibben and Bartlett (2001) and Bartlett and Dibben (2002) explored the role both of leadership and user empowerment in service innovations in local government services in the UK.

All these studies provided good descriptions of the work undertaken and provide many valuable lessons for future practice. The best (particularly Goldberg and Warburton, Dibben and Bartlett, and Bartlett and Dibben) also produced some evaluation of the implementation of innovation. However, overall, there is a lack of any attempt to analyse innovation as a process itself, or to borrow from the organization studies literature for an understanding of the nature of the phenomenon.

The exception to this has been the work of Osborne (1998a, 1998b, 1998c), who explored the innovation capacity of voluntary organizations in the field of the PSS. He developed a model of this capacity which drew explicitly on the management and organization studies literature and which emphasized the significance of environmental and institutional factors in the release of this innovative capacity. Walker (2001) subsequently expanded this work to explore innovative activity by PSOs in the field of housing. It will be returned to below.

Important work has been carried out in the US. Daft and Becker (1991) was an early important study that focused attention on the political nature of the innovation process, whilst Berry (1994) produced an early study on strategic approaches to innovation and public management. More recently, at a descriptive level, Altshuler and Behn (1997) pulled together a series of case studies of innovation in public management in the UK and Donahue (1999) described 'tales' of innovation in the federal government in the US. There has also been a particular focus on issues of leadership in relation to PSOs and innovation. Roberts and King (1996) explored the nature of entrepreneurship in American PSOs, whilst, both Cohen and Eimicke (1998) and Light (1998) have explored the managerial challenges of leadership for innovation in the PSS.

By far the greatest contribution, though, has come from Sandford Borins. In a series of studies (Borins 2000, 2001a, 2001b, 2001c, 2001d, 2002) Borins has explored the contingent factors that impact upon the innovative capacity of PSOs. Based upon extensive quantitative analysis (both in North America and across the Commonwealth counties) he argues that innovation is difficult to achieve in PSOs because the rewards for it are 'meagre' whilst the consequences of unsuccessful innovation are 'grave' (Borins 2001a: 6). He produces a set of five characteristics of successful innovations in PSOs (Box 7.4a) as well as seven principles to guide managers in developing innovation in them (Box 7.4b)

Innovation in community care services

The 1980s saw a series of innovations in the delivery of community care services in the UK. At the most general level, the work of the PSSRU in piloting and evaluating community care innovations has already been noted. Some more recent

BOX 7.4 (a) CHARACTERISTICS OF SUCCESSFUL INNOVATIONS

- The use of systems approach.
- The use of new technology.
- Process improvement.
- The involvement of private/voluntary bodies in public services.
- The empowerment of citizens and PSO staff.

(b) GUIDELINES FOR THE MANAGEMENT OF INNOVATION IN PSOs

- Support a culture of innovation from the top of it.
- Increase rewards for innovation.
- Establish an innovation fund to support innovative projects.
- Encourage diversity inside the organization, in order to engender differential perspectives on issues.
- Use information effectively.
- Draw on ideas from staff at all organizational levels.
- Value experimentation – and learn from it.

Based on Borins (2001a)

studies have also examined specific aspects of this initiative, such as the work of Barritt (1990) on innovations in community care in non-metropolitan areas, and Barnes and Wistow (1992) on the problems of sustaining initiatives beyond the pilot stage.

There have also been studies of innovations within particular client-based services:

- Marks and Scott (1990) and Ramon and Giannichedda (1991) have both reviewed innovative approaches to the delivery of mental health services.
- Grant and McGrath (1987) examined a community-based approach in Wales to services for people with learning difficulties (the All Wales Strategy).
- Connelly (1990) and Ross (1995) have looked at services for people with disabilities.
- Morris and Giller (1987) and Schall (1997) explored systemic approaches to the community care of young offenders.
- Parker *et al.* (1991) and Connelly (1994) evaluated approaches to the community care of children and families.

Undoubtedly the largest group of studies, though, concern services for elderly people. Ferlie and his colleagues have produced almost a library of such studies on their own (for example, Davies and Ferlie 1982; Ferlie 1983; Davies and Ferlie 1984; Ferlie *et al.* 1984a, 1984b, 1989). The emphasis in all Ferlie's studies is upon the efforts of the statutory authorities to produce more efficient ways of meeting the needs of elderly people within their own communities.

More generally, Marshall and Sommerville (1983) and Isaacs and Evers (1984) have evaluated innovative community-based services for elderly people, in Liverpool and Birmingham respectively, and Fisher (1994) has looked at the specific issue of the role of male carers. Butler (1985), Kraan *et al.* (1991) and Myrtle and Willer (1994) have also provided overviews of a range of developments of community care services for elderly people in different national contexts. Once again, though, *the innovation process* itself is ignored.

Understanding innovation in public services

All of the studies reviewed above provide both valuable insights into the new types of services developed in this field, and an invaluable source literature for those wanting to design new services. The best have also evaluated the impact of these innovations in the field. However, as should now be apparent, there have been few attempts to address the issue of understanding the nature of the process of innovation in social welfare services. An early study had found this to be the case in the 1970s (Delbecq 1978), and little seems to have changed since then.

Perhaps this is to do the literature an injustice; no doubt many of its authors would argue, quite rightly, that this was not their purpose. If not their purpose, however, it is still a task essential to the greater understanding of the provision of social welfare services. This section will therefore review that limited number of attempts to develop such an understanding.

Four approaches to understanding innovation in social welfare can be identified from the literature. Hasenfeld and Schmid (1989) have pinpointed the lifecycle of social services organizations as the key parameter of the development of innovative services. In doing so they were drawing upon a sizeable theme in organization studies (for example, Bessant and Grunt 1985). However, their approach was a discursive one, with little evidence produced to support their position and with no attempt to develop the implications of their framework for the actual management of innovation in the PSS.

A second approach to understanding innovation was taken by those studies that concentrated upon the role of strategic management and planning. Work in the 1970s by Rothman (1974) and Rothman et al. (1976) proposed a planning based model of innovation in the PSS which emphasized the importance of such: strategic planning in developing innovative services. The 1976 study took the form of a manual for service managers to use in developing innovation in the organization. This work was later brought together in the social marketing model of Rothman (1980; see also Berry 1994), which provided a rationalist model of planning to produce innovation.

This rationalist approach has been explicitly challenged by later studies, influenced by the work of the management 'guru' Tom Peters (for example, Peters and Waterman 1982). In particular, Golden (1990) has argued that her empirical studies have indicated that, far from requiring careful planning, successful innovation in human services is the result of 'groping along'.

Both these approaches draw attention to the managerial and strategic role in innovation in the PSS, and the Golden study was also based upon empirical evidence. Yet both approaches were too narrow in their focus to provide a holistic understanding of innovation. In particular, they ignored the impact of the social environment upon human service organizations in the development of innovative services, and the Peters and Waterman study also, by its commitment to the rationalist model, ignored the often irrational (or at least, arational) and apparently paradoxical nature of change within organizations.

The third approach was one taken by a number of studies and was to relate innovation specifically to the need to counter the bureaucratic nature of public services. Young (1976) has argued that this bureaucratic nature of public services inhibited their ability to innovate, which required entrepreneurial exercise. Gershuny (1983), in polemical vein, has also argued that innovation in public sector welfare services was required to make them more efficient so that they could meet the growing needs of service recipients rather than provide job security for public

147

sector employees. However, once again, no evidence was produced to support these implications. Moreover, the argument was structured in the form of exhortations to practising managers, rather than within a conceptual or analytic framework. Brodtrick (1998) does take a less polemical view of the issue. He argues for the explicit adoption of a 'learning organization' approach (see the earlier discussion in this volume, above) by PSOs and a focus on communication as a response to the bureaucratic tendencies of PSOs.

The fourth approach, of Ferlie *et al.* (1989), did produce such a framework, embedded within the production-of-welfare model discussed above. It also produced evidence to support its analysis of the relationship between innovation and the need for efficiency. The major drawback with this analysis is that it was limited to examining a subset of innovations within the PSS: that is, those concerned with the need to innovate in established mature services where environmental factors (in this case, demography and funding) had produced pressure for change. Thus, it ignored a whole range of innovative developments that spring not from the need for efficiency but rather from other imperatives, such as the need to address a newly defined need (a good recent example of this being services for people with AIDS).

These points were well drawn together by Baldock (1991) and Baldock and Evers (1991). These studies pointed to two possible pressures to innovate. The first was for 'bottom-up innovation', where a social or demographic change led to pressure for a new form of service in one locality, and which produced *ad hoc* innovation. This was often on a small scale, and was hard to replicate elsewhere or to integrate into the existing statutory services. It was based explicitly, however, upon meeting the expressed needs of the local community and frequently used existing resources in a new way. It thus expanded choice, but often at the cost of efficiency to the welfare system as a whole.

This was contrasted with 'top-down innovation', which sprang directly from the growing resource constraints of the statutory welfare services. This was directed at meeting an already recognized need more efficiently, by targeting existing services more accurately, by sharpening the boundaries between different services so as to utilize the cheapest, or by developing new cost-efficient forms of service.

The approach of Baldock is undoubtedly a helpful one in understanding innovation in public services, in that it takes account both of organizational and of environmental factors in the development of innovation. He does not take the approach sufficiently far, though. In presenting a simple dichotomy between needs-led and efficiency-led innovation, he ignores the intermediary cases, where the parameters of innovation could derive from both imperatives. A good example of this is the development of community-based living arrangements for adults with learning difficulties. Here there is both a needs-led pressure, because of the recognition that this is a far more appropriate way in which to provide homes for such adults, and an efficiency-led pressure, derived from the increasing number of adults requiring such community living options to be organized by SSDs, as a result of the closure of hospital-based accommodation.

In conclusion, it is suggested that the above attempts at understanding innovation within the PSS suffered from three faults. First, as has been a common refrain in this chapter, many of the studies lacked an empirical base and were often framed in a polemical or discursive manner. Second, they frequently adopted a simple linear and/or rationalist model of innovation, which belied its dynamism and complexity. Even the work of Baldock, which is probably the most complex attempt, was based on a simple dichotomy.

Third, several of the studies were so narrow in their approach as to ignore the breadth of innovative activity in the PSS. Finally, the majority of studies were constructed in almost total isolation from the organization studies literature. Ferlie *et al.* (1989; see also Perri 6, 1993) did discuss the implications of the work of Burns and Stalker (1961), whilst Rothman also referred to the work of Rogers and Shoemaker (1971). However, this is but to touch upon the range of material available and not necessarily upon the most sophisticated.

If a proper understanding of innovation in the PSS is to be developed it is suggested here that it is necessary to take greater cognizance of the managerial and organization studies literature. This is essential in order both to construct a meaningful conceptual framework for the understanding of innovation and to develop effective tools for its analysis, in constructing a framework. This task has best been achieved by Osborne (1998a).

COMBINING THE LITERATURES: DEVELOPING A THEORETICAL FRAMEWORK FOR UNDERSTANDING INNOVATION IN PUBLIC SERVICES

Overview

This section examines the extent to which it is possible to combine the insights from the organizational/innovation studies literature together with those from the dedicated literature on innovation in public services, in order to develop further our understanding of innovation in public services. Underpinning this discussion will be the work of Osborne (1998a), who drew extensively upon the managerial and organization studies literature in developing his theoretical model of the innovative capacity of VNPOs.

Three general issues from the managerial and organization studies literature about innovation are particularly relevant to understanding innovation both within VNPOs in particular – and PSOs in general. First, with regard to the nature of innovation, it is important to be clear about the significance of *discontinuity* as a core element of innovation. One issue to be teased out in the research discussed below is the differing roles and impacts of service *developments* (that is, the gradual improvement of, or changes to, existing services to the existing users of an organization) compared to actual *innovation*. This distinction is never really drawn out in public management literatures. However, its import is clear from the organization studies literature, in terms of its impact both upon its host organizations and upon their relationship with their end users.

Second, with regard to the nature of the innovators, it is important that the insights of the contingency approach be appreciated. The interrelationship between the host organization of an innovation and its environment is one that often seems to be lacking in the existing public management literature. It is true that some studies discussed above do talk about the role of end users in influencing innovation, as in the *bottom-up* innovation of Baldock and Evers (1991). However, this is but one element of the overall environment. The managerial and organization studies literature has provided some useful guidance over the full range of factors to be considered in this context.

Finally, the managerial and organization studies literature has provided a crucial conceptual framework for considering the causal factors involved in the innovative capacity of PSOs. Where these issues have been considered previously in the public management literature, they have been raised on a purely empirical, or even normative, basis. The managerial and organization studies literature gives a conceptual clarity to these issues that has been missing from the discussion till now. Significantly, it has also allowed the development of both a conceptual typology of innovation in public services (Osborne 1998b) and a research tool for studying its impact within PSOs – the modified Aston Measures (Osborne 1998c).

Developing a classification of change and innovation in public services

As discussed above, the issue of discontinuity is a core element of any definition of innovation. This is important in differentiating gradual organizational development, which may nonetheless produce major changes in service delivery over a period of time, from the actual process of innovation. This conceptual clarity will be important for this study, in differentiating *genuine* innovation from *ascribed* innovation. As Carter (1974) made clear, the term 'innovation' is often used in a pejorative and normative sense by the staff and supporters of voluntary activity and organizations, whilst the public management literature has frequently used a lax definition of it. It is argued here that, by reference to the managerial and organization studies literature, one can develop more rigour in the understanding and classification of the innovative capacity of PSOs, which delineates it from the organizational developmental activity identified above.

It is argued here that a useful approach to classifying and understanding organizational change and innovation in PSOs can be evolved by modifying the approach of Abernathy *et al.* (1983), discussed above. There is a developing managerial literature which is concerned both with understanding public services in terms of the markets that they serve (Crompton and Lamb 1988) and with viewing their management within a general management context rather than a service or professional one, such as social work or nursing (Nutley and Osborne 1994, McLaughlin *et al.* 2002). This literature suggested that it could be possible to develop a classification of change and innovation by adapting the model of Abernathy *et al.*

In terms of public services, therefore, the *method of production* is not (usually) a technological process that is transformed by the application of new scientific knowledge. Rather it is frequently an interpersonal (or sometimes inter-organizational) process, but one which can nevertheless be changed by the introduction of new knowledge – whether it be about, for example, the needs of service users, or the efficiency and effectiveness of methods of care. Similarly the actual users, or clients, of social services are the *market* for these services.

The typology presented here was developed by Osborne (1998a, 1998b) upon the basis of these assumptions and by the modification of the original model of Abernathy *et al.* to take account of them. This modified typology is displayed in Figure 7.2. The typology situates innovation as part of organizational change in general, allows different modes of innovation to be clarified, and distinguishes it from incremental organizational development. The x-axis now becomes concerned with the impact of an organizational change upon the actual services

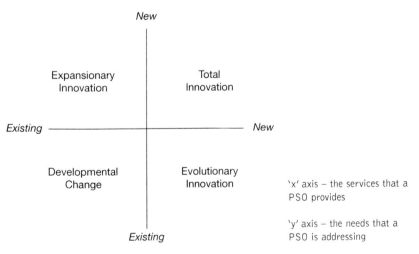

Figure 7.2 *A classification of innovation in public services.*

Source: Based on Osborne (1998a).

Baldock, J. and A. Evers (1991) On social innovation – an introduction. In R. Kraan et al. (eds), Care for the Elderly. Significant Innovations in Three European Countries. Campus Verlag, Frankfurt, pp. 87–92.

Barnes, M. and G. Wistow (1992) Sustaining innovation in community care, Local Government Policy Making 18(4): 3–19.

Barnett, H. (1953) Innovation: The Basis of Cultural Change. McGraw-Hill, New York.

Barras, R. (1989) Towards a theory of innovation in services, Research Policy 15(4): 161–74.

Barritt, A. (1990) Innovations in community care. Family Policy Studies Centre, London.

Bartlett, D. and P. Dibben (2002) Public sector innovation and entrepreneurship: Case studies from local government, Local Government Studies 28(4): 107–21.

Beck, S. and T. Whistler (1967) Innovative organizations: a selective view of current theory and research, Journal of Business 40: 462–9.

Becker, S. and F. Stafford (1967) Some determinants of organizational success, Journal of Business 40: 511–18.

Beekum, R. and G. Ginn (1993) Business strategy and inter-organizational linkages within the acute care hospital industry: an expansion of the Miles and Snow typology, Human Relations 46(11): 1291–318.

Beer, M. and A. Walton (1987) Organizational change and development, Annual Review of Psychology 38: 339–67a.

Berry, F. (1994) Innovation in public management: the adoption of strategic planning, Public Administration Review 54(4): 322–30.

Bessant, J. and M. Grunt (1985) Management and Manufacturing Innovation in the United Kingdom and West Germany. Gower, Aldershot.

Best, M. (1990) The New Competition. Polity Press, Cambridge.

Bhoovaraghaven, S., A. Vasudevan and R. Chaudran (1996) Resolving the process vs product innovation dilemma: a consumer choice theoretical approach, Management Science 42(2): 232–46.

Blau, P. and W. Scott (1963) Formal Organizations. Routledge and Kegan Paul, London.

Boeker, W. (1997) Strategic change: the influence of managerial characteristics and organizational growth, Academy of Management Journal 40(1).

Borins, S. (2000) Loose cannons and rule breakers, or enterprising leaders? Some evidence about innovative public managers, Public Administration Review 60(6): 498–507.

Borins, S. (2001a) The Challenge of Innovating in Government. Price Waterhouse Cooper Endowment for the Business of Government, Arlington.

Borins, S. (2001b) Innovation, success and failure in public management research: some methodological reflections, Public Management Review 3(1): 3–18.

Borins, S. (2001c) Encouraging innovation in the public sector, Journal of Intellectual Capital 2(3): 310–19.

Borins, S. (2001d) Public management innovation: toward a global perspective, *American Review of Public Administration* 31(1): 5–21.

Borins, S. (2002) Leaders and innovation in the public sector, *Leadership and Organisational Development Journal* 23(8): 467–76.

Brodtrick, O. (1998) Organizational learning and innovation: tools for revitalizing public services, *International Review of Administrative Sciences* 64(1): 83–96.

Burgelman, R. and L. Sayles (1986) *Inside Corporate Innovation*. Free Press, New York.

Burns, T. and G. Stalker (1961) *Management of Innovation*. Tavistock, London.

Burt, R. (1982) A note on co-operation and definitions of constraint. In P. Marsden and N. Lin (eds), *Social Structure and Network Analysis*. Sage, Beverly Hills, pp. 219–33.

Burt, R. (1992) The social structure of competition. In N. Nohria and R. Eccles (eds), *Network and Organizations*. Harvard Business School Press, Boston, pp. 57–91.

Butler, A. (ed.) (1985) *Ageing. Recent Advances and Creative Responses*. Croom Helm, London.

Butler, R. and D. Wilson (1990) *Managing Voluntary and Non-Profit Organisations*. Routledge, London.

Camagni, R. (1991a) From the local 'mileau' to innovation through cooperation networks. In R. Camagni (1991b) (ed.), *Innovation Networks, Spatial Perspectives*. Belhaven Press, London, pp. 1–9.

Carson, J. (1989) *Innovation. A Battle Plan for the 1990s*. Gower, Aldershot.

Carter, N. (1974) *Trends in Voluntary Support for Non Governmental Social Services Agencies*. Canadian Council on Social Welfare, Ottawa.

Cho, H.-D., J.-K. Lee and K.-K. Ro (1996) Environment and technology strategy of firms in government R&D programmes in Korea, *Technovation* 16(10): 553–60.

Clark, P. (1987) *Anglo-American Innovation*. de Gruyter, Berlin.

Clark, P. and N. Stanton (1989) *Innovation in Technology and Organization*. Routledge, London.

Cohen, S. and W. Eimicke (1998) *Tools for Innovators. Creative Strategies for Strengthening Public Sector Organisations*. Jossey-Bass, San Francisco.

Colville, I. and C. Packman (1996) Auditing cultural change, *Public Money and Management* (July/September): 27–32.

Connelly, M. (1994) An act of empowerment: the Children, Young Persons and the Family Act (1989), *British Journal of Social Work* 24(1): 87–100.

Connelly, N. (1990) *Raising Voices*. Policy Studies Institute, London.

Cooper, R. and E. Kleinschmidt (1993) Major new products: what distinguishes the winners in the chemical industry? *Journal of Product Innovation Management* 10(2): 90–111.

Crompton, J. and C. Lamb (1988) *Marketing Governmental Social Services*. John Wiley, New York.

Cyert, R. and J. March (1963) *Behavioural Theory of the Firm*. Prentice-Hall, Englewood Cliffs, NJ.

Daft, R. and S. Becker (1978) *Innovation in Organizations*. Elsevier, New York.

Damanpour, F. (1996) Organizational complexity and innovation, *Management Science* 42(5): 693–716.

Da Rocha, A., C. Christensen and N. Paim (1990) Characteristics of innovative firms in the Brazilian computer industry, *Journal of Product Innovation Management* 7(2): 123–34.

Davies, B. and D. Challis (1986) *Matching Resources to Need*. Gower, Aldershot.

Davies, B. and E. Ferlie (1982) Efficiency prompting innovations in social care: social services departments and the elderly, *Policy and Politics* 10(2): 181–203.

Davies, B. and E. Ferlie (1984) Patterns of efficiency improving innovations: social care of the elderly, *Policy and Politics* 12(3): 281–95.

Davies, B., A. Bebbington and H. Charnley (1990) *Resources, Needs and Outcomes in Community Based Care*. Gower, Aldershot.

Delbecq, A. (1978) The social political process of introducing innovation in human services. In R. Sarri and Y. Hasenfeld (eds), *The Management of Human Services*. Columbia University Press, New York, pp. 309–39.

Despres, C. (1991) Information, technology and culture, *Technovation* 16(1): 1–20.

Deutsch, K. (1966) *The Nerves of Government*. Free Press, New York.

Dibben, P. and D. Bartlett (2001) Local government and service users: empowerment through user-led innovation?, *Local Government Studies* 27(3): 43–58.

DiMaggio, P. and W. Powell (1988) The iron cage revisited. In C. Milofsky (ed.), *Community Organizations*. Oxford University Press, New York, pp. 77–99.

Donahue, J. (1999) (ed.) Making Washington work, *Tasks of Innovation in the Federal Government*. Brookings Institute, Washington, DC.

Doudeyns, M. and E. Hayman (1993) Statistical indicators of innovation, *Economic Trends* (September): 113–23.

Downs, G. and L. Mohr (1976) Conceptual issues in the study of innovation, *Administrative Science Quarterly* 21: 700–14.

Drucker, P. (1985) *Innovation and Entrepreneurship*. Heinemann, London.

Eshima, Y., T. Katayama and T. Ohmo (2001) Public management innovation in Japan: Its characteristics and challenges, *International Review of Administrative Sciences* 67(4): 699–714.

Feller, I. (1981) Public sector innovations as 'conspicuous consumption', *Policy Analysis* 7(1): 1–20.

Ferlie, E. (1983) *Source Book of Innovation in the Community Care of the Elderly*. PSSRU, University of Kent.

Ferlie, E., D. Challis and B. Davies (1984a) Models of innovation in the social care of the elderly, *Local Government Studies* 10(6): 67–72.

Ferlie, E., D. Challis and B. Davies (1984b) *A Guide to Efficiency Improving Innovations in the Care of the Frail Elderly*. PSSRU Discussion Paper 284, University of Kent.

Ferlie, E., D. Challies and B. Davies (1989) *Efficiency Improving Innovation in the Social Care of the Elderly*. Gower, Aldershot.

Fischer, W., W. Hamilton, C. McLaughlin and R. Zmud (1986) The elusive product champion, *Research Management* 29(3): 13–16.

Fisher, M. (1994) Man-made carers: community care and older male carers, *British Journal of Social Work* 24(6): 659–80.

Freeman, C. (1973) A study of success and failure in industrial innovation. In B. Williams (ed.), *Science and Technology in Economic Growth*. Macmillan, London, pp. 227–55.

Freeman, C. (1982) *Economics of Industrial Innovation*. Frances Pinter, London.

Frost, P. and C. Egri (1991) Political process of innovation, *Research in Organizational Behaviour*, 229–96.

Gershuny, J. (1983) *Social Innovation and the Division of Labor*. Oxford University Press, Oxford.

Goldberg, E. and R. Warburton (1979) *Ends and Means in Social Work*. George Allen & Unwin, London.

Golden, O. (1990) Innovation in public sector human service programs: the implications of innovation by 'groping along', *Journal of Policy Analysis and Management* 9(2): 219–48.

Gomulka, S. (1990) *The Theory of Technological Change and Economic Growth*. Routledge, London.

Grant, G. and M. McGrath (eds) (1987) *Community Mental Handicap Teams*. British Institute for Mental Health, Kidderminster.

Hage, J. (1980) *Theories of Organizations*. John Wiley, New York.

Hage, J. and M. Aiken (1967) Program change and organizational properties: a comparative analysis, *American Journal of Sociology* 7(2): 503–19.

Hage, J. and R. Dewar (1973) Elite values versus organizational structure in predicting innovation, *Administrative Science Quarterly* 18: 279–90.

Hannan, M. and J. Freeman (1989) *Organizational Ecology*. Harvard University Press, Cambridge, MA.

Hardy, B., A. Turrell and G. Wistow (1989) *Innovations in Management Arrangements*. CRSP, Loughborough University.

Hasenfeld, Y. and H. Schmid (1989) The life cycle of human service organizations. In Y. Hasenfeld (ed.), *Administrative Leadership in the Social Services*. Haworth Press, New York.

Haveman, H. (1993) Organizational size and change: diversification in the savings and loan industry after deregulation, *Administrative Science Quarterly* 38(1): 20–50.

Healy, P. (ed.) (1989) *Innovatory Management Practice in Social Services Departments*. Local Government Management Board, Luton.

Heap, J. (1989) *The Management of Innovation and Design.* Cassell, London.

Herbig, P. (1991) A cusp catastrophe model of the adoption of an industrial innovation, *Journal of Product Innovation Management* 8(2): 127–37.

Holloman, J. H. (1980) Life cycle, early market conditions and policy implications. In B.-A. Vedin (ed.), *Current Innovation,* pp. 103–12.

Huxham, C. (1993) Collaborative capability, *Public Money and Management* 13(3): 21–8.

Huxham, C. and S. Vangen (1996) Managing inter-organizational relationships. In S. Osborne (ed.), *Managing in the Voluntary Sector.* International Thomson Business Press, London, pp. 202–16.

Isaacs, B. and H. Evers (eds) (1984) *Innovations in the Care of the Elderly.* Croom Helm, London.

Iwamura, A. and V. Jog (1991) Innovation organization structure and the management of the innovation process in the securities industry, *Journal of Product Innovation Management* 8(2): 104–16.

Jelinek, M. and C. Schoonhoven (1990) *The Innovation Marathon.* Blackwell, Oxford.

Kamien, M. and N. Schwartz (1982) *Market Structure and Innovation.* Cambridge University Press, Cambridge.

Kamm, J. (1987) *Integrative Approach to Managing Innovation.* Lexington Books, Lexington, MA.

Kanter, R. (1985) *The Change Masters.* Unwin, London.

Kimberly, J. (1981) Managerial innovation. In P. Nystrom and W. Starbuck (eds), *Handbook of Organizational Design.* Oxford University Press, Oxford, pp. 84–104.

Kimberly, J. (1987) Organizational and contextual influences on the diffusion of technological innovation. In J. Pennings and A. Buitendan (eds), *New Technology as Organization Innovation,* pp. 237–59.

Kinder, T. (2002) Good practice in best practice: the use of best practice case studies in service innovation global public administrations, *Science and Public Policy* 29(3): 221–33.

Knapp, M. (1984) *The Economics of Social Care.* Macmillan, London.

Knapp, M., P. Cambridge, C. Thomason, J. Beecham, C. Allen and R. Darton (1990) *Care in the Community. Lessons from a Demonstration Project.* PSRU, University of Kent.

Knight, K. (1967) A descriptive model in the intra-firm innovation process, *Journal of Business* 40: 478–96.

Knight, R. (1987) Corporate innovation and enterpreneurship, *Journal of Product Innovation Management* 9(4): 284–97.

Knokke, D. and D. Prensky (1984) What relevance do organization theories have for voluntary organizations? *Social Science Quarterly* 63: 3–20.

Kondratiev, N. (1978) The long wave in economic life (translated by W. Stolper) in *Lloyds Bank Review* 129: 41–60.

Kraan, R., J. Baldock, B. Davies, A. Evers, L. Johansson, M. Knappen, M. Thorsland and C. Tunissen (eds) (1991) *Care for the Elderly. Significant Innovation in Three European Countries*. Campus Verlag, Frankfurt.

Kreiner, K. and M. Schultz (1993) Informed collaboration in research and design. The formation of networks across organizations, *Organizational Studies* 14(2): 189–209.

Langrish, L., M. Gibbons, W. Evans and F. Jervons (1972) *Wealth from Knowledge*. Halsted, New York.

Lawrence, P. and J. Lorsch (1967) *Organizations and Environment: Managing Differentiation and Integration*. Harvard University, Boston.

Le Grand, J. (1991) Quasi-markets and social policy, *The Economic Journal* 101: 1256–67.

Light, P. (1998) *Sustaining Innovation: Creating nonprofit and government organisations that innovate naturally*. Jossey-Bass, San Francisco.

McLaughlin, K., S. P. Osborne and E. Ferlie (2002) (eds) *New Public Management. Current Trends and Future Prospects*. Routledge, London.

Mansfield, E. (1963) Size of firm market structure and innovation, *Journal of Political Economy* 71: 556–76.

Marks, I. and R. Scott (1990) *Mental Health Care Delivery*. Cambridge University Press, Cambridge.

Marshall, A. (1966) *Principles of Economics*. Macmillan, London.

Marshall, M. and A. Sommerville (1983) *New Services for Old People*. Liverpool University Press, Liverpool.

Marx, K. (1974) *Capital [Vol. 1]*. Lawrence & Wishart, London.

Mensch, G. (1985) Trends in perspectives in innovation policies. In R. Merrit and A. Merrit (eds), *Innovation in the Public Sector*. Sage, Beverly Hills, pp. 253–67.

Miles, R. and C. Snow (1978) *Organization Strategy Structure and Process*. McGraw-Hill, New York.

Mohr, L. (1969) Determinants of innovation, *American Political Science Review* 63: 111–26.

Mohr, L. (1987) Innovation theory: an assessment from the vantage point of new electronic technology in organizations. In J. Pennings and A. Buitendan (eds), *New Technology as Organizational Innovation*, pp. 13–31.

Mole, V. and D. Elliot (1987) *Enterprising Innovation: An Alternative Approach*. Frances Pinter, London.

Morris, A. and H. Giller (1987) *Understanding Juvenile Justice*. Croom Helm, London.

Morris, T. and R. Westbrook (1996) Technical innovation and competitive advantage in retail financial services, *British Journal of Management* 7(1): 45–61.

Mort, J. (1991) The applicability of percolation theory to innovation, *Journal of Product Innovation Management* 18(1): 32–8.

163

Myrtle, R. and K. Willer (1994) Designing service delivery systems: lessons from the development of community based systems for care of the elderly, *Public Administation Review* 54(3): 245–52.

Nadler, D. (1988) Concepts for the management of organizational change. In M. Tushman and N. Moore (eds), *Readings in the Management of Innovation*. Harper Business, New York, pp. 718–32.

Nelson, R. (1993a) *National Innovation Systems*. Oxford University Press, New York.

Nelson, R. (1993b) Technological innovation: the role of non-profit organizations. In D. Hammock and D. Young (eds), *Nonprofit Organizations in a Market Economy*. Jossey-Bass, San Francisco, pp. 363–77.

Nelson, R. and S. Winter (1982) *An Evolutionary Theory of Economic Change*. Belknapp Press, Cambridge, MA.

Nohria, N. (1992) Is a network perspective a useful way of studying organizations? In N. Nohria and R. Eccles (eds) (1992) *Networks and Organizations*. Harvard Business School Press, Boston, pp. 1–22.

Normann, R. (1971) Organizational innovativeness, *Administrative Science Quarterly* 16: 203–15.

Normann, R. (1991) *Service Management*. John Wiley, Chichester.

Nutley, S. and S. Osborne (1994) *Public Sector Management Handbook*. Longman, London.

Nystrom, H. (1979) *Creativity and Innovation*. John Wiley, Chichester.

Osborne, S. (1998a) *Voluntary Organisations and Innovation in Public Services*. Routledge, London.

Osborne, S. (1998b) Naming the beast. Defining and classifying service innovations in social policy, *Human Relations* 51(9): 1133–54.

Osborne, S. (1998c) Organisational structure and innovation in voluntary associations: applying the Aston Measure, *Voluntas* 9(4): 345–62.

Osborne, S. (1998d) The innovative capacity of voluntary organisations. Implications for local government, *Local Government Studies* 24(1): 19–40.

Osborne, S. and N. Flynn (1997) Managing the innovative capacity of voluntary organisations in the provision of public services, *Public Money & Management* 17(4): 31–40.

Parker, R., H. Ward, S. Jackson, J. Aldgate and P. Wedge (eds) (1991) *Assessing Outcomes in Childcare*. HMSO, London.

Paton, R. (1993) Organisation and management studies on voluntary and non-profit organisations in the UK: achievements and prospects. *Paper to the Researching Voluntary and Non-profit Organisations in the UK: the State of the Art Symposium*. University of the South Bank, London.

Pavitt, K. (1991) Key characteristics of the large innovating firm, *British Journal of Management* 2(1): 41–50.

Pelz, D. (1985) Innovation complexity and the sequence of innovatory stages, *Knowledge: Creation, Diffusion, Utilization* 1985: 261–91.

Perri 6 (1993) Innovation by non-profit organizations: policy and research issues, *Nonprofit Management and Leadership* 3(4): 397–414.

Peters, T. (1988) *Thriving on Chaos*. Macmillan, London.

Peters, T. and N. Austin (1985) *A Passion for Excellence*. Fontana, Glasgow.

Peters, T. and R. Waterman (1982) *In Search of Excellence*. Harper & Row, New York.

Pettigrew, A. (1973) *Politics of Organisational Decision Making*. Tavistock, London.

Pfeffer, J. and A. Salancik (1978) *The External Control of Organizations*. Harper & Row, New York.

Pinchot, G. III (1985) *Intrapreneuring*. Harper & Row, New York.

Pinto, R. (1998) Innovations – the provision of public goods and services, *Public Administration & Development* 18(4): 387–98.

Poole, M. S. (1981) Decision development in small groups I: a comparison of two models, *Communication Monographs* 48: 1–24.

Poole, M. S. (1983a) 'Decision development in small groups II: a study of multiple sequences in decision making' in Communication Monographs (50), pp. 206–32.

Poole, M. S. (1983b) Decision development in small groups III: a multiple decision sequence model of group decision development, *Communication Monographs* 50: 321–41.

Poole, M. S. and J. Roth (1989) Decision development in small groups IV: a typology of group decision paths, *Human Communication Research* 15(3): 323–56.

Porter, M. (1985) *Competitive Advantage*. Free Press, New York.

Powell, W., K. Koput and L. Smith-Doew (1996) Inter-organizational collaboration and the locus of innovation: networks of learning in bio-technology, *Administrative Science Quarterly* 41(1): 116–45.

Ramon, S. and M. Giannichedda (eds) (1991) *Psychiatry in Transition*. Pluto Press, London.

Rickards, T. (1985) *Stimulating Innovation*. Pinter, London.

Robert, M. and A. Weiss (1988) *The Innovation Formula*. Ballinger, Cambridge, MA.

Roberts, N. and P. King (1996) *Transforming Public Policy. Dynamics of Public Entrepreneurship and Innovation*. Jossey-Bass, San Francisco.

Robertson, M., J. Swan and S. Newell (1996) The role of networks in the diffusion of technological innovation, *Journal of Management Studies* 33(3): 333–59.

Rogers, E. and F. Shoemaker (1971) *Communication of Innovation*. Free Press, New York.

Rosner, M. (1967) Economic determinants of organizational innovation, *Administrative Science Quarterly* 12: 614–25.

Ross, K. (1995) Speaking in tongues: involving users in day care services, *British Journal of Social Work* 25(6): 791–804.

Rothman, J. (1974) *Planning and Organizing for Social Change*. Columbia University Press, New York.

Rothman, J. (1980) *Social Research and Development: Research and Development in the Human Services*. Prentice-Hall, Englewood Cliffs, NJ.

Rothman, J., J. Erlich and J. Teresa (1976) *Promoting Innovation and Change in Organizations and Communities*. John Wiley, New York.

Rothwell, R. (1975) Project SAPPHO – some hypotheses tested. *Paper to the Innovation Symposium*, Royal Swedish Academy of Engineering Science, Stockholm.

Rothwell, R. and W. Zegveld (1981) *Industrial Innovation and Public Policy*. Pinter, London.

Rowe, L. and W. Boise (1974) Organizational innovation: current research and evolving concepts, *Public Administration Review* 34: 284–93.

Salamon, L. and H. Anheier (1994) *The Emerging Sector*. Johns Hopkins University, Baltimore.

Sapolsky, H. (1967) Organizational structure and innovation, *Journal of Business* 40: 497–510.

Schall, E. (1997) Public sector succession: a strategic approach to sustaining innovation, *Public Administration Review* 57(1): 4–10.

Schon, D. (1963) Champions for radical new inventions, *Harvard Business Review* (March/April): 77–86.

Schumpeter, J. (1939) *Business Cycles*. McGraw-Hill, New York.

Singh, J., D. Tucker and A. Meinhard (1991) Institutional change and ecological dynamics. In W. Powell and P. DiMaggio (eds), *The New Institutionalism in Organizational Analysis*. University of Chicago Press, Chicago, pp. 390–422.

Smale, G. and G. Tuson (1990) Community social work: foundation for the 1990s and beyond. In G. Darvill and G. Smale (eds), *Partners in Empowerment. Networks of Innovation in Social Work*. NISW, London, pp. 151–63.

Smith, A. (1910) *Wealth of Nations*. Dent, London.

Starkey, K. and A. McKinlay (1988) *Organizational Innovation*. Avebury, Aldershot.

Stroetman, K. (1979) Innovation in small and medium sized industrial firms – a German perspective. In M. Baker (ed.), *Industrial Innovation: Technology Policy and Diffusion*. Macmillan, London, pp. 205–25.

Thompson, V. (1965) Bureaucracy and innovation, *Administrative Science Quarterly* 10: 1–20.

Tidd, J. (1995) Development of novel products through intraorganizational and interorganizational networks: the case of home automation, *Journal of Product Innovation Management* 12(4): 307–22.

Tushman, M. and P. Anderson (1985) Technological discontinuities and organizational environments, *Administrative Science Quarterly* 31: 439–65.

Twiss, B. (1987) *Managing Technological Innovation*. Pitman, London.

Urabe, K. (1988) Innovation and the Japanese management style. In K. Urabe, J. Child and T. Kagono (eds), *Innovation and Management. International Comparisons*. de Gruyter, Berlin, pp. 3–26.

Van de Ven, A. (1988) Central problems in the management of innovation. In M. Tushman and W. Moore (eds) (1988) *Readings in the Management of Innovation*, Harper Business, New York, pp. 103–22.

Van de Ven, A., H. Angle and M. Doole (1989) *Research on the Management of Innovation*. Harper & Row, New York.

Von Hippel, E. (1978) A customer active paradigm for industrial product idea generation, *Research Policy* 7: 240–66.

Von Hippel, E. (1982) Appropriability of innovation benefits as a predictor of the source of innovation, *Research Policy* 11(2): 95–116.

Walker, R., E. Jeanes and R. Rowlands (2001) *Managing Public Services Innovation*. Policy Press, Bristol.

Williams, H. and A. Webb (1992) *Outcome Funding*. Rensselaerville Institute, New York.

Wilson, D. (1992) The strategic challenge of cooperation and competition in British voluntary organisations, *Nonprofit Management and Leadership* 2(3): 239–52.

Wilson, J. (1966) Innovation in organization: notes towards a theory. In J. Thompson (ed.), *Approaches to Organizational Design*. Pittsburgh University Press, Pittsburgh, pp. 193–218.

Young, D. (1976) *If not For Profit, For What?* Lexington Books, MA.

Zahria, S. and J. Pearce (1990) Research evidence on the Miles-Snow typology, *Journal of Management* 16(4): 751–68.

Zaltman, G., R. Duncan and J. Holbek (1973) *Innovation and Organizations*. John Wiley, New York.

FURTHER READING

On the nature of innovation

This topic has been explored extensively in this chapter. However, for those readers wanting to take their understanding further, there are three excellent collections on the topic. These three edited collections are all perhaps slightly ageing now, but still essential reading!

M. Tushman and W. Moore (eds) (1988) *Readings in the Management of Innovation*. Harper Business, New York and J. Henry and D. Walker (eds) (1994) *Managing Innovation*. Sage, London, are excellent collections for furthering your reading about innovation. At a more specialized level, the collection edited by A. Van de Ven, H. Angle and M. Doole (1989) *Research on the Management of Innovation*. Harper & Row,

New York, pulls together the findings and insights that emerged out of the seminal Minnesota studies on innovation.

On innovation in public services

Two books are essential reading here. First, Stephen Osborne (1998) *Voluntary Organizations and Innovation in Public Services*. Routledge, London, explores in more detail the nature of the innovation process in public services. Drawing extensively upon institutional theory, he develops a model of the innovative capacity of public services. His work is explored further, in the context of housing policy in the UK in R. Walker and E. Deanes (2001) Innovation in regulated service: the case of English housing associations, *Public Management Review* 3(4): 525–50.

Second, Sandy Borins (2001) *The Challenge of Innovating in Government*. PriceWaterhouseCoopers Endowment for the Business of Government, Arlington, deals in more depth with the development and sustenance of innovators within PSOs. His work is dealt with in more detail in the next chapter of this volume.

Chapter 8

Developing and supporting innovators in public service organizations

LEARNING OBJECTIVES

By the end of this chapter you should have:

■ understood the different models of the role of the individual in the innovation process; and

■ developed an evaluation of how individuals might best be supported in innovation in PSOs.

KEY POINTS OF THIS CHAPTER

■ The innovation studies literature places great store by the role of individual agency in the innovation process. This might be as 'an advocate' of innovation (usually a senior manager), 'a supporter' (usually a politician or other key external stakeholder) or 'a champion' (usually a lower level manager, sometimes called a 'hero innovator').

■ In PSOs, it is possible to understand the role of individual agency in the innovation process through three models: 'the individual characteristics model' (which emphasizes the importance of entrepreneurial action by key individuals in the organization); 'the structural model' (which emphasizes the importance of the organizational context of the individual); and 'the contingency model' (which brings the above two models together).

■ Managing the role of the individual in the innovation process requires balancing the impact of individual agency with that of organizational culture and the relationship of the PSO to its external environment.

KEY TERMS

- **Individual agency** – the actions that an individual takes to have an impact upon a situation or process.
- **Entrepreneur** – an individual who, in the context of PSOs, acts to bring resources together in a way that creates new resources or opportunities for the organization.
- **Hero innovator** – a (usually) lower level manager in a PSO who champions an innovation against the strength of conservatism and the status quo in a PSO.
- **Innovation champion** – a manager who promotes an innovation inside a PSO.
- **Innovation advocate** – a politician or other influential external stakeholder of a PSO who supports the development of an innovation within it.
- **Innovation sponsor** – a senior manager who legitimates the development of an innovation within a PSO.
- **Boundary spanning** – a PSO acting to link its work to that of other relevant organizations, by staff crossing over and working across organizational boundaries.
- **Boundary maintenance** – a PSO acting to maintain its organizational integrity and identity in a situation that involves it working across organizational boundaries and in collaboration with other organizations.

THE ROLE OF THE INDIVIDUAL IN INNOVATION

There is a particular subset of the innovation studies literature that concentrates upon the role of the individual as the agent of innovation within organizations. Brief elements will be reiterated here.

In this literature the role of the individual as the agent of innovation is prime. Some locate this primarily as an entrepreneurial role, acted out by charismatic or 'strong' individuals. Robert and Weiss (1988: 8) state simply 'innovation is the tool of entrepreneurs'. Others conceptualize the role more as an enabling one, acting as a manager to create an organizational culture which privileges innovation against other possible activity (Jelinek and Schoonhoven 1990). Finally, the 'hero-innovator' role focuses upon a lower level, often middle management, figure who supports and promotes an innovation, frequently against strong organizational opposition from entrenched interests within the organization (Schon 1963; Fischer *et al.* 1986; Peters and Waterman 1982).

All these three approaches have a strong normative element to them, as their use of language suggests. The innovator is the 'champion' or 'hero' (rarely heroine!) who promotes innovation against the lethargy and status quo of the 'organisation-as-villain' (Frost and Egri 1991).

In the public services management literature, there is a similar concern with the role of the individual – particularly as manifested through organizational leaders and managers (such as Light 1998). However, a weakness of this approach is that its focus on the individual alone, to the exclusion of their organizational context, ignores the impact of this context – both on their behaviour and upon the import of their actions. In a UK Health Services example, Praill and Baldwin (1988) have shown how the role of the individual can only be understood within this organizational context. They graphically describe how the 'dragon' of the UK National Health Service invariably 'eats for breakfast' any would-be 'hero innovators', who are isolated within this vast organization and unable to sustain their ideas.

More pragmatically, an over-emphasis on the individual to the exclusion of the organizational context risks the collapse of the innovation once that individual leaves the organization. A good example of this in the UK was in the early 1970s, in the field of the diversion of juvenile offenders from custody and towards community care. Many such 'intermediate treatment' schemes were set up around charismatic individuals, and which schemes often had profound initial successes. However, they depended for their success upon these charismatic individuals for their inspiration and sustainability. Consequently, when these individuals moved on to other developments, these projects invariably collapsed (Thorpe et al. 1980; Morris and Giller 1987). Even hero innovators, it seems, ignore their organizational and/or institutional context at their peril. Further, the hero innovator literature invariaibly ignores the significance of the relationship of a PSO to its wider environment, as discussed in the previous chapter.

This chapter will first highlight some of the key elements of this organizational and institutional context, and their import for innovation in PSOs. It will then present three approaches to understanding the role of the individual in innovation in PSOs – the *individual characteristics model*, the *structural model*, and the *contingent model*. Finally, key lessons will be drawn out for the development and sustenance of innovators in PSOs.

THE ORGANIZATIONAL AND INSTITUTIONAL CONTEXT AND CONSTRAINTS OF INNOVATION IN PUBLIC SERVICES

As has been indicated throughout this volume, there are important environmental and contingent factors in and around PSOs that militate against innovative activity within them. Osborne (1998) locates the innovative capacity of VNPOs within the relationship between these organizations and this institutional environment. Borins (2001a) summarizes these institutional factors as:

- the political context of PSOs which locates the final focus of power in the political rather than the organizational system;

- the need for PSOs to constrain individual flexibility in order to provide both for accountability for the use of public money and for the protection for vulnerable service users;
- the focus of the media on PSO failure, as newsworthy (and in contrast to PSO successes); and
- the lack of rewards for innovation in PSO career structures.

In fact, Borins argues, despite these very real constraints, innovators can and do flourish within PSOs, at a variety of organizational levels. Sometimes this happens in spite of the organization itself and sometimes it happens through the active support of the organization. This issue is explored further below. However, given that innovators clearly do exist in PSOs, notwithstanding the constraints, the central question is: 'how to develop and support them within PSOs?'

THREE MODELS OF THE INNOVATOR IN PSOs: AND THEIR IMPLICATIONS

The 'individual characteristics' model

Following Drucker (1985) this model argues that the innovator in a PSO is essentially *an entrepreneur* who is able to promote innovation because of a set of personality traits that they possess. The most significant of such studies in the public sector is undoubtedly that of Roberts and King (1996) who built a model of the 'public entrepreneur' on the basis of extensive research. They portray the public entrepreneur as:

- tenacious;
- working long hours;
- goal driven;
- willing to take risks;
- confident; and
- skilled in using political connections.

Roberts and King carried out extensive psychological testing of such entrepreneurs and isolated a set of core personality traits which they argued were essential of such a 'hero innovator'(see Box 8.1 and Box 8.2). Despite a robust defence of their approach, though, Roberts and King are comparatively ambivalent about the implications of their findings. On the one hand, to the question 'can anyone become a public entrepreneur?' they respond with an unequivocal 'no', arguing for the existence of an 'entrepreneurial identity':

BOX 8.1 THE PERSONALITY CHARACTERISTICS OF THE PUBLIC ENTREPRENEUR

- is highly intuitive;
- uses critical analytic thinking;
- is able to instigate constructive social interaction;
- has a well integrated personality and highly developed ego;
- possesses good leadership skills;
- is creative.

Based on Roberts and King (1996).

BOX 8.2 KEY HEURISTICS OF INNOVATIVE BEHAVIOUR IN PSOs

1 Know where you want to end up and don't lose sight of where you are heading.
2 Say 'no' rather than compromise.
3 Wait for the right political conditions.
4 Use outside pressure to move bureaucratic lethargy in PSOs.
5 Do not expect to gain a consensus – change never comes through consensus.
6 Money and resources are needed so be active in the acquisition.
7 Stay with issues that you have had some kind of advantage on.
8 Keep change at the forefront of people's minds.
9 Co-opt opponents.
10 Be willing to be bold.

Based on Roberts and King (1996).

Individualistic, intuitive, innovative and analytical, they excel at critical thinking and problem solving. They appear to be change agents, alert to new possibilities and solutions and constantly searching for ways to convert their visions into reality. Such an orientation often requires them to assume leadership positions, for which they seem to have a distinct talent.

(Roberts and King 1996: 145)

However, if such public entrepreneurs are born, Roberts and King (1996: 158) also subsequently argue that it is possible for people to learn innovational behaviour:

> We believe that a person can learn to behave more entrepreneurally even without an entrepreneurial identity, just as one can learn to behave more creatively even without strong natural abilities.

Subsequently, they develop a set of ten 'key heuristics' which they argue need to guide the behaviour of individuals seeking to develop their entrepreneurial and innovative behaviour (Box 8.2).

This study is an important examination of the nature and role of the individual in innovation in PSOs. However, it does have four important drawbacks. First, it assumes a lack of potential for innovation in PSOs, as organizations, which it presents as traditional 'hidebound' bureaucracies – and which the innovator must strive against. Arguably, this may have been the case in the past but PSOs have increasingly evidenced a range of organizational configurations – some of which are highly conducive to innovation (the development of matrix style organizations in the public sector has been particularly important here).

Second, and following on from this point, this individualistic approach lacks an organizational perspective. As Osborne (1998) has argued, individuals described as 'hero innovators' do indeed often possess distinctive and strong personalities. However, the key issue is not to define these personality traits in isolation. Rather it is to question why these individuals, in their organizations at a particular time, have turned their skills to innovation rather than to, for example, fund raising, sustaining specialist services or marketing (in which such strong individuals can also be found). This contingent approach is vital to really understanding the role of the individual in stimulating and supporting innovation in PSOs.

Third, this approach does not consider sustainability. A key issue that has to be addressed for PSOs is – 'what happens when the innovator moves on – what organizational systems are in place to sustain the innovation for the future?' As the earlier example of Intermediate Treatment in the UK made clear, PSOs ignore this point at their peril. Finally, and notwithstanding the work of Roberts and King above, this espoused role of the 'hero innovator' in PSOs still suffers from a dearth of empirical evidence to substantiate its import.

The structural model

This model, whilst acknowledging the influence of individuals, places more emphasis upon their organizational context than upon their personality alone. At the most basic, in their seminal study of innovation, Frost and Egri (1991) point to the 'mythic' role that 'hero innovators' can play inside organizations, in creating a normative vision of innovation. It is this interaction of the individual and the organization that is at the heart of innovation in public services, they argue.

More concretely, Bartlett and Dibben (2002) do look at the actual interplay between individuals and their organizational context. Echoing the individual characteristics model, they start by identifying individuals who act as 'champions' and 'sponsors' of innovation. However their study then:

> . . . moves away from a bias towards individual characteristics of entre-preneurs by focusing upon the roles played by people within organisa-tions . . . [w]e suggest that, in contrast to the stereotype of local government organisations and large bureaucracies which stifle innovation and for which there is little room for the entrepreneurial spirit, the public sector entrepreneur is critical to the successful implementation of recent policy initiatives in an international public sector context. We see entre-preneurship and innovation as necessarily going hand in hand in the local government context and we have pointed towards the ways in which the entrepreneurial roles we have identified serve to generate, develop, implement and consolidate innovations in the public sector.
>
> (Bartlett and Dibben 2002: 119)

Based upon their study of innovation in UK local authorities, and echoing some of the earlier studies by researchers within a private sector context, Bartlett and Dibben identify two key organizational roles – that of *innovation champion* and *innovation sponsor*. They are at pains to point out that these are not personality arche-types. Rather they are roles within the organization that are required for effective innovation. Thus this approach moves the focus away from the personality traits of individual entrepreneurs and towards the role of the entrepreneur inside an organ-ization, emphasizing the interplay between the individual and their organizational context.

According to Bartlett and Dibben, the *innovation champion* role was invariably taken by a manager within a PSO who supported the innovation inside that organ-ization. This role itself splits into two sub-roles. The 'public champion' was someone who sponsored innovation because of a desire to improve the quality of public services. The 'empowered champion' was someone who sponsored innova-tion because of a desire for personal fulfilment and a desire to make their mark.

The *innovation sponsor*, in contrast, was someone in the political context of the PSO who provided a political mandate for their activity. Bartlett and Dibben (2002: 119) argue further that this model 'moves away from a bias towards the individual characteristics of entrepreneur' and inside focuses on organizational roles – and in particular upon how innovation champions and sponsors worked together.

175

This model is indeed strong in moving the focus away from the individual alone to the organization – though it by no means dismisses the role of the individual entirely. However, its practical implication for developing innovation inside PSOs are limited, beyond a general call for managers and politicians to work together.

A variant on this structural model, that focuses more on the external rather than the internal organizational environment, is provided by Osborne (1998) who examined the innovative capacity of voluntary and non-profit organizations (VNPOs) in the UK. His study found no single organizational factor, including leadership, which could alone explain the innovative capacity of VNPOs. However, he did find significant differences in the way that the innovative VNPOs related to their environment, compared to their non-innovative counterparts. The innovative VNPOs took a more proactive and open relationship with their environment and also tended to work in more complex environments with a multiplicity of organizational networks. This environment, he argued, provided an innovative 'milieu' (Camagni 1991), or network, within which 'open-systems' VNPOs interacted in order to achieve their core goals.

According to Osborne, this network provided seven roles for developing innovation in PSOs. These were:

- as a general context for innovation, by identifying an unmet need;
- as a legitimating network for the innovative work of the PSO;
- as a source of new ideas for innovation;
- as a facilitator of inter-agency planning of new services;
- as an aid to resource acquisition;
- as an agent of innovation itself; and
- as a key element in sustaining and enhancing the innovation in the wider service system.

In this model, the role of the 'innovation champion' thus becomes one of a 'network manager' for the PSO. The role involves both *boundary spanning* (linking the ideas and work of different PSOs together) and *boundary maintenance* (ensuring that the distinctive identity, mission and contribution of their PSO does not get lost in the wider network). Such a role draws as much on insights from theories of collaboration (see for example Hudson *et al.* 1999, Huxham 2003) as it does from the innovation studies literature.

This approach provides the strongest support for the outward-looking network management role for the manager, in terms of developing the innovative capacity of their PSO. It emphasizes the need for the external orientation for a PSO, in order to provide and sustain innovation with it (see also Beekum and Ginn 1993, for a Health Services example). However, it does perhaps underplay the role of the innovator 'per se' within a PSO. These approaches are brought together in the Contingent Model.

176

The contingent model

This model explores the interaction between the innovator within a PSO and its wider organizational environment. The strongest advocate of this approach is undoubtedly Borins (2001a, 2001b, 2001c). As was indicated earlier, Borins starts by considering what motivates innovation in PSOs. There is no venture capital available and no personal rewards for taking the risk of innovation. However, there is the counter-risk of public (and media documented) failure, as well as an ongoing concern within PSOs with control and accountability rather than flexibility. As a consequence, argues Borins, innovative individuals often reject careers in PSOs.

Despite this rejection, however, innovation does continue to occur in PSOs. Further, Borins explicitly rejects the view of those such as Bartlett and Dibben (2002) who argue that the innovators are primarily senior managers and politicians. Rather Borins contends that they come from across the organizational spectrum – from front-line staff through to political actors. Echoing the organizational learning perspective discussed earlier in this present volume, Borins (2001b) concludes that this finding:

> . . . that innovative ideas emerge from all levels of an organisation – has important implications. If innovative ideas can come from anywhere in an organisation, rather than from a senior elite, then organisations will be most innovative if they can stimulate innovation throughout.

Borins found five such stimuli to innovation in PSOs:

- political policy initiatives;
- new organizational leadership;
- an organizational crisis;
- internal organizational problems (including resource constraints or a failure to meet demand); and
- new opportunities for growth.

He argues that such diverse stimuli for innovation require PSOs to be able to respond at a variety of levels. Far from being the domain of the 'hero' or the 'champion' alone, innovation should be the focus for all organizational staff. To achieve this, Borins (2001a) outlines seven steps to creating an innovation-rich organizational milieu inside PSOs.

Step 1   Whilst middle managers and front-line staff can initiate innovation, sponsorship from senior managers and political leaders is an essential prerequisite to such individual agency. This should establish organizational priorities, provide a conduit for communication between the strategic and operational levels of a PSO, and provide active recognition and legitimacy for innovation inside PSOs.

177

Step II   A key issue for PSOs is often how to reward innovative activity in a noto-riously risk-aversive environment and where PSOs do not have a past history of large financial rewards for innovation (in contrast to parts of the private sector). Borins argues for the use of innovation awards or prizes which can be offered either by the government itself or by private foundations These awards offer little finan-cial incentive but do provide public recognition of innovation – and such recogni-tion has itself been argued previously to be an effective motivation of staff (for example, Kanter 1988).

Step III   Innovation requires resources. The private sector can have access to venture capital, but PSOs do not. Often they have had to resort to carefully made budget savings to finance innovation. Borins argues for the financial reform of PSOs that would give them the power to 'vire' funds more easily for innovative devel-opments, as well as to be able to carry surplus income from one financial year to the next in order to fund innovation.

Step IV   Again drawing on Kanter (1988) Borins argues for organizational diver-sity (of staff backgrounds, professions and personalities) as essential for the inno-vative PSO. Echoing the learning organizational perspective once again, Borins suggests that PSOs can stimulate on-the-job diversity by keeping job descriptions as broad rather than as narrow as possible, by giving staff a mandate to diversify rather than narrowly specialize their skills and by promoting cross-professional, cross-departmental and cross-agency working groups.

Step V   Echoing Osborne (1998), Borins contends that PSOs that are effective innovators have an external orientation and are prepared to learn from the exper-ience of other organizations. The innovative PSO needs to develop a strategy for working across organizational boundaries and by looking for innovative solu-tions which bring together different expertises. Key approaches here can be encouraging inter-organizational working groups, and encouraging staff both to attend both external conferences and events and to participate in professional networks.

Step VI   Significantly, Borins explicitly rejects the idea of dedicated innovation champions or heroes. This marginalizes the innovation role within the PSO. Rather he proclaims that innovation 'is everyone's responsibility'. Consequently condi-tions need to be created for all staff to contribute to the innovation process.

Step VII   Innovation often involves trial and error (or 'groping along', as Golden (1990) called it). Innovative PSOs need therefore to encourage experimentation. Traditionally they have been risk aversive, however, because of the public account-ability and protection of vulnerable people imperatives outlined above. Borins does not argue against the need for such accountability and responsibility within PSOs. Rather he suggests that PSOs should take risks *but* only when they have evaluative

> ## EXERCISE 8.1 APPLYING THE BORINS' 'SEVEN POINT PLAN'
>
> Take the PSO that you currently work for, or one that you are very familiar with. Consider how you might apply Borins' *Seven Point Plan* to develop an innovation-rich environment in this organization. You should:
>
> - Consider the practicalities of implementing each step – what would it actually mean and how would it change organizational practices?
> - Consider what blocks to this plan might arise both within and without the organization and how would you act to minimize their impact?
> - Having created such an innovation-rich environment within this PSO, what would need to happen to allow this environment to sustain itself and to grow?

mechanisms in place to monitor and learn from these experiments. He believes that the current trend towards decentralization can support experimentation by PSOs, but that often the evaluation, which is the crucial element here, is lacking. Consequently the lessons of either success or failure are not learned. Experimentation and evaluation need to go hand-in-hand together.

The approach of Borins is a strong one. It brings together the concept of individual agency together with that of the organizational and institutional context. However, it can tend towards the normative (the 'should' word is perhaps too prevalent in his writings) and can offer rather generalized prescriptions for innovation that belie the complex ecology of PSOs. Exercise 8.1 will help to clarify your own thinking towards this approach and its utility.

CONCLUSIONS

Lessons for promoting innovators

Three key lessons can be drawn out of the models presented above. These are the role of individual agency, the impact of organizational culture and the import of the organizational orientation to its environment.

Individual agency

This is a necessary, but not sufficient, condition for innovation. Moreover, the key issue is not so much one about encouraging dynamic individuals into an organization but rather one about why/how they focus on innovation rather than another organizational roles/goals. It may also be that organizational roles are as, or more, important than personality traits.

Different types of individual agency have also been identified including:

- the *champion* of an innovation, at a variety of organizational levels;
- the *supporter* (usually a senior manager) of an innovation; and
- the *advocate* (usually a political or external stakeholder of an innovation).

The key issue for a PSO is the right balance between these different roles.

Organizational culture

A common theme coming through the work of Borins, in particular, is the need to develop an organizational culture which is not risk aversive, which encourages exploration *and* learning and which rewards innovation. This is a real challenge for PSOs and it can be at odds to their 'traditional' cultures.

Organizational culture can often be hard to engage with inside organizations. It comprises the values, beliefs and expectations that the members of an organization share, as well as providing unwritten rules governing behaviour both within the organization and with the external environment. Approaches to changing organizational culture were explored in Chapter 6 of this present volume. However, it is important to reiterate that, although the need for cultural change can be easy to identify, it is much more difficult to implement such cultural change, as Colville and Packman (1996) have well demonstrated in the context of the UK Customs and Excise Service.

An external orientation

Finally, Osborne (1998) has demonstrated the need for an external orientation for the innovative PSO – in theoretical terms, it needs to be an open rather than a closed system (Scott 1992). This requires both strategic positioning by the PSO to be open to its environment and effective network management skills for PSO managers – the boundary spanning and boundary maintenance skills outlined above.

DISCUSSION QUESTIONS

1 Which of the models of individual agency in innovation public services (the individual characteristics, the structural and the contingency models) do you find most convincing and why? What evidence can you find to support this belief from your knowledge of public services provision in your region?

2   To what extent do you believe that it is possible to bring about innovation by individual agency alone, as envisaged in the 'hero innovator' concept? What evidence for and against this role can you find from your knowledge of public services provision in your region?

3   In what ways might an innovation supporter try to engender a culture of innovation inside their organization, and what potential blocks might exist to this?

4   Drawing upon your own experiences of public services provision, how important do you think is the relationship of a PSO to its environment in developing its innovative capacity?

REFERENCES

Bartlett, D. and P. Dibben (2002) Public sector innovation and entrepreneurship: case studies from local government, *Local Government Studies* 28(4): 107–21.

Borins, S. (2001a) *The Challenge of Innovating in Government*. Price Waterhouse Cooper Endowment for the Business of Government, Arlington.

Borins, S. (2001b) Innovation, success and failure in public management research: some methodological reflections, *Public Management Review* 3(1): 3–18.

Borins, S. (2001c) Encouraging innovation in the public sector, *Journal of Intellectual Capital* 2(3): 310–19.

Beekum, R. and G. Ginn (1993) Business strategy and inter-organizational linkages within the acute care hospital industry: an expansion of the Miles and Snow typology, *Human Relations* 46(11): 1291–318.

Camagni, R. (1991) From the local 'mileau' to innovation through cooperation networks. In R. Camagni (ed.), *Innovation Networks, Spatial Perspectives*, Bellhaven Press, London, pp. 1–9.

Colville, I. and C. Packman (1996) Auditing cultural change, *Public Money & Management* (July/September): 27–33.

Drucker, P. (1985) *Innovation and Entrepreneurship*. Heinemann, London.

Fischer, W., W. Hamilton, C. McLaughlin and R. Zmud (1986) The elusive product champion, *Research Management* 29(3): 13–16.

Frost, P. and C. Egri (1991) Political process of innovation, *Research in Organizational Behaviour*: 229–96.

Golden, O. (1990) Innovation in public sector human service programs: the implications of innovation by 'groping along', *Journal of Policy Analysis and Management* 9(2): 219–48.

Hudson, B., B. Hardy, M. Henwood and G. Wistow (1999) In pursuit of inter-agency collaboration in the public sector: what is the contribution of theory and research? *Public Management Review* 1(2): 235–60.

Huxham, C. (2003) Theorizing collaboration practice, *Public Management Review* 5(3): 401–24.

Jelinek, M. and C. Schoonhoven (1990) *The Innovation Marathon*. Blackwell, Oxford.

Kanter, R. (1988) When a thousand flowers bloom: structural, collective and social conditions for innovation in organisations, *Research in Organisational Behaviour* 10: 169–211.

Light, P. (1998) *Creating Nonprofit and Government Organisations that Innovate Naturally*. Jossey-Bass, San Francisco.

Morris, A. and H. Giller (1987) *Understanding Juvenile Justice*. Croom Helm, London.

Osborne, S. (1998) *Voluntary Organisations and Innovation in Public Services*. Routledge, London.

Peters, T. and R. Waterman (1982) *In Search of Excellence*. Harper & Row, New York.

Praille, T. and S. Baldwin (1988) Beyond hero-innovation: real change in unreal systems, *Behavioural Psychotherapy* 16(1): 1–14.

Robert, M. and A. Weiss (1988) *The Innovation Formula*. Ballinger, Cambridge, MA.

Roberts, N. and P. King (1996) *Transforming Public Policy. Dynamics of Public Entrepreneurship and Innovation*. Jossey-Bass, San Francisco.

Schon, D. (1963) Champions for radical new inventions, *Harvard Business Review* (March/April): 77–86.

Scott, R. (1992) *Organisations. Rational Natural and Open Systems*. Prentice Hall, Englewood Cliffs, NJ.

Thorpe, D., D. Smith, C. Green and J. Paley (1980) *Out of Care. The Community Support of Young Offenders*. George Allen & Unwin, London.

FURTHER READING

The classic text from the business sector upon the role of individuals in innovation is that of T. Peters and R. Waterman (1982) *In Search of Excellence* (Harper & Row, New York) – though the seminal paper by D. Schon (1967) Champions for radical new inventions, *Harvard Business Review* (March/April): 77–86 is also important. A final approach worthy of attention is that of W. Fischer, W. Hamilton, C. McLaughlin and R. Zmud (1986) The elusive product champion, *Research Management* 29(3): 13–16.

The key work in terms of innovation in public services is undoubtedly that of S. Borins (2001) *The Challenge of Innovating in Government*. PricewaterhouseCoopers Endowment for the Business of Government, Arlington. However, despite his extensive work across the Commonwealth in testing out his model, it could still be criticized as being rooted too much in North American experience. You may well want to consider the applicability of all its elements in your own national or regional context (for example, the US is particularly fond of award type schemes, but this fondness is not necessarily shared in all cultures). An alternative approach is that of D. Bartlett and P. Dibben (2002) Public sector innovation and entrepreneurship: case studies from local government, *Local Government Studies* 28(4): 107–21. Finally a healthy antidote to too much of this 'cult of the hero innovator' is found in T. Praill and S. Baldwin (1988) Beyond hero innovation: real change in unreal systems, *Behavioural Psychotherapy* 16(1): 1–14.

Chapter 9

Managing the process of innovation in public services

LEARNING OBJECTIVES

By the end of this chapter you should have:

- understood the nature and stages of the process of innovation;
- considered the skills required to manage this process; and
- developed a strategy for sustaining innovation beyond its initial stages.

KEY POINTS OF THIS CHAPTER

- There are four distinct impeti to innovation by PSOs – research, market demand, political imperatives and the need to be seen to perform ('conspicuous production').
- The management of risk is a key element of the innovation process.
- Innovation is also a political process as well as a design and managerial one.
- A particular challenge for PSOs in the innovation process is the potential for learning from failure and mistakes, when the political and media cost for these can be quite high.
- This chapter identifies four approaches to managing the process of innovation – the rational management, political negotiation, building blocks and learning organization approaches.
- Resistance is a natural part of the change process; the challenge for managers is to differentiate such 'process resistance' from resistance that is derived from a fault in the intended innovation.

KEY TERMS

■ **Conspicuous production** – this is where PSO managers pursue innovation as a proxy for their own productivity and/or success, because of the difficulty of demonstrating success against the multiple and complex goals of PSOs.

■ **Top-down innovation** – this is innovation instigated by senior managers of a PSO, often for cost efficiency reasons.

■ **Bottom-up innovation** – this is innovation instigated by front-line managers of a PSO, often in response to a change in demand or to develop more effective service delivery.

■ **Stakeholder** – this is someone who has an interest, direct or indirect, in the work and serices of an organization.

INTRODUCTION: THE PROCESS OF INNOVATION

This chapter will commence by developing your understanding of the process of innovation and by reviewing some key elements of this in relation to public services in particular. It will then outline some of the key issues to be addressed in managing this process. The core of the chapter will explore the two most common approaches to managing the innovation process – the rational approach and the political approach. It will also draw out some of the key elements in terms of good managerial practice for managing this process. The chapter will conclude by discussing the issues of diffusion and the sustainability of innovation.

Of course, there are some key common themes between the management of the process of change in general and the management of the innovation process. Many of the issues identified in the earlier chapter on the process of change are thus also highly relevant here. However, innovation does also have some distinctive challenges and these are addressed in this chapter.

Earlier in this book, we differentiated three broad phases of the innovation process. These were

■ invention (the creation of new knowledge or the adaptation of existing knowledge – sometimes characterized as a separate process from innovation and sometimes as an initial stage of innovation);

■ implementation (the adoption of this new knowledge by an organization – the core of the innovation process); and

■ diffusion (the adoption of new knowledge developed within one organization or within an industry/sector as a whole).

This chapter commences by exploring the nature of the impetus for innovation in public services, before going on to explore the innovation implementation process in detail, as well as the diffusion of innovation.

THE INNOVATION IMPETUS

In the private sector, innovation is about taking knowledge, in the form either of a new product/service or of a new production process and using it to increase the market share and/or profit margins of a firm. As we have seen earlier (in Chapter 7) innovation in the field of public services is rather more complex. One issue in particular makes innovation more complex in public services and in PSOs – the nature of the impetus to innovate.

Chapter 7 drew upon the broad innovation studies literature to differentiate two major impeti for innovation – the development of new knowledge through the research and development process (such as in the pharmaceutical industry) and the development of new knowledge about the needs/wants of the consumer, usually through market research. These were denoted to the *research push* and *market pull* impeti.

Both these impeti to innovation exist in relation to public services also. Medical research can, for example, lead to innovation in surgical or nursing practice, whilst market research can lead either to a new way to provide an existing service (such as in relation to the collection and recycling of domestic waste) or to the design of a new service based on demand (the development of carer support services for people caring for an adult with special needs is a good example of this). However, to these two impeti must be added two more, distinctive, public service impetus. These might be called the *political imperative* impetus – that is, innovation required by the political context of a public service or a PSO – and the *conspicuous production* impetus – that is innovation required as a proxy for organizational or managerial performance in public services. These latter two impeti are explored in more detail here.

The political imperative impetus

This impetus is distinctive to public services and may be manifested in one of two ways. First there may be *a substantive change in public policy* requiring profound change in the nature of a public service. The policy shift in the UK in the 1980s and 1990s, from residential to community care services for adults with special needs, is a good example of this. The political requirements for the service changed, including the legislative requirements, and this required the design, development and implementation of a whole raft of new services for this user group.

Similarly a change of political will towards environmental sustainability (this time as a result of a global change in political will, embodied in the Kyoto Accords) has required the design of a host of new environmental services ranging from refuse collection and disposal through to the development of new ways to create sustainable public resources (such as forests and parks).

Second, there is also another element to the political requirement to innovate. This is *the elevation of innovation to a policy goal in its own right*. This was especially marked in the UK during the Conservative governments of the 1980s and 1990s, with their commitment to the hegemony of the market and of private sector management techniques over those in the public sector.

Rightly or wrongly, public services were perceived as being poorly managed, compared with their private sector counterparts, leading to inefficiency and ineffectiveness. Heavily influenced by the work of Michael Porter (1985) on competitive advantage, these governments perceived the absence of innovation as an impediment to improved performance and productivity in public services. Consequently innovation itself became a touchstone of the development and funding of public services. It was not uncommon, for example, for the opening section of an application for a government funding programme to be one that required the applicant to specify the innovative features of their application. Needless to say, such an approach not only stimulated genuine innovation, it also stimulated the ability of public service managers to describe their services using the language of innovation, irrespective of their actual nature (Osborne 1998).

The conspicuous production impetus

The term was coined by Feller (1981). He argued that it was becoming increasingly difficult for the managers within PSOs to demonstrate their effectiveness, because of the indeterminate nature of the goals of public services and the subjective and often contested nature of performance monitoring and evaluation (Osborne *et al.* 1995). However hard it was to demonstrate effectiveness, however, one could always be seen to innovate. Consequently innovation became adopted by many PSO managers as a *proxy* for their own or their organization's effectiveness.

These four different impeti for innovation are brought together in Box 9.1. Clearly each of these impeti places its own requirements upon public services managers – innovation as a result of research push is very different to innovation as a result of the need for conspicuous production, for example. Before continuing with this chapter, you should complete Exercise 9.1 to help you clarify the differences involved.

KEY ISSUES IN THE INNOVATION PROCESS

There are a number of key issues that will determine the managerial challenges for innovation in public services, irrespective of their impetus. These are explored in more detail below and are also displayed in Box 9.2.

BOX 9.1 THE IMPETUS FOR INNOVATION IN PSOs

Impetus	Nature
Research push	Innovation through the generation of new knowledge
Market pull	Innovation through the identification of new needs
Political imperative	Innovation through change in the public policy environment
Conspicuous production	Innovation as a proxy for individual or organizational performance

EXERCISE 9.1

This exercise is to help you understand the differences between the four impeti to innovation in public services described above. First, taking your own PSO (or one that you are familiar with), try to identify an example of innovation from each of these four impeti. Then attempt to tease out the differences between the innovation processes as a result of these different impeti. You should then be able to identify what is common across the four impeti and what is distinctive to each.

BOX 9.2 KEY ISSUES IN INNOVATION IN PUBLIC SERVICES

- Do you need top-down or bottom-up innovation?
- Is the innovation a planned or emergent one?
- How do you manage/share risk?
- What do you do about resistance?
- What sort of learning do you need inside the organization?
- What obstacles might you foresee and how will you overcome them?
- Who will be the winners and losers in the innovation and how will you deal with this?

Top-down and bottom-up innovation

The distinction between these two types of innovation was well made by Baldock and Evers (1991) in their study of innovations in care of the elderly across Europe.[1] By *bottom-up* innovation they meant an innovation that was developed at the 'front line' of service provision, often as a local response to a social or demographic change (such as the growing elderly population across Europe). Such bottom-up innovations were invariably led by practitioners in one locality and would be explicitly focused on the effectiveness of a service in relation to user need.

Bottom-up innovations require a facilitative approach from managers that allows and supports the development of these innovations by front-line staff. However, the manager also has a key role in controlling the cost of these innovations – they may often expand the quality and choice available of a public service, but at a greater unit cost. The PSO manager thus needs:

- to support front-line staff in developing bottom-up innovations;
- to ensure that such innovations do not lead to inequity across the service as a whole (by paying attention to diffusion);
- to ensure that these innovations become embedded and sustainable within the service as a whole; and
- to control their costs.

Top-down innovation, by contrast, invariably springs directly from the resource constraints of a public service or a PSO. It is directed to meeting an already recognized need more efficiently – perhaps by targeting existing services more accurately, by sharpening the boundaries between different services so as to utilize the most cost-efficient, or by developing new cost-efficient forms of service. Here the managerial role is rather different – it is primarily that of the advocate for the new service. In this context therefore it requires him/her:

- to identify where cost-efficiency needs to be enhanced;
- to plan/develop the innovation for such cost-efficiency;
- to persuade staff and service users of the necessity for the innovation; and
- to monitor and evaluate its actual impact upon the cost-efficiency – and effectiveness – of a service.

Planned and emergent innovation

The differences between planned and emergent change and innovation have already been discussed above. Broadly, they are concerned with whether the innovation is one that a manager or a PSO has planned for themselves or whether it is being imposed upon them – either as a result of the political imperative impetus discussed above or because of decisions taken higher up in the organization.

In reality, public service managers need to be able to cope with both types of innovation. However, as discussed earlier, it is important to recognize that emergent innovation imposes especial constraints on the service manager. S/he will not have control over the design or objectives of the innovation, for example. This is especially challenging.

Innovation and risk

All innovation involves risk – the new service may fail, it may be too expensive or its users may simply not like it. A key question for a PSO and its managers, therefore, is how to manage risk. In the private sector, it is the successful management of this risk element that provides a firm with its competitive advantage (Porter 1985). For public service organizations, though, it is not simply its own profitability, or performance, that is at stake. PSOs often either provide services to the most vulnerable groups in society (the sick, the frail and those with special needs) – or provide services where their performance has an impact upon the health and safety of all citizens (roads, for example). Three examples will illustrate this point. First, an innovation in surgical procedures could easily lead to an increase in deaths if it is a more effective, but risky, procedure. Second, social workers are often cautious in introducing new approaches to child abuse – if such an approach leads to the death of a child then a public inquiry, and loss of jobs, will surely follow. Finally, a new method of producing tar for roads may be more cost efficient, but if it leads to the road service crumbling then it may well also lead to road traffic accidents and loss of life. These very public, and important, risks often make PSOs inherently cautious and conservative when considering innovation. Box 9.3 gives two concrete examples of the unexpected risk that can incur in the innovation process.

A key managerial challenge for innovation in public services is therefore the management of risk. Beyond the obvious risk of the failure of an innovation,[2] other risks that need to be considered are:

- the risk that the innovation may render the skills of the staff or service manager of the organization obsolete;
- the risk that the innovation will cost more than was intended;
- the risk that the innovation will have unintended consequences;
- the risk that the innovation is seen as a normative/ideological good and may be pursued by external (political) stakeholders, irrespective of its actual impact on the efficiency and/or effectiveness of a public service;
- the risk that the innovation may be successful but not attract sufficient take-up to ensure its financial viability; and

BOX 9.3 PUBLIC SERVICE INNOVATION AND RISK: TWO CASE EXAMPLES

A hospital in the UK introduced an innovation in the 1990s, intended to increase the efficiency of its in-patient services by increasing throughput – that is, the patients would occupy beds for a shorter period, increasing the throughput of the services. Managers were surprised though, when their unit costs increased drastically. This was because the admission/discharge elements of a hospital stay are the most expensive elements. By decreasing length of stay and increasing throughput, they actually decreased the overall efficiency of the service, although with increased throughout!

A residential home for teenage children hit the headlines in the UK in the 1990s when its radical approach to dealing with disturbed behaviour produced uproar. This became known as 'pin-down' and involved the physical restraint of children. The evidence on the effectiveness of the approach was mixed – some experts argued that it did actually have a positive impact on the behaviour of the children. However, the experiment was brought to a quick conclusion (with job losses) because the public was not prepared to see children so restrained, no matter how effective the service might be.

■ the risk that the innovation might be successful but that the PSO could not cope with the subsequent increased level of demand for the service.

None of these are reasons not to engage in the innovation process. However, they are risks that need to be evaluated and managed. They also have implications for the relationship between risk and the funding of an innovation in public service. There are three options for a PSO engaged, willingly or unwillingly, in innovation:

■ that it funds the innovation wholly itself, bearing all the risk but with the potential of reaping all the benefits (in terms of future funding and of reputation);
■ that the innovation is funded solely by an external funder, who would then bear these risks but who would also dictate the direction of the innovation – and take any credit for it; or
■ that the innovation is jointly funded by a PSO and external funder – this approach allows the sharing of the risks (and benefits) of innovation, but it does require a degree of trust between the parties involved.

191

Resistance to innovation

The issue of individual resistance to change has been raised already, and many of the same issues apply here. Staff may feel (often rightly) that their existing legitimacy, skills or even their jobs may be at risk from an innovation and will oppose its introduction. However, it is a mistake to see resistance simply as a blockage, to be 'managed' out of the way. Whilst it is a natural part of the change process, resistance can also be right! It may identify a fundamental flaw in an innovation previously overlooked. A core challenge for managers is thus to differentiate 'normal' resistance from resistance which is identifying clear problems to be resolved.

Organizational learning

An earlier chapter discussed the work of Argyris and Schon (1996) who developed the concept of single-loop and double-loop learning. Single-loop learning occurs when the existing services of an organization are improved through incremental change. Double-loop learning, by contrast, involves the questioning of organizational values, behaviour and services at their most basic. This is the type of learning involved in innovation.

Double-loop learning is an iterative process involving four basic stages: acquiring information; generating knowledge by the analysis of this information; applying the new knowledge to the organization; and encoding the knowledge into the routine behaviour of the organization. This approach to learning has led some authors to argue for a post-modernist approach to managing innovation, based on the concept of the 'learning organisation' (Argyris and Schon 1996). This has been discussed previously and is also returned to below.

Obstacles to innovation

Another task for the manager is to identify potential obstacles to the innovation process and to plan how to respond to these. This is not easy. Many obstacles do not become apparent until they are encountered and can be unexpected. It is vital, therefore, that the timetable for any innovation has sufficient 'slack' built in to it to enable such obstacles to be dealt with.

Borins (2001) has identified three types of obstacles to innovation. These are displayed in Table 9.1, together with typical examples of each. He argues that the most effective approach to resolving obstacles are *persuasion* (such as showing the benefits of an innovation, establishing demonstration projects and social marketing) and *accommodation* (such as consulting with affected parties, co-opting them onto the governance structures for an innovation and providing appropriate training for staff). Both these approaches, he argues, are more successful than *power politics*

Table 9.1 *Obstacles to innovation in public services*

Obstacle	Examples
Bureaucratic obstacles	Bureaucratic attitudes
	'Turf wars'
Internal organizational obstacles	Coordination problems
	Logistical problems
	Staff burn-out
	Technology failure
	Union opposition
	Middle management opposition
	General opposition to 'new innovations'
Political obstacles	Doubts of external stakeholders
	Failure to reach target groups
	Influential interest groups negatively affected
	Public opposition
	Private sector competition

Source: Based on Borins (2001).

(such as changing the staff a PSO employs and using authority and/or superiority to stifle opposition).

Winners and losers

As with any organizational change, innovation is bound to have winners and losers. As Pettigrew (1973) noted in his famous study on innovation in the automobile industry, some departments will have their role and resources enhanced by an innovation, whilst others will see their role and resources diminish. This is also true at the individual level – some staff will have their positions enhanced whilst others will have their position diminished. This has two implications for the management of innovation in public services.

First, it is important *to embrace the concept of innovation as a political process* (Frost and Egri 1991). This has profound implications for how to manage innovation inside a public organization and is returned to below in much greater detail. Second, as with any change, it is important *to pay attention to the individual level of*

193

analysis. Individual members of staff will be winners and losers. It is essential for the credibility of the manager that this is not glossed over, or an attempt is made to portray everyone as a winner. Staff will know that this is not the case and the attempt to portray it as so will only damage the credibility both of the innovation and of the manager concerned. Finally, it is also a key role for the manager to enable staff to move through the change process at the individual level. Some of the issues that a manager needs to consider in managing individuals through innovation are:

- To ensure early involvement of staff in the innovation process. Do not delay it to later in the hope that this will reduce resistance. It is likely to produce more resentment and resistence, and to not give staff the time they need to make their own decisions and adjustments.
- If possible, provide staff with help in facing up to changes. Few PSOs can afford to employ counsellors to support staff, but it may be possible to identify an organizational source for this or to develop peer-support groups.
- Remember to work through face-to-face communication. Staff will be more prepared to listen to what you have to say if you do personally, rather than through a memo or email, or through a subordinate.
- Remember that communication involves listening as well as talking – you need to do both!
- Take a proactive stance in working to gain commitment to an innovation and to enabling staff to see the opportunities that it poses, as well as its threats.

Drawing a balance sheet of risk and innovation

Depending upon the innovation intended, the comparative weight that each of these issues carries will be different – some innovations will engender more losers than winners, for example, whilst others might carry greater risk or need great attention to organizational politics. The successful management of innovation in public services requires the manager to have a clear understanding about how these issues will impact upon their particular innovation. As a way to think through these issues, you should now undertake Exercise 9.2 before proceeding further.

A final point in this section is to emphasize *the need both to tolerate and to learn from failure*. Innovation requires the chance to fail. However, as discussed above, PSOs are famously intolerant of failure and are risk-aversive – yet this is highly counter-productive for fostering innovation in public services. Staff will not take the risks required for innovation if they believe that they will be blamed individually for failure (Colville and Packham 1996). A key task for the PSO manager, therefore, is the development of an organization culture that promotes and allows

EXERCISE 9.2

Consider an innovation that you feel needs introducing into your organization or service, or one that you are familiar with. Draw up a balance sheet for this innovation against each of the issues identified above. Then consider what the implications are of this balance sheet for how you will manage the process of innovation. Finally, on this basis then draw up an initial action plan for the introduction and sustainability of the innovation.

You may also find it helpful to undertake this exercise for two or three different potential innovations. This will allow you to discover what issues are generic ones for all innovations and which are specific to one type of innovation.

for an acceptable level of risk and failure. This is very difficult for public service organizations, as discussed in the chapter on changing culture above. It requires a careful balancing act.

Further, it is essential that organizations do learn from failure and mistakes when they happen. This is a core element of the innovation process but one that is often neglected in public services – not least because the cost of failure can often be quite high profile media and/or political criticism. This makes learning from failure especially challenging in PSOs. At the very least, however, monitoring and evaluation should always be built in from the offset of a project and be set up to clearly identify lessons for the future from it.

APPROACHES TO MANAGING THE INNOVATION PROCESS

This section of the chapter reviews four approaches to the management of the innovation process in public service organizations. These are:

- The *rational management* approach.
- The *political negotiation* approach.
- The *building block* approach.
- The *learning organization* approach.

The lessons of these approaches are then pulled together within a *contingent* approach to managing public service innovation. First, though it is important to recognize some of the common fallacies abut the management of the innovation process in PSOs.

Fallacies about the management of innovation[3]

Before proceeding onto these substantive approaches, however, it is worth considering some of the common fallacies that abound about managing the innovation process. Eight fallacies in particular are often found and can be quite seductive – in part because each contains an element of truth, but which element is then elevated to the status of a principle by reputation.

Fallacy No. 1. The 'cascade' fallacy

This fallacy says that innovation must always be led from the top of an organization. It is consistent with the traditional pyramidal organizational structure of many PSOs and casts managers at each successive organizational level of the organization as 'heroes' who must spread the innovation across their level and who deal assertively with any resistance. Organizational staff are seen as purely passive in this process.

This fallacy is much beloved by Chief Executives, for obvious reasons. However, there is limited evidence for its effectiveness and it also ignores the existence of the bottom-up innovation discussed above. Moreover, its portrayal of organizational staff as passive 'sponges' absorbing innovation in the cascade, bears little relation to reality.

Fallacy No. 2. The 'anthropomorphic' fallacy

This fallacy talks of 'ideas spreading' or 'innovators developing' as if they had some life of their own. In reality, of course, they do not. The sloppy use of language ignores the reality and complexity of how, for example, ideas are spread *from person to person* within an organization.

Fallacy No. 3. The 'natural selection' fallacy

This asserts that good ideas will always succeed. In the long run this may be true – but then few managers live in the long run. Consider the case of scurvy amongst sailors. In 1601 an English sea captain demonstrated the effectiveness of lemon juice in preventing scurvy amongst ocean-going sailors. Some one hundred and fifty years later British Navy doctors confirmed this – but it was a further forty years before the navy introduced lemon rations onto their ships in 1790. Finally it took a further seventy years before, in 1860, the English Board of Trade introduced lemon juice as a preventative to scurvy on civil ships. The 'good idea' did indeed succeed – it just took two hundred and sixty years for it to happen!

Fallacy No. 4. The 'Trojan Horse' fallacy

This fallacy concerns using pilot projects to 'smuggle' an idea into an organization, on the basis that once the innovation is inside the organization, it cannot be got rid of. Pilot projects are indeed important for the innovation, for testing and 'debugging' potential innovations. But they are not a good way to initiate or diffuse an innovation. Mainstream staff will often be jealous of the attention (and extra resources) that a pilot project can garner and will invariably be prone to both the *NIH* ('not invented here') *Syndrome* and the *DATA* ('do all that already') *Syndrome*. Moreover, running a pilot project is not the same thing as integrating an innovation into a mainstream public service and it can result in a dangerous sense of acceptance and accomplishment before the real tasks of implementation have begun.

Fallacy No. 5. The 'charismatic individual' fallacy

This fallacy focuses on the role of charismatic individuals, or heroes, in introducing innovation into an organization or service, by force of their personality. Such forceful individuals can be an important source of innovation, but to rely on them alone is an error, for two reasons, as discussed in Chapter 7. First, if the success of the innovation is linked too closely to the advocacy of one individual, then when that individual leaves the organization the innovation invariably collapses – because there is no systemic organizational support for it. Second, the language of the innovator as 'hero' by implication casts the resisters as villains who must be overcome. It denigrates the important lessons that resisting may have to offer, as well as the importance of supporting staff through the innovation process.

Fallacy No. 6. The 'people want to avoid reinventing the wheel' fallacy

This fallacy assumes that, if an innovation has been successfully introduced in one PSO, area or team, then it can simply be taken in that finished form, and introduced elsewhere – the output of the innovation process in one area becomes an input in another. However, this misses the point that *innovation is a process* that has to be gone through. Staff have to leave old beliefs behind and learn new ones. An innovation cannot simply be 'plugged in' from elsewhere. Each team or organization has to make its own *innovation journey*.

Fallacy No. 7. The 'more of the same' fallacy

This argues that if a particular approach to introducing innovation has been successful, for one innovation or in one PSO, then that method will be successful for other innovations or PSOs. This will not necessarily be the case though.

197

Different approaches may well be necessary for different types of innovation, or in different PSOs.

Fallacy No. 8. The 'innovation must be led by restructuring' fallacy

This fallacy is much beloved by PSOs and their chief executives – who often seem ready and willing to restructure their organization at the drop of a hat. Indeed sometimes restructuring is an important part of the innovation process. However, it can also be a diversion away from confronting the real issues of innovation – and invariably also consumes vast amounts of organizational resources that might be used more productively in a different way.

MANAGING THE INNOVATION PROCESS

Approach No. 1. The rational management approach to innovation in PSOs

This approach is rooted in the rational systems perspective (Scott 1992). This sees organizations as 'instruments designed to attain specified goals' (Scott 1992: 29). According to Scott, the defining characteristics of this perspective are:

■ the specificity of organizational goals, which are assumed to be the basis for all decision making; and
■ the formalization or organizational structure and its impact upon behaviour within the organization.

This approach to the management of innovation sees it as a linear series of stages to be managed sequentially. A typical model of innovation in this approach is displayed in Figure 9.1.

The process starts with the identification of a performance problem, or 'gap', for the organization – such as the failure to provide sufficient affordable social housing in a rural community (Stage I). This leads to the need to assess the reason for this failure (Stage II) and subsequent attempts to mobilize organizational support around attempts to innovate to respond to the identified problem (Stage III).

The organizational management team then turn their attention to generating alternative options to dealing with the identified problem and the selection of the desired option for innovation (Stages IV and V). This then leads to the development of a concrete plan for implementation (Stages VI and VII). Finally the process is evaluated for its impact – possibly leading to the identification of a further performance gap to be addressed (Stage VIII).

Three important tools are commonly associated with the approach. The first is the *repetitive why analysis*, and involves the persistent interrogation of a

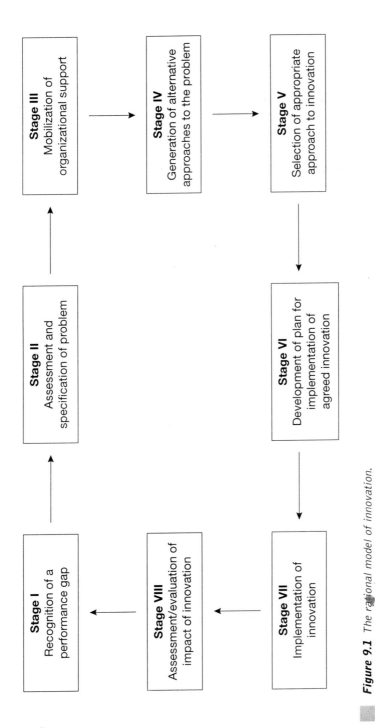

Figure 9.1 *The rational model of innovation.*

performance gap by use of the 'why' question. This is often used at Stage II to try to move from the recognized performance gap to the actual problem that needs to be addressed. Although this is a rational tool it inevitably involves the exercise of judgement in deciding when to stop asking 'why' and to accept the presented response as *the* problem to be addressed.

An example of a repetitive why analysis is given in Figure 9.2. This is based upon a real example from the UK from a few years ago, concerning the introduction of a new vocational qualification (the National Vocational Qualification, or 'NVQ') into a Local Authority Social Services Department. This innovation was proving problematic and this analysis was used to identify where the problem actually lay in the innovation process. In this case, the Department decided that the

NVQ is becoming devalued as a method of training

Which is caused by

Demotivation and dissatisfaction expressed by candidates

Which is caused by

Slow candidate progress with assessments

Which is caused by

Assessors not managing the process

Which is caused by

The time investment for NVQ being perceived as too great/costly

Which is caused by

Relative newness of NVQ and assessors not fully conversant with requirements of assessment,
therefore, large amounts of time being spent on familiarization

Which is caused by

The care standards being complex combined with assessment specifications that do not quantify candidate evidence or required depth, therefore, variance between candidates creates confusion

Figure 9.2 *Repetitive why analysis.*

actual performance problem that the NVQ was 'becoming devalued as a method of training' and concluded that this was because of the complexity of training standards and the variation in their implementation.

The second useful tool in this approach is the *Fishbone Diagram*.[4] It is used to plan the implementation process (Stage VI). To take our above example further, Figure 9.3 presents a fishbone diagram in relation to this innovation. Subsequent to the identification of variance in standards as being the key problem in the implementation of this training innovation, the Social Services Department involved decided that it needed to establish an effective assessment system, to provide more equity and credibility for the NVQ award. This fishbone diagram then split this aim into three sub-objectives, that needed to be achieved in order for this aim to be successful, and then split these sub-objectives down to the micro-steps that must be taken for each of these sub-objectives (the 'bones' of the fish).

Finally, in this example, a *Bar-chart* was constructed (Figure 9.4). This took the objectives and micro-steps from the fishbone diagram and tracked them across time to produce a plan for implementation (Stage VII).

Inevitably, these are only selected examples of the tools available with the rational management model of innovation. However, they do give a good example of the tenor of this approach.

The rational management approach to innovation is certainly useful for managers. It can provide an 'ideal type' of innovation process – this is how it should look if everything goes to plan. It also has a deal of resonance with the Weberian hierarchic-bureaucratic structure of many PSOs, which itself is rooted within the rational systems paradigm, and it provides managers with reassurance about positive ways in which to manage innovation, in the otherwise often chaotic organizational environment in which they live.

Equally, though, this approach has significant drawbacks. Most fundamentally, it ignores the frequently paradoxical and arational (if not irrational) reality of organizational life. PSOs are not rational entities but collections of individuals with differing goals. The rational model can quickly come unstuck in confronting this reality. Second, there is an assumption in the model of inevitable progression from one stage to another, leading to final implementation of the innovation. This can belie the complexity of the process in reality. Third, it over-emphasizes the role(s) of managers in the innovation process, but has little to say about other organizational staff or stakeholders.

The implementation stage in this model (Stage VII) is itself something of a 'black box'. Simply asserting that this stage involves the 'implementation' of the innovation misses out on the sheer interpersonal and organizational complexity of implementation. In the popular television series, *Star Trek: The Next Generation*, Captain Picard is able to say 'Make it so' and it happens – whatever it is. For the manager of the PSO, however, life is rather more complex. 'Make it so' simply will not do!

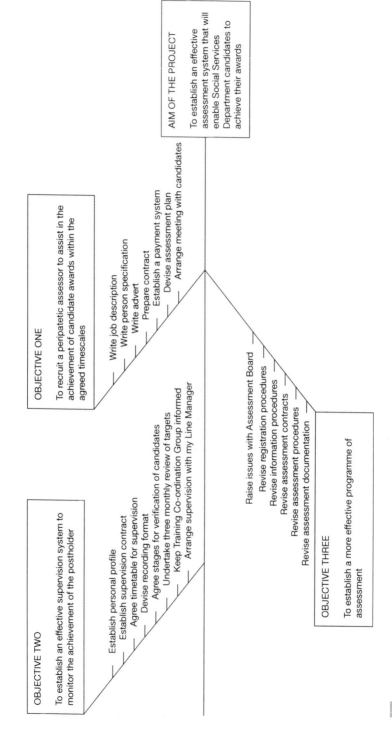

Figure 9.3 *Ishikawa diagram used for planning purposes.*

OBJECTIVE TWO

To establish an effective supervision system to monitor the achievement of the postholder

Establish personal profile
Establish supervision contract
Agree timetable for supervision
Devise recording format
Agree stages for verification of candidates
Undertake three monthly review of targets
Keep Training Co-ordination Group informed
Arrange supervision with my Line Manager

OBJECTIVE ONE

To recruit a peripatetic assessor to assist in the achievement of candidate awards within the agreed timescales

Write job description
Write person specification
Write advert
Prepare contract
Establish a payment system
Devise assessment plan
Arrange meeting with candidates

AIM OF THE PROJECT

To establish an effective assessment system that will enable Social Services Department candidates to achieve their awards

Raise issues with Assessment Board
Revise registration procedures
Revise information procedures
Revise assessment contracts
Revise assessment procedures
Revise assessment documentation

OBJECTIVE THREE

To establish a more effective programme of assessment

Activity	May	Jun	Jul	Aug	Sep	Oct	Nov	Dec	Jan	Feb	Mar	Apr	May	Jun
1. Recruitment and selection of assessors														
a) Prepare job description, advert and person specification	▪													
b) Arrange interview, appoint and prepare contract		▪												
c) Set up payment system		▪												
d) Prepare programme of induction to include meeting candidates/assessors and familiarization with organization and relevant personnel			▪											
e) Identify goals and expectations for achievement and establish plan of action			▪											
2. Candidate assessment														
a) Candidate learning agreements established														
b) Formal assessment commence			1st	2nd	3rd	4th	5th	6th	7th	8th	9th	10th	11th	12th
c) Internal verification of assessments				▪										▪
3. Progress monitoring														
a) Establish supervision profile, contract and timetable														
b) Review progress through supervision					▪	▪	▪	▪	▪	▪	▪	▪	▪	▪
c) Reports to Training Co-ordination Group														▪

Figure 9.4 Bar chart to demonstrate action plan.

Approach No. 2. The political negotiation approach

This approach takes its lead from the famous sixteenth-century writer Machiavelli who argued that the innovator would make enemies of all those who had thrived under the old system, and receive only lukewarm support from those who would prosper under the new, because of their innate sense of caution.

More recently, Andrew Pettigrew has given a clear enunciation of the approach in his classic text on the political negotiation approach to innovation. Innovation is a process beset by organizational politics, he argues:

> [Innovation] decisions are likely to threaten existing patterns of resource sharing. New responses are created and appear to fall within the juris-diction of a department. This department or its principal representative may see this as an opportunity to increase his or her status and rewards in the organisation. Those who see their interests threatened . . . may invoke resistance in the joint decision making process. In all these ways new political action is released and ultimately the existing distribution of power is endangered.
>
> (Pettigrew 1973)

The political negotiation approach is rooted within the natural systems perspective on organizations (Scott 1992). This perceives organizations as collections of individuals and interest groups, which all have their own goals, often distinctive from the espoused organizational goals. This approach to organizations emphasizes goal complexities with them, and the significance of informal structures and organizational subgroups.

The political negotiation approach to innovation thus concerns itself not so much with the design of the innovation, as the rational management model does, but rather with managing the micro-political process within an organization to ensure the successful adoption of an innovation. Thus the key processes in this are:

- identification of the key stakeholders who impact upon an innovation;
- negotiation between individuals and/or power-blocs within an organization;
- the influencing of key decision makers; and
- using ceremony/ritual to reinforce the importance and/or adoption of an innovation, and the use of experts both as 'flak catchers' (to deflect criticism from the innovation itself on external experts) and/or to provide 'expert mystique' for the innovation.

Unlike the rational management model, there is no one 'process' involved here. Rather it requires the selection of the appropriate tactics to successfully carry through an innovation from a 'tool box' of such tactics. The most common of these tactics are illustrated in Box 9.4.

204

BOX 9.4 COMMON TACTICS USED IN THE POLITICAL NEGOTIATION APPROACH TO INNOVATION

- controlling information flow within the organization to ensure that the right message gets through;
- selecting the performance criteria against which the innovation will be judged to ensure it is viewed as a success;
- using outside experts to provide credibility and/or to deflect opposition;
- co-opting key opponents of the innovation onto its management team;
- controlling the agenda at key meetings, to keep control of the discussion;
- building alliances and coalitions with key stakeholders;
- using organizational incentives/rewards to reinforce the importance of the innovation for organizational life; and
- using group pressure to persuade individuals to 'buy in' to an innovation.

At the core of this approach is the concept of persuasion – that the successful manager of an innovation needs to *persuade* the key stakeholders that the innovation is in their best interest. Box 9.5 gives examples of some of the core approaches to persuasion which characterize the political negotiation approach.

A central technique in this approach to innovation for PSOs is that of *stakeholder analysis* (Bryson 2004). A stakeholder is usually defined as anyone who has an interest in a particular organization (or innovation). For public service organizations this is usually said to comprise four groups:

- those who control resources (such as government departments or funding foundations);
- those who have political influence (such as the media or pressure groups);
- those who have involvement in the service delivery process (such as staff, the trade unions or other service contractors); and
- those who have an impact on the wider environment of the organization/innovation (such as regulatory bodies, local industry or local authorities).

Stakeholder analysis is a systematic approach to identify these key stakeholders for a particular innovation and seeking to influence them. There are many variants on stakeholder analysis, but typically it will involve six steps:

Step 1   List all the political stakeholders for the proposed innovation (usually through a 'brainstorming' exercise).

**BOX 9.5 PRINCIPLES OF PERSUASION
IN THE POLITICAL NEGOTIATION APPROACH
TO INNOVATION**

1   Keep the message simple – not stupid but do not overload it with
    unnecessary detail that detracts from the core message.
2   Make the message real to people by explaining how the innovation will
    affect them (positively) rather than talking in generalities.
3   Listen to (and hear) the fears and expectations of people before you
    speak.
4   Repeat the message for as many times as it takes for people to hear it.
5   Talk to people personally, not through intermediaries or by memoranda.
6   Choose your words of persuasion carefully and recognize what they will
    mean to other people as well as yourself. Once they have been uttered they
    can *never* be taken back.

Step II   Assess the strengths of influence of each stakeholder in relation to this
              particular innovation.
Step III   Select the four or five most influential stakeholders who you believe will
              impact on the innovation and which you wish to influence.
Step IV   Clarify the criteria by which they will assess the success of your proposed
              innovation
Step V   Develop a plan to influence these criteria for each stakeholder so that
              they judge the innovation a success.
Step VI   Use the positive support from these key stakeholders to influence other
              stakeholders and staff to support the innovation.

On the positive side, this approach to managing the innovation process recognizes
the complex reality of decision making and innovation within PSOs. It also
provides concrete tactics by which to take forward your identified innovation.

   However, with its emphasis on practicality, it can sometimes lead to the introduction of innovations that are politically easy to manage within the organization
instead of those which are politically risky – but perhaps much more needed –
innovations. Moreover, in its most extensive version, this approach can lead to a
manipulative and unethical approach to people management. It is conceivable that
a manager could succeed in such a way once, but the legacy of mistrust and suspi-
cion engendered by such manipulation would seriously damage their ability to
manage within their organization in the future.

Approach No. 3. The building block approach

This approach to the management of innovation in PSOs has been developed by Borins (2001), on the basis of his own extensive research, discussed previously in this book. Borins premises his approach on seven principles about innovation in PSOs. These are:

- that innovation in PSOs requires an 'innovation friendly' culture, supported from the top of the organization;
- that innovative individuals should be rewarded appropriately;
- that innovation is resource-hungry and requires special innovation funds (and conversely, that lack of resources is often the most serious constraint on innovation);
- that an innovative culture needed to embrace diversity of backgrounds and of thinking, in order to generate new thinking about delivering public services;
- that innovative PSOs are 'information hungry' and actively seek out information about the needs of their users and about their service;
- that innovative PSOs draw ideas from people at all levels of the organization; and
- that innovative PSOs put a premium on evaluation and on learning from both innovation success and failure.

From these principles, Borins developed five 'building blocks' for innovation in public services. Whilst his work is based specifically upon governmental organizations alone, they are nevertheless applicable to all PSOs.

Building Block I is the use of a systems approach. This involves both actively embracing the entire public service 'industry' that a PSO inhabits as a system of inter-locking partnerships and seeing public services as holistic rather than as a series of discrete elements.

Building Block II is the use of information technology (IT). This is often an innovation in its own right, presaging new ways of working inside an organization and a powerful tool with which to process and analyse the information upon which innovation is based.

Building Block III is process improvement. This refers to paying attention to the *process* of delivering public services as well as their actual design.

Building Block IV is the involvement of the private and non-profit sectors in service delivery. This can not only challenge the traditional ways of working of governmental agencies, but can also open new alliances and information channels that can lead to innovative approaches to service delivery.

Building Block V is the empowerment of communities, citizens and organizational staff. This emphasizes the importance of bottom-up innovation and of engaging as wide a constituency as possible in developing public service innovations.

The approach of Borins is an important one. It is rooted in detailed empirical research and is one of the few approaches to innovation that is actually based upon the experience of PSOs. It does not offer an easy 'menu' of tactics for managing the process of innovation and requires significant effort and input from those charged with innovation. This is both its greatest strength and weakness.

Approach No. 4. The learning organization approach

Based within the post-modernist organizational paradigm, this approach argues that organizational life is now too complex to be managed by traditional means, whether within the rational or natural systems paradigm: change is happening too fast to plan for and so planning based models are always bound to fail. Rather, the management of innovation requires embracing the complexity of the modern organization and its environment – what Tom Peters has called 'thriving on chaos' (Peters 1988).

A typical example of this approach argues against the idea of planning individual or isolated innovations. Rather, it argues for creating a 'learning environment' where staff can respond to change with innovation, without the need for managerial planning. Such a model usually has four stages:

Stage I is intended to develop a 'chaotic' approach to management within an organization, by frequently changing management style, by encouraging job rotation and by encouraging a plethora of sub-cultures to thrive.

Stage II then takes the organizational fluctuations and anomalies created in Stage I and amplifies them by creating artificial crises in order to stimulate creativity in the organization (for example, by asking for a 30 per cent budget cut when only a 3 per cent one is required!).

Stage III encourages interaction between the different parts of the organization and across specializations. It sees managers as catalysts rather than controllers (the analogy of a sports team and its captain is often used here) and seeks to encourage different subgroups to interact – through this interaction new ways of work are generated.

Stage IV involves the final establishment of the 'learning organization' that provides the perfect environment for the development of innovation. Front-line staff are empowered to make decisions and to develop new responses as the environment changes, rather than waiting for their managers to do so.

This approach to change certainly recognizes and enhances the uncertainty and speed of change and chaos that is endemic to most PSOs and their environment and does not try to impose rational models onto this complexity. It also includes some dynamic tactics for encouraging bottom-up change. However, it has nothing to say about the management of emergent innovation, imposed from the political environment. Further, it provides little security or support for public service staff already buffeted and exhausted by the constant change around them. It should come as no surprise that this approach to innovation developed in 'Silicon Valley' in California in the 1970s and 1980s, as the IT revolution was taking off and was popular with the young dynamic staff of these small firms. Its applicability to larger scale more traditional organizations is, however, still open to question. Nonetheless it is becoming an increasingly influential model.

Pulling it together: a contingent approach

This section has so far reviewed a range of approaches and tactics towards the management of innovation in public services. As should have become clear, no one approach is privileged here above the others. Rather, it is argued that what is needed is a contingent approach rooted in open systems theory (Scott 1992). This argues that there is no one right way to manage (innovation, in this case) but that not all alternatives are equally effective in any one situation. The management task thus, is the selection of the appropriate approach and skills (or mix of these) for a specific innovation. Exercise 9.3 will help in applying this contingent approach to your own PSO or one that you are familiar with.

EXERCISE 9.3

It is important now to take some time to think through the implications of each of the approaches described here for your own PSO or ones that you are familiar with.

Identify a particular innovation that you feel your organization or service needs to introduce in the near future. Then take each of the approaches identified above, in turn, and apply it to the management of this innovation. When you have completed this:

- consider the strengths and weaknesses of each approach; and
- identify what is the correct mix of the approaches and tools for implementing your identified innovation.

BOX 9.6 TEN 'GOLDEN RULES' TO GUARANTEE THE FAILURE OF AN INNOVATION

1   Introduce an innovation but do not provide training to support it.

2   If you must train staff then do it in isolation, both from each other and from their jobs.

3   Make use of meaningless statistics to alienate staff.

4   Invent cosmetic performance indicators that support the status quo.

5   Ensure that management–staff communication channels break down or work imperfectly.

6   Utilize as much jargon as possible to further alienate staff.

7   Appoint a 'hero innovator' but do not support them – when they fail the innovation will be discredited with them.

8   Ensure that the grounds for internal promotion and reward are linked to the status quo.

9   Exclude critics of the innovation from the decision-making process to encourage further resistance.

10 If in doubt use the 'Sir Humphrey' technique – procrastinate and/or set up a committee.

A FINAL WORD: SUSTAINING INNOVATION IN PUBLIC SERVICES AND IN PSOs

Finally in this chapter, a word must be said about the sustainability of innovation. A constant theme of much criticism of government and foundation-based funding schemes is that they are only interested in innovation and are less inclined to provide the longer-term revenue support needed for an innovation to become part of the main stream fabric of public services. This is not the only block to sustainability, however. Indeed, it is quite easy to think of ways to ensure that an innovation will fail (Box 9.6 gives a rather tongue-in-cheek view of this).

Notwithstanding this, the core principles to building sustainability into an innovation are not difficult, as long as they are addressed from the outset, rather than in retrospect. Some key principles of sustainability are outlined in Box 9.7.

BOX 9.7 APPROACHES TO THE SUSTAINABILITY OF PUBLIC SERVICE INNOVATIONS

- Choose visible goals for the innovation that you know will be met early on and which will reinforce to staff its effectiveness.
- Create organizational subsystems to support the innovation after its initial introduction and which do not rely on one or two individuals alone for their sustenance.
- Ensure a wide spectrum of organizational staff and stakeholders receive credit from the innovation.
- Take personal responsibility for mistakes rather than blaming them on, and discrediting, the innovation.
- Provide regular 'breathers' for staff to catch up with the pace of change and assimilate the implications of the innovation for themselves.
- Ensure that an innovation-friendly culture is engendered and which exists beyond the initial period of innovation, and which can allow lessons to be learned and further innovations to be engendered.
- Provide an evaluation mechanism from the outset which is about learning positive lessons and supporting innovation, rather than being negatively oriented and concerned with blaming individuals for mistakes.

DISCUSSION QUESTIONS

1   Consider the four approaches to the process of innovation discussed above. Putting them in the context of your own knowledge and experience of PSOs, which of these do you believe will be most effective and why? What pre-conditions might have to exist to ensure its success?
2   What different issues might a PSO manager have to consider when supporting bottom-up innovation, compared to top-down innovation?

NOTES

1   See also Ferlie *et al.* (1989).
2   Andrew Van de Ven has famously remarked that there is no such thing as an unsuccessful innovation – there are only 'innovations' and 'mistakes'! The self-defining nature of innovation can make it hard to estimate the real risks involved.

3   I am indebted to a seminar by, and subsequent discussion with, Gerry Smale at
     the Tavistock Institute in the mid-1990s, for his insight into the fallacies about
     the management of innovation.
4   This is sometimes also called an *Ishikawa diagram* after Kaoru Ishikawa
     (1915–1989) who pioneered this technique.

REFERENCES

Argyris, C. and D. Schon (1996) *Organizational Learning 2, Theory Method and
    Practice*. Addison Wesley, Reading, MA.

Baldock, J. and A. Evers (1991) On social innovation – an introduction. In R. Kraan
    and Associates (ed.), *Care for the Elderly. Significant Innovation in Three
    European Countries*, Campus Verlag, Frankfurt, pp. 87–92.

Borins, S. (2001) *The Challenge of Innovating in Government*. PricewaterhouseCoopers
    Endowment for the Business of Government.

Bryson, J. (2004) What to do when stakeholders matter: stakeholder identification and
    analysis techniques, *Public Management Review* 6(1): 21–54.

Colville, I. and C. Packham (1996) Auditing cultural change, *Public Money &
    Management* (July/September): pp. 27–32.

Feller, I. (1981) Public sector innovations a 'conspicuous production', *Policy Analysis*
    7(1): 1–20.

Ferlie, E., D. Challis and B. Davies (1989) *Efficiency Improving Innovations in the
    Social Care of the Elderly*. Gower, Aldershot.

Frost, P. and C. Egri (1991) Political process of innovation, *Research in Organizational
    Behaviour*, 229–96.

Osborne, S. (1998) *Voluntary Organizations and Innovation in Public Services*.
    Routledge, London.

Osborne, S., T. Bovaird, S. Martin, M. Tricker and P. Waterston (1995) Performance
    management and accountability in complex public programmes, *Financial
    Accountability and Management* 11(1): 19–38.

Peters, T. (1988) *Thriving on Chaos*. Macmillan, London.

Pettigrew, A. (1973) *Politics of Organisational Decision Making*. Tavistock, London.

Porter, M. (1985) *Competitive Advantage*. Free Press, New York.

Scott, R. (1992) *Organizations. Rational, Natural and Open Systems*. Prentice Hall,
    New Jersey.

FURTHER READING

Much of the further reading germane to the management of the process of innovation in PSOs has already been covered in the previous chapters on innovation. The studies referred to there are relevant to this chapter also.

Part IV

Conclusions

Chapter 10

Sustaining change and innovation in public services and public service organizations

LEARNING OBJECTIVES

By the end of this chapter you should be able to:

■ identify key elements of change programmes that sustain innovation and change in public services and public service organizations;

■ understand the influences on change and innovation that affect the ability of a change programme to survive and flourish;

■ critically analyse the differing approaches to maintaining change and innovation in public services and public service organizations; and

■ outline and interpret common themes in approaches to sustain change and innovation.

KEY POINTS OF THIS CHAPTER

■ Initiating and implementing change agendas and programmes is only one aspect of a change initiative; change needs to be embedded.

■ Traditional models of change are the punctuated equilibrium and planned change models of 'unfreeze-freeze-refreeze'; but continuous change has emerged as a new model of change.

■ PSOs are susceptible to change resistance and change fatigue in adopting change initiatives.

KEY TERMS

■ **Punctuated equilibrium** – this posits that organizations are mostly stable but at a critical point a single cataclysmic event will dramatically alter the operating and values systems.

■ **Continuous change** – this is emergent and results from external conditions of turbulence and volatility. Change is ongoing and does not have an end-point.

■ **Change readiness** – this is the ability and propensity of organizational members to either engage in behaviours that offer resistance to, or support for, a change effort.

Initiating and implementing change initiatives and innovation in public service organizations are key aspects in the change process. However, these facets are only a part of the change effort. Fostering a climate receptive to change and innovation and maintaining the ongoing momentum of change and innovation are critical elements in the change equation.

Over time, more diverse bodies of research, and a greater variety of perspectives have been advanced to account for the greater complexity of change. Weick and Quinn (1999) argue there has been a shift of research interest and attention from change that is discontinuous, episodic and intermittent to change efforts that are continuous, evolving and incremental. It is argued that newer models of change acknowledge that volatile contextual factors affect organizational calculations about change whereas existing models and interventions had little to offer firms operating under conditions of rapid growth and uncertainty in a continuously changing environment (Edelmann and Benning 1999).

MODELS OF CHANGE AND INNOVATION

Traditional models of change and innovation have tended to operate on a premise of planned change. Lewin (1951) formulated the widely cited and often used change model that conceptualized change as occurring in the three-step process, 'unfreeze-change-refreeze' and was introduced as part of his Field Force Theory. This theory represents forces for change as opposing those forces for stability, with the greater force affecting equilibrium. According to this model, a period of refreezing occurs in which the new design or pattern of behaviour is set following the change. Weick and Quinn (1999: 363) suggest the majority of organizational change models can be attributed to an underlying three-step process of unfreeze, move, refreeze as postulated by Lewin (1951).

However, in a continuous change context there is no 'refreezing' and therefore the workforce struggles to create norms of values and behaviours. Continuous change is driven by organizations engaging in competition on the 'edge of chaos'

(Peters 1989), and using both reactive and proactive strategies, the change is driven by disequilibrium. Weick and Quinn, (1999: 361) suggest that the process of 'freeze, rebalance and unfreeze' is more appropriate to successfully achieving change in a continuous change environment. This amended process, however, results in the workforce undergoing a heightened state of transition. During the 'freeze' stage, organizational members are aware of impending change, then rebalance requires change, and unfreeze requires greater change again. Continuous change is considered emergent because the outcomes emerge without having a pre-set agenda of steps to systematically work through and without a predetermined way to achieve outcomes.

Punctuated equilibrium (Gersick 1991; Tushman and Romanelli 1985) is a conventional framework within which to analyse organizational change. This model is based on the premise that organizational change is a singular event with a discrete beginning and end, and interventions for achieving change reflect this approach. However, Brown and Eisenhardt (1997) suggest that organizational change is not a discrete, episodic event as conceptualized by the punctuated equilibrium approach. Brown and Eisenhardt (1997) argue that firms engage in change efforts according to a continuous change continuum rather than implement change as a discrete episodic event. However, critics of the concept of continuous change challenge the utility of the continuous change rhetoric as being ever present in the change discourse (Zorn *et al.* 1999, Kirkpatrick and Ackroyd 2003, du Gay 2003).

It is argued (Baden-Fuller and Volberda 1997) that continuous change environments result from external conditions of turbulence and volatility that can be attributed to changing technology, increased globalization of markets and increasing pressure on public sectors to undergo reform initiatives derived from the private sector. These aspects are found in the global and cultural environmental governance level outlined by Lynn (2001). Continuous change is emergent and 'the outcome emerges from a series of seemingly trivial small-scale changes which enable a firm to adapt to their environment' (Edelman and Benning 1999: 79). Thus continuous change is adaptive and is a response to conditions of uncertainty in the external environment. The notion of planning for a particular set of stages and steps to undertake as part of a change initiative is not appropriate in this type of context. The management of ambiguity and uncertainty are core skills in an approach that hinges critically on being adept at responding to unpredictable environments.

Different types of change require differing strategies to sustain the change momentum; however, all change programmes are susceptible to dysfunction, stalling and failure. Consequently, a change programme requires elements of both emergent change and planned change to maintain the impetus of a change programme. Emergent and continuous change initiatives may need to adopt some degree of formalized structure, and planned change initiatives may need to incorporate some degree of flexibility to allow for unanticipated and unexpected events and outcomes.

219

Sustaining change and innovation

Lewis and Thompson (2003) argue that organizational change is a complex process that requires further effort than just ensuring that the change processes are in place; embedding the change initiative is also a vital aspect of any change agenda. Patrickson and Bamber (1995) suggest that sustaining the change effort requires more than senior managers identifying a vision and new direction but relies on a programme of change that is reinforced by systems and procedures that reflect the new approach and is accompanied by cultural change. Schneider *et al.* (1996) contend that a programme that changes the mindset of people within the organization must accompany a programme of structural change. The authors argue that programmes of change need to contain elements of structure and function, but the adoption of new technologies together with the forging of new kinds of relationships between employees, stakeholders and consumers are also vital for successful change initiatives (Schneider *et al.* 1996).

Lewis and Thompson (2003) suggest that leadership, communication and vision are common elements in change strategies, but that in order to sustain change initiatives, there is a need for supplementary and more sophisticated responses to change. It is argued that communicating the change initiative should involve two-way communication, leadership of change should include acknowledgement of the importance of building organizational social capital to assist sustaining change efforts, networks rather than hierarchy deliver better change outcomes, and there is a need to develop reward systems that support the desired change (Lewis and Thompson 2003). In this way, there are 'higher order' activities and processes that are required to maintain change efforts and these need to be considered as a critical part of the change process.

Sustaining change in public service organizations: a 'special case'?

To determine whether the public sector responds to change efforts with the same degree of success as the private sector, Robertson and Seneviratne (1995) conducted a meta-analysis of planned change in a range of public and private organizations. According to their study, there is little reported difference in the success of change interventions between the sectors. However, it was found that while change efforts had greater ease of implementation in private sector organizations, performance was enhanced 'more readily' in public service organizations (Robertson and Seneviratne 1995: 547). These results indicate that the potential for undertaking successful change initiatives in public service organizations, while complicated by the difficulty of establishing appropriate performance and outcome measures, appears to be more conducive to improving performance when change programmes are initiated.

Quinn (1996) argues that formal and systematic procedures, while creating consistency of action and predictable responses, also routinize and stagnate activities. It is suggested that change must be continuously moving through a cycle of initiation, uncertainty, transformation and routinization (Quinn 1996). The transformational process happens at both an organizational and individual level and is based on a mix of organizational learning and personal learning and an adaptation approach combining learning, empowerment, vision, strategic fit between environment and organization and an engagement with broader goals.

Failure of change initiatives occurs when there is a mismatch between the preferred change strategy and the ability of organizational members to absorb or understand the effort. There is also a difference between the change in behaviour required for the change and in the adoption of values and principles of the desired change and this is the arena in which culture is implicated in the design and ongoing support of change. Armenakis *et al.* (1993) argue that change readiness is an important stage in determining the success of change efforts. Change readiness denotes 'the cognitive precursor to the behaviours of either resistance to, or support for a change effort' (Armenakis *et al.* 1993: 681).

Barriers to change

Beer and Eisenstat (2000) contend that there is a range of barriers to achieving organizational change and have identified the 'silent killers' of organizational learning and change strategies as:

- top-down or laissez-faire senior management style;
- unclear strategy and conflicting priorities;
- an ineffective senior management team;
- poor vertical communication;
- poor coordination across function, businesses or borders; and
- inadequate down-the-line leadership skills and development.

The factors that are important to developing effective change strategies involve setting clear organizational goals, adopting appropriate communication strategies and linkages across the organization and high-quality leadership and management. One of the major barriers to change, particularly in public service organizations, is the inability to change the culture of public service organizations from the 'old' culture, signifying a conception of underlying culture as resistant to change efforts and counter-productive to efficiency. Prior studies of change and managing change demonstrate that perceptions of fairness are positively related to change receptivity (Folger and Skarlicki 1999).

Change strategies that rely on the cooperation of organization participants usually suggest that these participants see a need for change (Bridges 1987; Lewin 1951). Unless there is a clear need for change then it is unlikely that organizational members will be 'change ready' (Armenakis *et al.* 1993) and will be unlikely to be motivated to implement change.

Resistance to change

This has been discussed to some extent earlier in this book. Getting a balance between fostering an adaptive organization wherein organizational members accept and work with continuous change and instigating a process that produces continual change that exhausts organizational members is not a simple task. Morgan (1997: 431) observes in relation to change initiatives that:

> One of the major paradoxes facing modern managers is that they need to combine a high tolerance of ambiguity and openness to competing views with the need to create a 'closure' that allows them to go forward in a positive way.

The emergent change scenario requires adaptive capacity but change that has an 'endless' or continual quality may result in unintended consequences of change fatigue or change resistance.

An area that is pertinent to the literature about issues relating to change within public services is the propensity of change initiatives to encounter resistance to change. In the continuous change context, a further problem that has been identified is that of change fatigue (Piderit 2000, Doyle *et al.* 2000, Dent and Galloway-Goldberg 1999). Organizational members' responses to change are a crucial aspect of a change programme. Moreover, resistance to change efforts prevents the successful implementation of change initiatives. An underpinning assumption of Lewin's (1951) model of change is the notion of resistance to change and the need to overcome employee resistance to change. However, there is greater attention given to unpacking the notion of employee resistance to change to determine whether resistance is a case of employees' reluctance to embrace change or this aspect relates to power relationships between managers and workers (Willmott 1993, Piderit 2000).

Emergent change has a dominant place in recent organizational change management literature. Morgan (1997: 38) argues that a focus solely on changing the technical aspects of organizations in order to achieve change is inadequate as it ignores the social and informal aspects of organizational life and thus re-engineering programmes that ignored the interaction of the technical systems with a human dimension resulted in high levels of worker resistance.

BRINGING IT ALL TOGETHER: SUSTAINING ORGANIZATIONAL INNOVATION AND CHANGE

Change can be mapped over many dimensions and the multitude of influences and factors impacting on change ensure that understanding and effecting change is a complex business. Waterhouse *et al.* (2002) observe that the literature on organizational change engages with questions of organizational change in three ways: first the literature seeks to understand the rationale for organizations to undergo change, second, it examines how organizations change, and third, it interrogates the relevant elements of the organization that may be changed. In order to sustain change and innovation, the authors argue that incremental change, a focus on fostering the core purpose and mission of an organization and envisioning the organizational objectives is required (Waterhouse *et al.* 2002). However, these elements work together with a leader who is able to display characteristics of both transactional leadership that focuses on systems and processes and the transformational approach that focuses on altering the beliefs and principles of their followers (Waterhouse *et al.* 2002).

Figure 10.1 outlines the different change options available to implement and sustain change agendas. Dawson (2003) highlights the change scenario as emanating from a series of points ranging across small-scale incremental change to the polar opposite of large-scale transformational change. Change is conceptualized as being located on a continuum that moves from disjuncture and discontinuous to

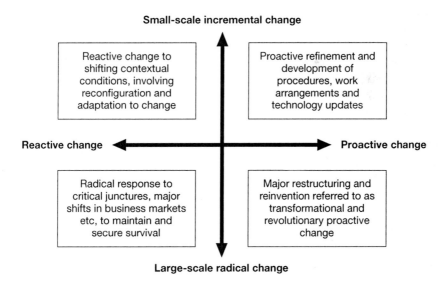

Figure 10.1 *Types of organizational change.*

Source: Dawson (2003).

evolutionary. The change effort may be reactive to the currents of environmental and organizational change or it may be anticipatory and proactively respond in terms of a long-term or strategic approach to pre-empt issues.

The notion of public service innovation has been regarded traditionally as an oxymoron (Borins 2002). Similar forces are at play in terms of conceptualizing public service organizations as resistant to change and possessing a 'bureaucratic' culture that is antagonistic to both change and innovation. Senge (1990) suggests that an invention becomes an innovation when it can be recreated in such a way that it is available to a wider group of users at a cost benefiting from exploiting economies of scale. The translation of an invention to an innovation occurs when an 'ensemble' of factors comes together (Senge 1990). Borins (2002) suggests that innovation is just as important to public sector managers as it is to those in the private sector because the pressures of reform together with increasing technology have required an orientation to innovation.

CONCLUSIONS

This chapter has examined the ways that change and innovation can be sustained in public services and public service organizations. While leadership, communication and vision recur as common themes in implementing change there is another set of considerations that are part of the change agenda. These elements are argued to be critical to ensure that the momentum for change and innovation is maintained. In order to sustain change initiatives, there is a requirement to develop higher order skills and approaches to change. Two-way or dialogic communication, building organizational social capital, operating according to networks and aligning reward systems with the desired change (Lewis and Thompson 2003) are elements of these higher order activities. Change and innovation initiatives need to be bolstered by implementing systems and procedures that align with the change approach but also require culture change (Patrickson and Bamber 1995). Schneider *et al.* (1996) concur, as they argue that structural change is inadequate to the task, the mindset of organizational members must changed as well. The higher order activities suggested by these authors include building new forms of relationships with employees, stakeholders and consumers (Schneider *et al.* 1996). In this way, 'higher order' activities and processes are required to sustain change and innovation efforts.

DISCUSSION QUESTIONS

1   What are the main features of change programmes? Which are the most relevant to achieve a successful change programme? Discuss.

2   Choose a change initiative in a public service or public sector organization with which you are familiar. How would you sustain organizational change and innovation in that organization?

3   The culture of public service organizations is becoming more like that of private sector organizations. Discuss.

REFERENCES

Armemakis, A., S. Harris and K. Mossholder (1993) Creating readiness for organizational change, *Human Relations* 46: 681–703.

Baden-Fuller, C. and H. W. Volberda (1997) Strategic renewal: How large complex organizations prepare for the future, *International Studies of Management and Organization* 27: 95–120.

Beer, M. and R. A. Eisenstat (2000) The silent killers of strategy implementation and learning, *Sloan Management Review*, Summer: 29–40.

Borins, S. (2002) Leadership and innovation in the public sector, *Leadership & Organization Development Journal* 23(8): 467–76.

Bridges, W. (1991) *Managing Transitions: Making the Most of Change*. Reading: Addison-Wesley.

Brown, S. L. and K. M. Eisenhardt (1997) The art of continuous change: linking complexity theory and time-paced evolution in relentlessly shifting organizations, *Administrative Science Quarterly* 42: 1–34.

Dawson, P. (2003) *Reshaping Change: A Processual Perspective*. London: Routledge.

Dent, E. and S. Galloway-Goldberg (1999) Challenging 'resistance to change', *The Journal of Applied Behavioral Science* 35(1): 25–41.

Doyle, M., T. Claydon and D. Buchanan (2000) Mixed results, lousy process: The management experience of organizational change, *British Journal of Management* 11 (Special Issue): S59–S80.

Du Gay, P. (2003) The tyranny of the epochal change: Epochalism and organizational reform, *Organization* 10(4): 663–84.

Edelman, L. F. and A. L. Benning (1999) Incremental revolution: Organizational change in highly turbulent Environments, *Organization Development Journal* 17: 79–93.

Folger, R. and D. P. Skarlicki (1999) Unfairness and resistance to change: Hardship as mistreatment, *Journal of Organizational Change Management* 12(1): 35–50.

Gersick, C. J. G. (1991) Revolutionary change theories: A multilevel exploration of the punctuated equilibrium paradigm, *Academy of Management Review* 16: 10–36.

Kirkpatrick, I. and S. Ackroyd (2003) Archetype theory and the changing professional organization: A critique and alternative, *Organization* 10(4): 731–75.

Lewin, K. (1951) *Field Theory in Social Science*. London: Tavistock Publications.

225

Lewis, D. and R. Thompson (2003) You've changed the culture: Now, how do you sustain it? *Human Resources and Employment Review* 1(1): 37–64.

Lynn, L. E. Jr (2001) Globalization and administrative reform: What is happening in theory? *Public Management Review* 3(2): 191–208.

Morgan, G. (1997) *Images of Organization* (2nd edn). Thousand Oaks, CA: Sage.

Patrickson, M. and G. Bamber (1995) Introduction. In M. Patrickson, V. Bamber and G. Bamber (eds), *Organisational Change Strategies, Case Studies of Human Resource and Industrial Relations Issues*, Melbourne: Longman.

Piderit, S. K. (2000) Rethinking resistance and recognizing ambivalence: A multidimensional view of attitudes towards an organizational change, *Academy of Management Review* 25(4): 783–94.

Quinn, R. E. (1996) *Deep Change: Discovering the Leader Within*. San Francisco: Jossey-Bass.

Robertson, P. J. and S. J. Seneviratne (1995) Outcomes of planned organizational change in the public sector: A meta-analytic comparison to the private sector, *Public Administration Review* 55(6): 547–58.

Schneider, B., A. Brief and R. A. Guzzo (1996) Creating a climate and culture for sustainable organizational change, *Organizational Dynamics Spring*: 7–19.

Senge, P. M. (1990) *The Fifth Discipline: The Art and Practice of the Learning Organization*. New York: Doubleday Currency.

Tushman, M. and E. Romanelli (1985) Organizational evolution: A metamorphosis model of convergence and reorientation, *Research in Organizational Behaviour* 7: 171–222.

Waterhouse, J., K. Brown and C. Flynn (2002) Change management practices: Is a hybrid model a better alternative for public sector agencies? *International Journal of Public Sector Management* 16(3): 230–41.

Weick, K. E. and R. E. Quinn (1999) Organizational change and development, *Annual Review of Psychology* 50: 361.

Willmott, H. (1993) Strength is ignorance; Slavery is freedom: Managing culture in modern organizations, *Journal of Management Studies* 30(4): 515–52.

Zorn, T. E., L. T. Christensen and G. Cheney (1999) *Do We Really Want Constant Change?: Beyond the Bottom Line*. San Francisco: Berrett-Koehler Communications.

FURTHER READING

Resistance to change

Agócs, C. (1997) Institutionalized resistance to organizational change: Denial, inaction and repression, *Journal of Business Ethics* 16(9): 917–31.

The paper argues that despite much literature about resistance, few studies actually give a definition of what is meant by it. Consideration of 'resistance to change' is raised from a personal psychological perspective to an institutional one. The paper uses a typology of resistance ranging from inaction to repression. It describes institutionalized resistance as 'the pattern of organisational behaviour that decision makers in organisations employ to actively deny, reject, refuse to implement, repress and even dismantle change proposals and initiatives'.

Dent, E. B. and S. Galloway Goldberg (1999) Challenging 'resistance to change', *Journal of Applied Behavioural Science* 35(1): 25–41.

This paper overviews the literature on 'resistance to change' and proposes that the concept needs to be overhauled. While Lewin initially described resistance to change as a systems problem affecting both management and employees, over time it has come to be depicted as a 'mental model', a psychological impediment affecting only employees and requiring management intervention to overcome it. Primarily the paper argues that employees do not resist change. They may be wary of or dislike certain elements of it, e.g. being dictated to by management or being cynical of the benefits of change, but there is little evidence to support the notion that employees actually resist change.

Piderit, S. K. (2000) Rethinking resistance and recognizing ambivalence: A multidimensional view of attitudes toward an organizational change, *Academy of Management Review* 25(4): 783–94.

As status differences erode in organizations, some employees are now *expecting* inclusion in decisions about organizational change. Wholesale labelling employee concerns for change as 'resistance' is therefore no longer credible. First, their concerns may be warranted, second calling them 'resistant' may only reinforce their beliefs through failure to alleviate their fears regarding proposed changes.

Chapter 11

Key lessons and issues for the future

LEARNING OBJECTIVES

By the end of this chapter you should:

■ understand that different types of change and innovation are required for achieving particular outcomes of change;

■ develop an understanding of the different elements of the change equation; and

■ identify the salient future issues in relation to change and innovation in public services and public service organizations.

KEY POINTS OF THIS CHAPTER

■ There are a myriad of approaches to understanding change and innovation in organizations but the main classificatory systems rely on contrasting small and large scale change and emergent and planned change.

■ Organizational change programmes need adaptation to the public services context.

■ Change can be mapped along three dimensions; scope, depth and pace.

KEY TERMS

▪ **The change cycle** – this is the conceptualization of change as continuously moving through a cycle of initiation, uncertainty, transformation and 'routinization'.

▪ **The change and innovation equation** – this is made up of the elements of leadership, communication, culture, type of change programme and context and relate to the scope, pace and depth of change required.

INTRODUCTION

There is a multiplexity of perspectives in relation to how and why change and innovation occurs in organizations. Managing organizational change and innovation relates to how to choose from competing theories and viewpoints on change and innovation, how to develop the appropriate analytic lens from which to view and understand the issues and to construct an agenda for change that accounts for the varied factors that make up the change equation. Coram and Burnes (2001) contend that organizational change is the 'core of organizational life'. In this way, change is conceptualized as an integral and ongoing part of an organization and inextricably tied to the day-to-day work undertaken by organizational members.

The lessons for public services and public service organizations are that change programmes may take many forms and flow from the Global, National and Institutional levels, but also change occurs at the macro- meso- and micro-organizational levels (Lynn 2001). Change may be either planned or emergent and occur in small, incremental steps or be undertaken on a large-scale basis that transforms organizations.

Particularly for public services and public service organizations with their orientation to public purpose and the lack of guiding principles offered by the profit motive, there is added complexity and uncertainty. For these public service organizations, developing an approach to change and innovation through research derived from private sector organizations is a complex task. Pressures on public services have driven institutional responses such as the adoption of market mechanisms as part of the attempt to deliver services more efficiently (Christensen and Laegreid 2003). For public service organizations, change has involved devolution of decision-making authority, downsizing and adopting private sector management techniques and principles such as re-engineering and Total Quality Management (Brown *et al.* 2003).

Choosing between sometimes competing approaches in order to develop an agenda and programme for change responding to and implementing change is a difficult undertaking. Adopting strategies for eliminating or minimizing the barriers to successful change adds another layer of complexity to an already complicated task.

In order to successfully implement change and foster an environment of innovation, the culture, communication and leadership issues need to be addressed. The change and innovation approaches need strategies not just at an organizational level, but should to be comprehensive and account for political, contextual and institutional factors. Achieving a successful change effort may be confounded by the inability of organizational members to be 'change ready'. It is important to recognize that change and innovation involve a broader construct of change than narrow notions of behaviour and structure. Cultural aspects as well as structures and processes are implicated in change and innovation. (Wise 1999).

THE CHANGE PROBLEMATIC

There has been greater acknowledgement in more recent times that there is no 'one best way' to initiate, lead and manage a programme of change. Dawson (2003: 6) suggests that conceptualizing organizational change involves being able to 'appreciate multiple and shifting views' and requires accepting that change can be understood from a variety of perspectives rather than adopting a single 'authentic' prescription for change. The OECD (2001, 2002) makes an explicit move away from 'template' and prescriptive models of change to those approaches that are diagnostic and account for particular circumstances, problems and challenges. However, at the same time, the OECD (2001, 2002) research publications note the change to less rather than a greater diversity in approaches to implementing change programmes and processes. The reality is that those researching and implementing change and innovation often look for and resort to step-by-step and formulaic approaches to change.

Problems in the characterization of change in organizational change management are identified as a narrow focus on the organizational aspects rather than examining broader social and environmental contexts that contribute to understanding change (Sturdy and Grey 2003). The authors argue there is a need to shift from a 'recipe book' approach to incorporating notions of power and politics, institutional approaches and resisting notions of a universalism of change.

Sturdy and Grey (2003) warn against an unproblematic adoption of the change motif as ever present in organizational discourse and an objective of organizational efforts to create system dynamism. In this way, the relationship of stability and change needs to be examined as stability has been ignored in the over-emphasis on incorporating a change agenda into organizations.

Sturdy and Grey (2003) cite Rogers (1995) who contended that a 'pro-innovation bias' existed that treated all innovation as inherently beneficial and argued that these accounts masked inherent contradictions in developing an informed response to organizational change strategies. It is argued (March and Olsen 1989) that the difficulties in planned change initiatives relate to the ways in which it is problematic to align and make consistent change at individual, institutional and environmental levels and, the inability to guide or predict specific outcomes or even, change initiatives may create the opposite of what was intended.

March and Olsen (1989) suggest that institutions are so complex as to defy predictable outcomes in planned change programmes and the interrelated layers of institutional members, institutions and context work against consistent outcomes of change. The stability of rules and formalized processes allow institutions to adapt to their context to create change rapidly in response to altered environmental conditions. Quinn (1996) however, argues that formal and systematic procedures, while creating consistency of action and predictable responses, also routinize and stagnate activities as change must be continuously moving through a cycle of initiation, uncertainty, transformation and routinization. According to Quinn (1996) the transformational process happens at both an organizational and individual level and is based on a mix of organizational learning and personal learning and an adaptation approach combining learning, empowerment, vision, strategic fit between environment and organization and an engagement with broader goals.

Organizational culture is implicated as a key element in organizational change efforts. However, the culture of an organization is difficult to identify and change. The artefacts and surface level of culture are usually altered in organizational change efforts, but the more difficult task is to change the underlying values and assumptions of organizational members.

Valle (1999: 249) argues that adaptive cultures establish the architecture for developing innovation and creativity within organizations and cites the example of General Patton's leadership strategy of 'Never tell people how to do things, tell them what to do and they will surprise you with their ingenuity' as an adaptive change approach suited to conditions of environmental volatility.

Dawson (2003) argues that change should be considered a process rather than a discrete event. In this way, the implementation and fostering of change and innovation have resonance with emergent and continuous models of change. According to Nadler and Tushman (1980) transformational change occurs in response to a high level of volatility in both the internal and external context, is driven from the top and middle levels of management, results in an organizational paradigm shift, and ushers in innovation and organizational learning.

Innovation emerges from developing creative tensions within organizations. Thus it is important to explore differences within an organization. Wheatley (1996) contends that conflict is a source of new ideas and that forthright conversations, capable teams, a clear organizational identity and well-functioning relationships create a new organizational dynamics that work to maintain organizational effectiveness in a turbulent environment. However, the record of managers in managing organizational change effectively and in management innovation is found to be poor (Maddock 2002). Kotter's research (1995) found that managers' response to change was reactive, ad hoc and internally driven and that innovation was rejected in favour of established ways of operating.

FURTHER RESEARCH

The ubiquity and inevitability of change is a compelling construct that has spawned an enormous body of literature, particularly in the organizational theory arena (Beer and Nohria 2000). However, more recently, scholars have turned their attention to unpacking the broad set of assumptions underpinning notions of change and highlighting the 'pro-change bias' of organizational research (Sturdy and Grey 2003, du Gay 2003, Kirkpatrick and Ackroyd 2003). Sturdy and Grey (2003: 659) argue that organizational change management research literature falls too easily into the over-generalized position that change is 'inevitable, desirable and/or manageable'. The authors call for alternative constructions of change that acknowledge the role and purpose of stability, that recognize the discontinuity of change and allow for broadening the issues relating to change by including other perspectives to provide a different 'authorial voice'. These areas suggest that further research would establish a new paradigm of change or at least dislodge the primacy of the change motif that change is inescapable and 'non-change' should be labelled 'resistance to change'.

An overview of the change and development literature found over one million references to the topic (Van den Ven and Poole 1995), and this large body of work establishes that the research subject has currency and topicality. The enormous volume of literature about change and innovation suggests that change may be an area that has exhausted the possibilities for developing new insights into the processes of change. However, Pettigrew et al. (2001) have alerted to the deficit in this research topic by outlining six significant areas that have defied investigation and research effort. It is argued that the investigation of change incorporating longitudinal, multi-layered and international comparative studies that focus on the relationship of receptivity, pace and type of change would extend knowledge and understanding about change more generally and specifically about the links between the approach to change and the change outcomes achieved (Pettigrew et al. 2001). Brown et al. (2003) suggest that while there is a huge body of research and understanding developed around the management of corporate change, there is less known about the different processes of change and their interaction in different settings. In addition, the interaction between individual and organizational influences and the combined effect of leadership, context and type of change when sub-cultures of the organization interact, has not been mapped or investigated in any depth.

While there is a vast amount of research in relation to corporate change in the private sector (Van den Ven and Poole 1995, Armenakis and Bedeian 1999) research relating to change in public service organizations is not as well developed. Common to research studies on public services is the contention that public service organizations are resistant to change and appear culturally antagonistic to change efforts, but there is little depth of investigation into the reasons for resisting change and the cultural attributes of public service organizations that may invoke the propensity to stability rather than change. It has also been argued that many public service organizations have been adept at adopting change and innovation is a significant feature of their operation. This anomaly needs further teasing out to escape the frequently drawn conclusion that public service organizations are reluctant to embrace or resistant to change efforts. The contention that 'bureaucratic culture' prevents change is a simplistic but widely held view that needs closer scrutiny, through informed debate and more evidence-based research.

The research effort into change has also ignored the question of the extent to which political choices drive the agenda for change or work to constrain change and innovation. Of particular note is the lack of evidence base to inform the imposition of change agendas at a political level. Rather than effecting a new regime of efficiency, political 'ideological commitment' may work against 'best practice' (Brown et al. 2003).

It was found that dialogic communication strategies assisted in constructing and shaping a change agenda that recognized and utilized employee input. Further research in terms of the type of skills, experience and organizational capabilities required to develop dialogue is needed. The strategic interplay of dialogic and monologic communication strategies to achieve successful change is also an area of further research. It is known that dialogic communication may stall change efforts and a top-down monologic stabilizing approach may be needed to allow an organization to consolidate change messages. Further refinements to understanding the appropriate mix of monologic and dialogic communication strategies are required.

CONCLUSIONS

The currents in public service change and innovation have been charted as emanating from the range of difference levels in the governance frameworks outlined by Lynn (2001). It is suggested that contemporary management practices articulate to the change agenda pursued in the public services and public service organizations. The interaction and interplay of institutional, policy and organizational levels have delivered a new paradigm of understanding and managing change and innovation.

The change and innovation equation is made up of leadership, communication, culture, change programme and context. Choices in relation to the type of change being undertaken rely on decision-making accounting for the scope, pace and depth of change required. Attempts to implement change agendas have often been unsuccessful due to a mismatch between the required goals and outcomes of the change programme and the type of change model adopted. Scant attention is often given to understanding the import and implications of context and culture to creating successful change initiatives. In response to the emergence of a more complex operating environment, public service organizations have adopted a range of new processes and ways of working. Continuous change is a recurring theme in public services, often displacing the conventional planned change approaches.

The different organizational orientation and accountabilities towards public purpose of public services to that of for-profit, private sector firms means that while the management of change will have commonalities across all sectors, change in the public sector will exhibit a range of differences to that of organizational understandings of change and innovation garnered from private sector models. The implementation of change is a difficult process that is confounded by problems of inattention to contextual factors, inadequate time, the lack of consensus about objectives, confusing or absent communication and the presence of competing objectives. For public service organizations, the importation of private sector management approaches have created tensions in relation to balancing the commitment to public purpose with techniques that deliver bottom line financial considerations and support a charter for profit.

It has been argued that it is not enough just to implement change, there is a need to institutionalize change and for the 'architects of change to mobilise the willing cooperation of staff' in order to orient successfully to the change agenda (Thompson *et al.* 2003).

DISCUSSION QUESTIONS

1   Choose a public service organization that is undergoing a change process. Briefly outline the type of change happening and identify the different elements of the change process.

2   In response to the change process outlined in your case example, discuss the following:

Organizational change
How do you know that you need to change?
What do you need to change?
How do you go about the change?

Organizational innovation
What are the prospects for organizational innovation?
What elements would foster an environment of innovation?

REFERENCES

Armenakis, A. A. and A. G. Bedeian (1999) Organizational change: A review of theory and research in the 1990s. *Journal of Management* 25(3): 293–315

Beer, M. and N. Nohria (2000) *Breaking the Code of Change*. Boston, MA: HBS Press.

Brown, K., J. Waterhouse and C. Flynn (2003) Change management practices: Is a hybrid model a better alternative for public agencies? *International Journal of Public Sector Management* 16(3): 230–41.

Christensen, T. and P. Laegreid (2003) Governmental autonomization and control – the Norwegian way. Paper presented to the *7th International Research Symposium on Public Management*, Hong Kong, 2–4 October.

Coram, R. and B. Burnes (2001) Managing organisational change in the public sector: Lessons from the privatisation of the Property Service Agency, *International Journal of Public Sector Management* 14(2): 94–110.

Dawson, P. (2003) *Reshaping Change: a processual perspective*. London: Routledge.

Du Gay, P. (2003) The tyranny of the epochal change: Epochalism and organizational reform. *Interdisciplinary Journal of Organization* 10(4): 663–84

Kirkpatrick, I. and S. Ackroyd (2003) Archetype theory and the changing professional organization: A critique and alternative. *Organization* 10(4): 731–50.

Kotter, J. P. (1999) The eight steps to transformation. In J. A. Conger, G. M. Spreitzer and E. E. Lawler III (eds), *The Leader's Change Handbook: An Essential Guide to Setting Direction and Taking Action*, San Francisco: Jossey-Bass.

Lynn, L. E. Jr (2001) Globalization and administrative reform: What is happening in theory? *Public Management Review* 3(2): 191–208.

Maddock, S. (2002) Modernization requires transformational skills: The need for a gender-balanced workforce, *Women in Management Review* 17(1): 12–17.

March, J. G. and J. P. Olsen (1989) *Rediscovering Institutions: The Organizational Basis of Politics*. New York: Free Press.

Nadler, D. and M. Tushman (1980) A model for diagnosing organizational behaviour, *Organizational Dynamics* 9(2): 35–51.

OECD (2001) *Public Sector Leadership for the 21st Century*. Parsi: OECD.

OECD (2002) *Regulatory Policies in OECD Countries: From Interventionism to Regulatory Governance*. Paris: OECD.

Pettigrew, A. M., R. W. Woodman and K. S. Cameron (2001) Studying organizational change and development challenges for future research, *Academy of Management Journal* 44(4): 697–713.

Quinn, R. E. (1996) *Deep Change: Discovering the Leader Within*. San Francisco: Jossey-Bass.

Sturdy, A. and C. Grey (2003) Beneath and beyond organizational change management: Exploring alternatives, *Organization* 10(4): 651–62.

235

Thompson, R., K. Brown and C. Flynn (2003) Changing tiger stripes: The complex task of producing change in a technically oriented professional organisation. Paper presented to the *7th International Research Symposium on Public Management*, Hong Kong, 2–4 October.

Valle, M. (1999) Crisis, culture and charisma: The new leader's work in public organizations, *Public Personnel Management* 28(2): 245–57.

Van den Ven, A. and M. Poole (1995) Explaining development and change in organizations, *Academy of Management Review* 20(3): 510–40.

Wheatley, M. (1994) *Leadership and the New Science: Learning About Organizations from an Orderly Universe.* San Francisco: Berrett-Koehler.

Wise, L. R. (1999) The use of innovative practices in the public and private sectors: The role of organizational and individual factors, *Public Productivity & Management Review* 23(2): 150–68.

FURTHER READING

Institutional level change

March, J. and J. Olsen (1989) *Rediscovering Institutions. The Organizational Basis of Politics.* New York: Free Press.

This book explores the institutional level of public sector change and aims to reinstate institutions into theories of politics by recapturing the place for formal organizations, and legal and bureaucratic institutions of government into considerations of change. Formal organizations are significant political actors. Institutions are a product of rules and formalized processes and the way individuals interact with those rules. In this way, politics does not rely solely on the reactions of individuals but is shaped by the obligations and functions of institutional roles taken up by those individuals. Institutional transformation is conceptualized in terms of an *evolutionary approach* as institutions adapt to contextual changes.

Planned change

Lewin, K. (1952) *Field Theory in Social Science.* London: Tavistock.

The mechanisms and enabling factors of *planned change* are examined. It is found there is greater success and less resistance to be encountered in instilling change in a group than it is to change any one individual. Organizational change proceeds in three steps: 'unfreezing, moving and freezing'.

Nutt, P. (1992) *Managing Planned Change.* New York: Macmillan.

The focus of the book is improving organizational performance using *planned change*. The processes, implementation and management of planned change initiatives within

236

organizations are examined. Case studies of different types of change initiatives outlining the pitfalls and success factors of undertaking planned organizational change are included. Strategies for initiating and implementing change are identified and a typology of change is outlined according to the internal drivers of change, the underlying assumptions about change and processes of change. The roles of those who 'sponsor' the change by identifying the need for change and starting the process and those who carry out the change, 'planners' are examined.

Morgan, G. (1997) *Images of Organization* (2nd edn). Sage: Thousand Oaks, CA.

The central premise of this book is that metaphors are powerful tools to understand organizations. 'Images' of organizations are drawn from a review of organizational development, politics, science and philosophy research and literature. *Metaphors of organizations* conceptualize firms as machines, brains, organisms, politics, or 'psychic prisons' and identifying the prevailing metaphor assists in shaping appropriate responses to change. Metaphors that construct organizations as machines, for example, focus on the different elements of organizational life as constituent parts that work together with precision to achieve predetermined goals, and efficiency is achieved by specialization and routinized tasks.

Emergent change

Quinn, R. (1996) *Deep Change: Discovering the Leader Within*. San Francisco: Jossey-Bass.

The book suggests that large-scale change can result from an individual's efforts to influence an organization. The role of the *change agent* is explored and the potential for altering the organization by an internal leader is examined. Deep change is conceptualized as transformational change that creates new knowledge and ways of acting and interacting and is contrasted with incremental change which is characterized as processual, easily reversed change that does not afford lasting or immutable change. The precepts of deep change centre on the ways that individuals within organizations can achieve change by changing their values and beliefs about themselves and their place in the organization. The principles rely on eschewing traditional control mechanisms and adopting persuasion, leading by example and lateral thinking techniques

Senge, P. (1990) *The Fifth Discipline: The Art and Practice of the Learning Organization*. Boston, MA: Doubleday Currency.

Understanding the ways that organizations adapt and change is a critical component of this work. Organizational learning as a competitive advantage and creating the conditions through which organizational learning can take place is a major theme, illustrated by examples from business practice. A '*learning organization*' is represented as an organic model comprising three interconnected levels: individual, group and organization. It relies on identifying and working with five 'disciplines' comprising values, shared insights and vision together with a systems and team approach to understanding organizational life. The five interrelated disciplines form the basis of the organizational learning model: a systems approach, individual learning, understanding and developing mental models of organizational life, developing a shared vision and finally, adopting a team learning mode.

Wheatley, M. (1996) *Leadership and the New Science: Learning about organization from an orderly universe*. San Francisco: Berrett-Kohler.

Organizations and organizational life are characterized as organic, self-organizing systems. Core organizational competencies for dealing with complex situations centre on relationship building, networking and teamworking in order to build trust and quality relationships. The skills for change in a chaotic environment are planning for an unknown future, establishing conversation and story telling capabilities and developing meaningful intra-organizational relationships.

Appendices

Appendix A

Managing change in public service organizations: a case study

Kerry Brown, Queensland University of Technology, Australia, and Christine Flynn, formerly Department of Main Roads, Queensland, Australia

THE DEPARTMENT OF MAIN ROADS, QUEENSLAND, AUSTRALIA

The appointment of the first non-engineer as the Director-General of the Department of Main Roads in Queensland, Australia, was always going to create controversy. In the eighty years since it came into existence there had been an engineer heading the department. Managers and employees alike could not have imagined the course and extent of the new wave of change resulting from the agenda for change pursued by the new Director-General.

The department had undergone large changes as part of the government commercialization reforms and had been amalgamated with another government agency in the mid-1990s and 'de-amalgamated' a couple of years later, so widespread change was not new. However, the scope, direction and outcomes of the change were not anticipated. Large-scale changes implemented in the ways the organization operated, related to and communicated with internal and external stakeholders and structured activities were far-reaching. Importantly, the principles and values espoused and adopted in the change programme built on and extended the existing organizational values in new ways.

The Department of Main Roads was a technically oriented public service organization seeking to change to a more responsive, relationship focused organization and adopting a whole-of-government approach to programme and service delivery. The Department of Main Roads provides an interesting study of a public sector organization undergoing an innovative change management process initiated and driven from within the organization. The department employs more than 4,000 staff and has an annual operating budget of A$1.6 billion. It is a geographically dispersed government department with large distances between the fourteen regional centres. While national road agencies have privatized or contracted out large

241

portions of their operations, and in some cases all road building and maintenance work, Main Roads has significantly retained their in-house 'build and maintain' capacity. This approach has been due in part to restructuring incorporating an approach that includes purchaser-provider arrangements within the department. The department divided along corporate/commercial lines with the creation of Roadtek, the commercialized business unit within the Department of Main Roads that may compete for certain types of construction work alongside private sector contractors as well as utilizing internal 'user pays' purchasing arrangements.

The department has focused on delivering and achieving engineering and technical excellence with the implementation of state of the art approaches to road construction, traffic management and intelligent transport systems. This case study examines how a highly technically oriented public service organization responded to a planned change initiative that focused on changing systems and structures as well as the values, culture and relationships. The change programme shifted the department from a 'builder and maintainer of roads' to a 'manager of the road network', and from a highly technical culture to a more customer-orientated and relational culture. It also adopted a hybrid model of public management rather than accept the New Public Management (NPM) model in its entirety.

The processes of the change effort began in 1998 when the newly appointed Director-General embarked on a process of planned change. The department had a history of undergoing change and was recognized as a leader in the public service, but the most recent change agenda was much broader and more comprehensive than previous change programmes and included culture change as a significant element of the change programme. In previous times, change was driven top-down by external forces such as central public service agencies or by government policy. The change programme was internally driven and was a proactive measure to ensure the continuing existence of the organization. However, as with all previous changes in Main Roads, the impetus was from the external contextual environment and aimed at efficiency and organizational survival.

The change agenda encompassed improving communication and relationships both within and without the organization. It also linked into achieving whole-of-government objectives with respect to engaging with the community, preserving the environment, recognizing indigenous cultural heritage and adopting principles of social justice within a commercialization context.

Prior to the arrival of the new Director-General, the culture of the Department of Main Roads was characterized as being dominated by poor internal relationships, especially in respect to personality conflicts within the senior management team. The culture was also previously dominated by a focus on the technical responsibilities of the organization, with a lack of attention given to other organizational needs such as management capabilities, policy analysis and business development. Accordingly, the organization was, at times, perceived as being inefficient and lacking accountability. The department was also perceived as being resistant to change, neglecting diversity and lacking common values. These characteristics were considered to be significant obstacles in its capacity to effect change. However, at the same time, Main Roads was also recognized as having a strong 'family' culture and a culture that assisted anyone (and their family) in times of need. Moreover, employees expressed a great sense of pride and achievement in working for Main Roads and voiced a great deal of satisfaction in belonging to the organization. The possibility of a high degree of organizational acceptance of the change agenda of the new Director-General related to several influences converging in the political landscape. Conditions for shifting to a new organizational paradigm were set when external and internal factors placed pressure on Main Roads to look not only to its continuation as a leader in the public service, but to its very survival.

Drivers of change

While the Department of Main Roads had developed a reputation for technical excellence in building and maintaining the road system, it also had acquired a reputation for being arrogant and as having a privileged position with government. A series of events changed the way the Department of Main Roads was perceived by government. Prior to the 1995 state election a new $680 million motorway was proposed, a section of which was to pass through a koala habitat. This planned route, while a technically superior road option, was abandoned after disaffected voters reacted angrily at the polls. An upgrade of the existing highway to eight lanes was proposed instead.

Part of the political 'fallout' of the failed motorway proposal led to the department being amalgamated with another government department. Staff thought that this period was a bleak time in the history of the department as it was felt strongly that the amalgamation resulted in 'de-engineering' the department and destroyed the identity of the Department of Main Roads. The Director-General of the amalgamated department was perceived by Main Roads managers as determined to suppress the former Main Roads culture and was described as 'anti-Roads, anti-engineers'. While the amalgamated agency was eventually split back into two departments, the possibility (and dread) of another amalgamation loomed large in the minds of Main Roads employees.

In relation to the external environment, the threat of re-amalgamation with the other government agency drove Main Roads to consider new ways of operating and be more responsive to alternative paradigms. In addition, it was clear that technical excellence alone could no longer sustain the department, as the political backlash against the alternate road route plainly demonstrated. New and broader areas of competency and organizational capabilities needed to be developed.

In 1998, a new Director-General, from a public service agency outside Main Roads and without an engineering background, launched the department into unknown and uncharted territory. The vision he formulated for Main Roads however, gave the department a strong sense of worth and achievement and was constructed as Main Roads being an internationally recognized road agency in South-East Asia. The existing culture of technical expertise was cultivated and promoted through encouraging the core purpose of providing roads by setting a vision of the department as 'a provider of roads that Queenslanders value'. Further, a long-range vision was also set for Main Roads as 'the premier road agency in Australia and the Asia Pacific'. While technical excellence was an important component of the vision, the Director-General established from the outset that a primary aim of his leadership was developing a department that was more responsive to community needs through consultation and communication.

After only two years, a new Director-General of Main Roads was appointed in 2000 when the Director-General was appointed as the head of another public service department. The incumbent possessed an engineering background and for some this was thought to signal a return to an engineering focus – 'the boys are back in town'. However, the story of change did not end there. The change programme was continued under the leadership of the second Director-General although with some modifications. The incoming Director-General outlined that his vision of the change task is a 'continuous process that is more characterized by considered evolution, rather than directed revolution'. Elements of change covered both systems change and values change and relied on a programmatic change model to guide the process.

Tools of change

The planned change approach involved implementing a change programme devised by the new Director-General that recognized a broader set of organizational concerns. The change process was initiated by identifying major barriers or 'blockages' preventing organizational members from achieving organizational objectives. A blockage was any aspect of departmental operations that hindered or prevented staff efforts to realize organizational objectives and goals and were grouped into three categories: people, structures and systems. This process was assisted by prioritization of the blockages and the creation of teams from senior management to deal with the most crucial five or six blockages in each of these groupings. The process was entitled 'unblocking for success' and created a leverage point for the introduction of change strategies in Main Roads. As part of the mapping process to understand the organizational structure, the Director-General discovered a departmental position that reported to no one and no lines of authority or supervision to any other staff members.

The key platform of the conceptual framework for implementing change became commonly known as the 'Three Frames' approach and was introduced in the early stage of the new Director-General's leadership. The Three Frames introduced a management approach that brought relationships with internal and external stakeholders, budgetary and financial considerations that also accounted for triple bottom line aspects of social and community responsibility and a balancing of systems and people aspects. The three management systems or 'frames' were conceived as working together simultaneously – alignment, relationships and a balanced performance scorecard. 'Alignment' referred to people, systems and structures working together and aligning with the Strategic Plan. 'Relationships' sought to ensure that Main Roads is based on principles of genuine communication and information-sharing both internally and externally. The 'Balanced Performance Scorecard' introduced a means of judging economic outcomes by broader measures than narrowly defined financial and technical performance, and depended on improved customer/stakeholder relationships as well as good management of people and learning.

A key feature of the Three Frames was the promotion of a cultural shift away from hierarchical and control-oriented management and communication towards the adoption of a networked, horizontal structure and open and two-way communication. As these elements of the change process filtered through Main Roads, expectations were developed in regard to communication and the right to be consulted and contribute to organizational direction and decision making. Within the relationship frame, and in the pursuit of open communication, the Director-General introduced the practice of 'calling behaviours' whereby it was encouraged to bring to an individual's attention any behaviour that was considered inappropriate. Such actions could be taken publicly and, under the auspices of the Director-General, without reprisal. Communication and consultation mechanisms were instituted through the development of a systematic committee system, an intranet information bulletin, 'Main Roads Junction', and the D-Gs Hotline. The D-Gs Hotline was introduced to enable employees to raise concerns, comments or provide feedback on the implementation of the Three Frames and the change strategies implemented in Main Roads. Adopting a range of initiatives and opportunities for employee participation and changing the adversarial and 'command and control' management practices signalled a seismic shift in thinking and action in a department that previously had a reputation for 'butt-kicking', sorting differences out 'behind the shed' and telling employees they were only needed to work 'from the neck down'.

Following the introduction of the Three Frames approach, staff of the department acknowledged the need for shifting from a sole focus on 'putting down the black stuff' to taking into account the needs of community, government and internal stakeholders in a relational way.

Before the changes could be bedded down throughout all levels and layers of the department, the Director-General moved to head another government. However, the new Director-General publicly committed himself to the 'Three

245

Frames' management approach initiated by the previous Director-General, and built on them with the Five Signposts. The Five Signposts reflected a vision of five change themes and directions for the future: listening, positioning, aligning, leading and learning.

Senior managers in Main Roads invested much effort into positioning Main Roads within a whole-of-government perspective, and road network management environment. With these issues in mind, Main Roads have developed (and are developing) a strategic context within which change efforts can be focused. This strategic context has so far consisted of Scenario Planning, a fifteen year plan – *Roads Connecting Queenslanders*, a departmental strategic plan, and operational plans. *Roads Connecting Queenslanders* (RCQ), the department's key policy document, was conceived in 2001–2002 to identify how Main Roads will operate in the next fifteen years. RCQ outlines policy directions and decisions that need to be made in order to make the transition from being a road builder to a road system manager.

The Strategic Plan outlines how these directions will be effected over a five year period. The Strategic Plan provides a blueprint for action and balances the needs of the organization to be economically efficient at the same time as responding to broader whole-of-government objectives. The Strategic Plan 2002–2007 outlines the importance of relationship building as a means by which Main Roads can increase its relevance to government and other stakeholders.

Project 21, a cultural change programme instigated by the commercial arm of the department, (RoadTek) is aimed at moving the commercial operations away from its hierarchical, functional structure to a structure based on project teams. The instigators claim it 'will develop a single, integrated business management system and create a commercial project management culture'. The elements of *Project 21* consist of an Information Technology platform to undertake standardized on-line purchasing, asset management and commercial business transactions.

Through the change programme, Main Roads improved its business performance. It was noted that a consequence of improved relationships was a clearer focus on achieving improved 'collective' outputs, as teams worked to common goals. Staff indicated that the department had improved business systems; developed more and streamlined flexible work practices and improved training opportunities. Other features of an improved business environment included a clearer focus on customers, improved costing systems, resource sharing and more transparent accountability systems.

The Roads Connecting Queenslanders initiative, scenario planning within the broader Transport portfolio, and memoranda to staff from the Director-General contribute to a better understanding of Main Roads desired future state. In addition to the work being done on positioning Main Roads, considerable emphasis has been given to providing departmental staff with roadmaps for moving towards the desired future, specifically, the Three Frames, the Five Signposts and *Project 21*. These roadmaps are practical tools for improving organizational performance.

A significant and distinguishing feature of *Project 21* is that its directors identified from the outset that not just a systems change was necessary, but that such changes also involve changing people and their culture.

The 'Three Frames' has remained the cornerstone of Main Roads' change philosophy and has continued to dominate the thinking of most of the senior management team. The five change themes in the Five Signposts model sought to build organizational capabilities that are seen to be essential to taking practical action addressing the challenges facing the department, particularly the challenge of 'being asked to do more with less'.

Subcultures

Consistent with the pluralistic nature of most large organizations, several subcultures were identified within the department. These subcultures provide a comparison of responses to change between commercial and corporate operations, engineering-technical and administrative functions, and change agents and 'traditionalists'.

Subcultures within the department were a source of both diversity and resistance. Some subculture groups became change agents within the organization, providing innovation and direction to the change process while other subcultures appeared besieged by the constant demands of continual change and changing skill requirements. The presence of change agents and adequate resources devoted to change processes appear to be important components of the capacity of subcultures to commit to organizational change. Tensions between subcultures within Main Roads were apparent. These subcultures include corporate and commercial operations, and head office and regions. While there had been some progress in addressing these tensions, the resolution of these conflicts was uneven across the organization.

With an engineer back in charge of the organization and willing to adopt the cultural changes of his predecessor, non-technical employees were hopeful that the changes would now gain greater credibility with technical and engineering staff within the middle management ranks. Some engineering and technical staff, however, were hopeful that the organization would return to the way they had been and that the Three Frames would now disappear.

Many welcomed the new way of operating as it gave permission to 'do things differently' and they were keen to rise to the challenge and enlarge their work skills and responsibilities. Others felt the burden of responsibility for implementing the new approach was too much and were stressed by the prospect of delivering what they considered was a 'cut price product' rather than the quality product they felt they had delivered previously. The technical officer stream appeared to be the most problematic in that a combination of traditional work practices, problems with career progression and a current trend towards outsourcing a great deal of technical work had reduced the morale of this group. Other groups were keen to adopt the new work practices and values offered by the relational approach but felt they were prevented by those 'higher up' in the organization, particularly in the middle management levels.

Recognition of this changed approach was not uniform throughout the department, as there were those who thought that in a tight budgetary situation they should just be able to get on with the job of building roads and not waste scarce time and resources on consultation, liaison and responding to non-technical organizational considerations. Consultative processes became difficult because, with shrinking budgets, money could be better spent away from the 'touchy-feely' stuff and towards building better roads. With an engineer back in the leadership position, there was some hope among technical employees that this would occur.

External relationships

The espoused necessity for new forms of consultation with external stakeholders presented a challenge for Main Roads to perform outside the 'old culture' and embrace new ways of operating. By proactively engaging stakeholders in decision making, Main Roads managers proposed that they would continually improve the reputation of the organization. In particular, Main Roads staff saw a need for greater proactivity in engaging in community decision making and for the community to come to a greater understanding of the need to prioritize work programmes and work together with Main Roads to achieve both social justice and quality community outcomes. A Community Consultation Framework was developed in order to improve communication and relationships with community members. Over time, the Department of Main Roads gained greater credibility with the wider community. Alliance building efforts with stakeholders resulted in a much more integrated approach to the delivery of community projects. One example quoted was that community members are now more receptive to discussing road and transport issues rather than departmental employees being confronted by a 'farmer with a shotgun'.

One significant area of improving stakeholder relationships has been the efforts to engage with Indigenous Australians and promote cultural heritage principles. Prior to undertaking roadwork, traditional landowners are consulted, the site is mapped, artefacts are preserved and cultural practices observed. This process is complex and requires high levels of cultural sensitivity, legal and cultural knowledge and communication skills.

Changing stakeholder relationships are demonstrated in a shift in mindset from 'we know best' to asking the public what they think is best for them and then negotiating an outcome among competing interests. However, it was acknowledged that forging these new relationships with external stakeholders caused work intensification, and increasing amounts of time involved in setting up projects particularly in relation to consulting with community stakeholders. Notwithstanding these concerns, the success in building good relationships with external stakeholders was seen to be a pivotal aspect of the future viability of Main Roads.

Efforts with respect to external relationships were considered a positive feature of the current organizational culture of the department. It was believed that there was a clearer focus on whole-of-government priorities, management of community relations and external negotiation. There was a sense that the public image of Main Roads had improved, and that the organization was taking a leadership with the Queensland public service with respect to civic engagement in policy development.

Internal relationships

A filter-down approach of the change process from the top of the organization meant that the change process was achieved more comprehensively at the top levels of the organization. However, significant areas of the department were familiar with the change process and the intention to adopt a more relational approach to operating. Previously, the tradition of technical excellence was also argued to have been allied with a 'command and control' approach to managing.

Division in the department related to different subcultures that appear to have emerged between corporate and commercial operations. Some regional commercial units were leading organization change and their complaint was that corporate functions have not embraced the same level of commitment to change and innovation.

To move change forward 'Change Champions' in the lower rungs of the organization worked to secure higher level management support to continue the change momentum. These 'Change Champions' looked to senior management and strong leadership to assist them in their efforts and they encouraged senior management to hold accountable those who failed to espouse the changes.

Some of the obstacles to the change process included higher workloads, a lack of clarity in the direction of corporate change within the organization and additional demands resulting from new consultation processes. The highest levels of dissatisfaction within the organization were recorded in some of the regional areas. Specific complaints and issues related to high levels of stress, low morale, increased work intensification and tensions between staff. These groups reported tensions between competing objectives such as cost and quality, reducing costs and increasing consultation processes, and organization building and private sector contracting.

In particular, the role of middle managers in some regions was perceived as being particularly instrumental in slowing change processes within various organizational work units. Although the strongest responses were positive with respect to the new internal relationships within the organization, some regional groups believed that they had become disempowered within the new organizational culture, mostly because of a lack of consultation and downsizing. Some also believed that the team model within Main Roads was ineffective in an unpredictable work environment while others considered the relational model being applied to be time consuming without necessarily improving outcomes. Although it was acknowledged that communication had improved, there were indications that communication should be better, especially as staff now had higher expectations with respect to communication. The change programme and the allied activity in relation to changing organizational performance and culture had heightened expectations about consultation and the ability of organizational members to intervene and contribute to the change process and staff members became discouraged when their efforts to engage with the change initiative were not apparent.

Some of the structural issues that staff believed still need to be addressed include the fragmentation and loss of identity within Main Roads, and organizational misalignments. Purchaser–provider split drove the commercial arm to a more commercial orientation and despite problems of maintaining quality in a competitive, cost-cutting environment, the commercial arm has been extremely successful in re-orienting to a commercial setting, and has developed a pride in their ability to compete in the 'quality' end of the market.

At the same time, the corporate arm struggled with pressures to be responsive to emerging public demands for greater egalitarianism in public service delivery including legislative imperatives in cultural heritage, environmental preservation and community participation. The corporate arm responded by instituting measures for greater public consultation, and developed greater sensitivity and capability in dealing with indigenous cultural heritage and environmental issues, however, these are necessarily slower in moving the agenda for change forward, residing at the interface of legislation, policy and intergovernmental relations. The commercial arm had become exceedingly flexible and 'lean' in its operations modelling approaches for operating from the private, for profit sector. The corporate arm adopted a range of business mechanisms including contractual arrangements, alliances and project management. There is thus a mismatch in operating constructs and *raison d'être* between the corporate, bureaucratic model and the commercial provider model. The tension in bridging this divide creates critical organizational issues.

There were also some areas identified as problematic across the organization. One strong theme was the perception that there are still strong divisions across the organization, limiting the capacity of Main Roads to achieve a common organizational culture. It has previously been noted that tensions between the regions and Brisbane, and commercial and corporate arms appear to be a feature of the recent-past culture of the department. Some interpreted different cultures within the organization as part of the change process as the Department of Main Roads moved from one culture to the next. These tensions are still apparent within the organization, and possibly more transparent as other tensions within the organization are resolved.

With respect to internal relationships, many organizational members noted the emphasis given to teams and relationship building. Staff noted improved personal relationships between senior executives, and improved negotiation processes at this senior level. Some commented on improved access of staff to senior management, and improved flows of information from the senior management group across the organization. In general, employees characterized the relationship culture within the organization as participatory and empowering, in comparison to the previous culture of the department. Many women noted that a higher priority is currently given to the role of women within the organization than has previously been the case. Staff also indicated that the organization was open to new ideas, questioning and innovation.

CONCLUSION

A new Director-General sought to drive large-scale change from the top of the organization through a planned change initiative he developed and called the Three Frames. The change initiative included the introduction of open dialogue, participative change practices, a fostering of relationships, developing systems thinking alongside risk taking and innovation, cultural change and, aligning vision and organizational structures. The change agenda was continued under the second Director-General although there was a purposeful slowing of the pace of change and a greater consideration of the technical core of the department.

The 'frame' of the Three Frames model that was most successfully translated into new ways of working in Main Roads was the relational approach. Over time, the Department of Main Roads developed a greater focus on consultation with external and internal stakeholders, although the initial successes in this area were achieved in relation to building better relationships with external organizations. However, forging new relationships with external stakeholders did not result in easily-won cost efficiencies as it caused work intensification, and increased the lead time in setting up projects.

Main Roads transitioned from a technical civil engineering culture to a new philosophy that recognized the importance of external and internal relationships. Some of the drivers of change included new leadership within the organization, challenges to the viability of Main Roads and the salience of the change agenda for organizational members.

Main Roads introduced more open communication and a change process that allowed the shift to a more relational, egalitarian culture. Tensions in managing large-scale change are inevitable. Transformational change in a complex organization such as the Department of Main Roads is always going to be a difficult task. The scale and scope of change achieved fundamental shifts in systems, structures, identity, values and shared understandings, although the outcomes of changes were not distributed evenly across the organization. Significant differences across subcultures, between organizational levels and dispersed over place and time were evident.

This case study illustrates the way in which a planned change programme aimed at developing a relational approach to managing change in the Department of Main Roads reoriented a highly technically-based organization. The planned change approach built on the competitive advantage of the technical expertise of the department but paved the way for a new approach to thinking and responding to the pressures of change. The integration of relationship-building with high quality technical service delivery gives new insights into public sector management strategies, as traditional internal strengths were built on at the same time as efforts to broaden and enhance organizational capabilities in different ways.

QUESTIONS

1 What model of change best describes the change programme and outcomes outlined in the case study?

2 What are the problems and possibilities of implementing change in public service organizations?

3 How does leading change differ from managing change?

4 What leadership issues did the two leaders in the case study face? How do models of leadership inform the case study?

5 What are the implications of the change programme outlined for other types of public service organizations?

6 How might an emergent change approach to managing change differ from planned organizational change efforts in terms of process, principles, effects and outcomes?

Managing innovation in public service organizations: a case study of Regional Action West Midlands (RAWM)

Chris Bonnard, Network Director of RAWM and founder member of its original Steering Group

THE ONLY THING CONSTANT IS CHANGE!

June 1997 saw the election of a Labour government in the UK with a strong 'regional agenda'. Devolution in Scotland and Wales, devolved power in London and opportunities for devolved administrative, strategic and democratic arrangements in the English regions were all key policy initiatives.

These policy approaches emphasized the importance of both 'social inclusion' as a focus for area regeneration and the need for the participation of the voluntary and community sector (VCS) and local communities – of both geography and interest – in area regeneration.

In the West Midlands of the UK, as elsewhere, the only thing constant was change! This is a rural and urban region with a population of over 5.2 million people, Black and Ethnic Minority (BME) communities reflecting diversity across the region, and a business sector including continuing manufacturing industries and growing service industries.

The regional devolution agenda affected many PSOs in this region. Regional Development Agencies (RDAs) with an economic development brief were set up in each region with the formal establishment of Advantage West Midlands in April 1999. The West Midlands Regional Chamber (Assembly) was launched in January 1999 and cabinet style government and scrutiny arrangements introduced locally as part of local government reform. Government Offices were strengthened as a regional arm of central government.

RAWM: a development process

Innovation can be defined as the introduction and testing of new ideas. With the introduction of the 'regional agenda' how was the voluntary and community sector (VCS) to engage?

Voluntary sector meetings with the Government Office provided the catalyst for a strategic meeting in March 1998, of Chief Officers from West Midlands VCS infrastructure organizations, and which reflected urban, rural, BME and regeneration interests.

Drawing on prior experience in the North West, discussion emphasized the critical importance of securing an influential VCS voice, contributing to regional decision making.

The terms of reference for a regional VCS Steering Group and a consultation process testing the need for a Regional Network were agreed. Meetings with the eight other such developing VCS networks across England and participation in a national conference with key national infrastructure organizations gave a further kick start to the process.

Grants from the Home Office and the Rural Development Commission supported a major Consultation Conference in September 1998. A 'full house' of 140 delegates attended. Participative workshops, focusing on the rationale, purpose and governance for a regional strategic network, overwhelmingly supported its establishment. The minutes of the meeting concluded that: *'A network has the potential to finally provide the sector with an opportunity for both recognition and influence'*. The year 1999 saw:

- publication of progress reports;
- discussion with potential funders;
- a Home Office/National Lottery Conference focusing on BME engagement;
- a joint conference of embryonic regional networks across England; and
- meetings with Ministers at the Home Office and the Department of Transport, Local Government and the Regions.

July finally saw approval of a six-year £2 million bid to AWM for a six-year strategic funding programme. In parallel, work with national VCS infrastructure bodies clarifying the distinctive roles of national and region networks was under examination.

Expectations, particularly from regional government agencies, were growing. Nominations were made to the new Regional Chamber; discussions were held with the West Midlands Local Government Association, and views were sought on policy matters including Regional Planning Guidance, sustainability, the Regional Economic Strategy, Urban and Rural White Papers, as well as a number of speaking engagements.

The second phase consultation with the VCS sector took place in the summer of 1999 and focused on reviewing the outcomes of the September 1998 Conference. It led to an agreement on statement of purpose, shared values, key objectives, membership and staffing profile and governance and accountability arrangements. Work was commissioned to produce business and regeneration delivery plans and to finalize the Network's Memorandum and Articles of Association.

February 2000 saw *Regional Action West Midlands (RAWM)* formally established as a Company, with a Board of Directors in place and a successful three year funding bid to the Active Community Unit of the Home Office for £149,000. Accountable Body arrangements and work on governance, recruitment, office, financial and administrative protocols and systems were put in place. Later in the same year a further £313,000 was secured from the National Lottery to support a programme of regional participation and research.

RAWM's Network Director, Operations Manager and Administrative Officer were in post by July 2000, and three Co-coordinators, with focus on Strategy and Policy, Participation and Development and Information and Communications, and RAWM's Office Manager were recruited over the following six months.

What were the critical factors contributing to RAWM's development?

- The commitment of the Steering Group, the VCS sector and other allies and partners.
- Collaboration and trust – focusing on wider rather than parochial interests and with a commitment to shared values.
- Availability of interim resources to support the development process.
- An ability to build on existing infrastructure operating locally and across communities of interest.
- Clear and accountable consultation processes allowing time for consideration, change and agreement.
- Use of existing political, negotiation and management skills within the VCS.
- Ownership of decisions across the sector on purpose, objectives and governance, providing a baseline for implementation.

Four years on, in 2004, with a staff of fifteen, additional resources to assist development and sustainability of the sector's engagement with the regional agenda, what have been the key messages from the stakeholders of RAWM? An external evaluation of RAWM, published in July 2003, included the following responses:

> RAWM is a highly regarded organisation uniquely placed to influence the cultural change needed to establish the sector as an equal partners on the regional stage . . .

> The majority of stakeholders see RAWM as 'effective', 'well organised', 'clear about its objectives', 'open and fair in its practices' and 'fully engaged with regional issues.'

There is a very real sense in which RAWM has demonstrated that it 'adds value'. We doubt that priority issues like social housing, social inclusion, older people, labour market capacity, sector and organisational capacity among others, would now be common currency without RAWM's contribution.

RAWM, a new innovation for the West Midlands, has found itself 'facing both ways', driven both by the VCS in order to influence policy and strategy and by government because of its 'regional agenda'. As a learning organization the key messages that have assisted its effectiveness are:

- 'RAWM – we don't do local!' A focus on a regional and subregional strategic participation and influencing role.
- A focus on 'reflection' and 'accountability', role rather than acting as a single 'representative' voice of the VCS.
- Clear defined roles of Board and Staff, a staffing structure reflecting key skills required in order to meet objectives and delivery of services and the ability to manage internal and external change.
- Building of cross-sectoral alliances to maximize impact of voluntary and community sector engagement.

Finally, in looking ahead, the following key challenges have been identified:

- Continuing difficulties in bringing about 'cultural change' in the behaviour of regional and other institutions in working with the VCS.
- Questions of strategic leadership across the region and across the VCS require examination and joint cross-agency working skills, to build the broad range of regeneration coalitions required.
- The importance of initiating changes in the current, 'risk adverse' culture, enabling measurement of long-term strategic impact by VCS derived outcomes rather than government driven outputs.
- The political will and effective coordination to build the sustainable engagement of the VCS, of RAWM and other regional strategic networks.

KEY QUESTIONS

1   How did the developing policy environment have an impact upon the innovation process in this case – and to what extent was it driving this process or being driven by it?

2   What key skills were required by those individuals and groups driving the innovation process here – and did they remain constant or change over time?

3   What do you think needs to happen now in order to ensure the sustainability of RAWM into the future?

Index